DEPRIVED DEVIS

DEPRIVED DEVIS
Women's Unequal Status in Society

Dr. V. Mohini Giri

GYAN

GYAN PUBLISHING HOUSE
NEW DELHI - 110002

Deprived Devis
Women's Unequal Status in Society

Rs. 540

ISBN : 81-212-0856-4

Published in 2006 in India by
Gyan Publishing House
5, Ansari Road, Daryaganj
New Delhi-110 002
Phones-23282060, 23261060, Fax-(011) 23285914
Email : books@gyanbooks.com
Visit our Website at : http//www.gyanbooks.com

Laser type Setting by: Tact Computer Graphics, Delhi
Printed at: Salasar Imaging System, Delhi

This book is dedicated to the memory of my mother Vani Bai Ram and my father Dr. V. S. Ram who made a larger life possible for me

Contents

	Foreword	9
	Author's Note	11
1.	Religious Interpretation the Greatest Obstacles to Women's Empowerment	13
2.	Caste and Women	21
3.	Dalits: Slavery in the Century	31
4.	Reinterpretation of Tradition	35
5.	The Sacred Fire	37
6.	Marital Counselling	45
7.	Threat to Women	49
8.	Changing Mindset's	59
9.	Gender Equity	67
10.	Powerfully Empowered	71
11.	Federation of Panchayati Women	79
12.	Giving Power to Women	87
13.	The Role of Women in the New Millennium	91
14.	Millennium Development Goals	101
15.	The Death Penalty: An Affront to Humanity	107
16.	Elderly and Policy-Making	117
17.	Second Widowhood	121
18.	Widows: Lifetime Prisoners of War	125
19.	The Unsung Brave	129
20.	Wish We Could Stretch Out and Touch Your Hand	135

21. Crossing Divides 141
22. War at What Cost 147
23. Religion is it Operate from Politics 151
24. Communal Peace 159
25. Creating a Culture of Healing 165
26. Courage, Peace and Diplomacy 171
27. Women and Torture 179
28. Shortlived Joy 191
29. Reassertion of Woman's Place in Society 199
30. Securing a Future 203
31. Domestic Violence 215
32. Imprisoned Women and Closed Society 223
33. Women and Education 233
34. Challenges — 21st Century 239
35. Women and Peace 247
36. Dammed to be Doomed 255
37. Binding and Bonding 269
38. Trafficking in Women and Children 279
39. Human Rights and Women 289
40. Transforming Approaches to Conflict Resolution 297
41. Women's Initiatives for Peace in South Asia 305
42. The Unsung Brave 313
43. Sustainable Development 319
44. Participatory Democracy 323

Appendices 329

Index 351

Foreword

There is a growing discussion in national and international fora on the causes for the "Indian Enigma" in areas such as gender discrimination, technology divide, economic disparities and widespread occurrence of undernutrition in the midst of substantial achievements in the areas of democratic systems of governance, science and technology and agricultural products. The reasons for such contrasting characteristics of the Indian social and economic scenario obviously vary from region to region and culture to culture. Both the growing female foeticide, particularly in the affluent parts of the country like Punjab and Haryana, as well as the widespread occurrence of maternal and foetal undernutrition resulting in babies characterized by low birth weight, are matters of great concern. There is increasing feminization of not only poverty and hunger but also of the agriculture and HIV/AIDS. At the same time, the worship of Goddesses and female role models in various areas of human endeavour is also widespread. Why then the is unpardonable discrimination against the girl child and women?

We owe a deep debt of gratitude to Dr. Mohini Giri for putting together in this book several of her articles on Threat to Women, Domestic Violence, Second Widowhood, Women and Peace, Women and Education etc., Dr. Mohini Giri's style is both direct and powerful and her vocabulary is tailored to give expression to her inner voice. Her struggle for gender justice and for ensuring equity in all areas of development is now inspiring and igniting the whole country, just as Mahatma Gandhi's struggle for freedom and gender justice did in the last century. There are many pieces of legislation to prevent violence to women both in the household and in work-places, but these have not been able to end serious atrocities. Obviously, we need education and social mobilization in addition to regulation for achieving the goal of a happy society where men and women play equally important roles in promoting human security and well-being.

Dr. Mohini Giri's article on Second Widowhood is a sad commentary on the prevailing social ethos where widows are discriminated and quite often exploited. Fortunately, women are getting organized in different groups including Self-Help Groups and Mahila Mandals. Only such organizations conferring "group power" can help to prevent injustice and sexual exploitation. This is where Dr. Mohini Giri's contributions in the area of empowerment of the socially and economically underprivileged women have been monumental. I hope this book will be read widely and will help to reverse current trends in sexual disparities and discrimination so that the totality of our human resource becomes our greatest strength.

M. S. Swaminathan

Author's Note

The 21st Century started with a bang with women pioneers making an indelible impression in various fields, whether it be Smt. Sonia Gandhi as an unparallel leader or Kalpana Chawla reaching new heights, or Sania Mirza conquering the courts.

Inspite of all these, the status of women did not see much change. To our great distress, the demographic count showed a significant in the man-women ratio and the girl child has become nearly invisible.

All these naturally provoked debates, discussions, demonstration at various levels. In some of the discussions and articles, I have tried to put together some ideas and thoughts so that we could find speedy solutions in the coming days.

Needless to say, patriarchy and discriminations against dalits will remain in India as long as we do not change the mindset of the social fabric. I do hope that some of these article will initiate the process of questioning in society to act on many issues pertaining to women and dalits.

Despite women comprising 50 per cent of the population, their voices are unheard at the policy-making level in the Parliament. Members of civil society are fighting for affirmative action in the Parliament. Patriarchy, which is an obstacle to the progress of women, also deprives them of a voice in the legislative process of the nation. Again and again I have been emphasizing through my articles and speeches, the vital need to create that critical mass in the legislative process. I am convinced that on the road to empowerment, political affirmation of the woman's status is the first milestone.

I am indeed deeply indebted to my respected brother.

Dr. M.S. Swaminathan, whose gracious wife Meena Swaminathan has been my Guru in many ways, who has kindly given the foreword to this book.

My thanks to the staff of Guild of Service especially to Mariamma Ponnachan for having diligently worked on the manuscripts; to Saida Thomas for proof reading, Shri Amit Garg, Director, Publication of Gyan Publishing House, for printing and publishing this book in an excellent manner in record time. My thanks are also due to all my colleagues and friends.

A million thanks to those unnamed, unsung, unknown women—who have inspired and taught me the meaning of empowerment. In the following pages is the story of their struggles, their aspirations, their dreams and their successes and failures. They are the unhonoured heroines in the Indian women's empowerment.

Dr. (Mrs.) V. Mohini Giri

1

Religious Interpretation the Greatest Obstacles to Women's Empowerment

As the darkness enveloped the village, Savitri wore a frightened look as it was time for her husband to come back home. In the morning before leaving he had threatened that the Tantrik had said that at midnight she must sacrifice her two year old son or else there will be calamity. She huddled her little child Ravi to her breast and prayed to God that the evening should never come.

In another village Rukhsana was equally frightened as matters between her and her husband had gone sour since the past several months. He had said that according to the Quran he has to only say talaq three times and that will be the end of the journey. She prayed to the Almighty Allah to save her from such a disgrace.

Ann, a devout Catholic, came to the public hearing held by the National Commission for Women in Kerala and cried out that her husband was beating her day and night. Isn't it an irony that even when a woman is beaten up her religion forbids divorce.

Dina Mai, a pure Agiary temple going Parsi, brought up her daughter into the pure Zoroastrian faith. When her daughter turned 22 she fell in love with a Hindu boy from an affluent family. Dina Mai and her husband Jamshed tried their best to prevent their daughter from getting married outside the community. According to the Zoroastrian tradition the daughters children would be debarred entry to the Agiary (fire temple) and also deprived of the Navjyot ceremony which is an initiation into the Zoroastrian faith. Although the Parsi priests are forward looking but they will not perform the marriage ceremony of an intercaste alliance, i.e., the girl marrying outside the community. Poor Dina Mai and Jamshed everyday pray that good sense prevails on the priest. They fear on their demise their daughter will not be able to perform their last rites. However, it is heartening to note that Parsi women are entitled to the half share in their parent's property and wealth.

It is indeed strange that the Sikh religion, which was formed on the basis of doing away with rituals, has succumbed to the same. Before installation of the Holy book at Darbar Saheb, Amritsar when the place is sanctified by milk and water even till today women are not allowed in the precincts. Similarly, while carrying the Holy book from the Kotha Sahib to the Sanctum Sanctorum in the Golden Temple women are not allowed to carry the palanquin. Sikhism which originally gives equal status to men and women has no women priests till date.

It was tragic to go to the Reshampura village in Rajasthan to see huge marble houses recently built. When I went round the whole village I found to my dismay only one 66 year old woman. I asked her the whereabouts of other women, upon which I was told that it was a tradition in the village that as soon as a girl attained maturity she had to be wedded to prostitution and at present all the women of the village were sent to Dubai, Mumbai etc. I found groups and groups of men sitting on the verandas of those palatial buildings, smoking and playing cards with the money that their women earned from selling their bodies. One of the men looked daggers at me and told me that was the religious tradition and who was I to interfere!!

In many parts of South India till today a woman is relegated to live outside the house during her natural monthly periods. In the name of religion she becomes untouchable for those 5-6 days. She is not given food and nutrition.

So where are we today? This is the story of the women's saga of trauma. She finds at her doorstep—violence because of religious interpretation and beliefs that hinder her progress.

Tragically, organized religion, whose very reason for being entails service to the cause of empowerment of women, behaves all too frequently as one of the most formidable obstacles in the path of women's empowerment.

Religions per se have come to establish and sustain human values in society. However, the religious interpretation by vested interests namely of religious leaders and others has almost sullied the name of religion. The greatest interpretations of Hindu sages like Adi Shankaracharya, Madhavacharya never indulged in discriminating women from men so much so that Adi Shankaracharya spoke about Aham Brahamasmi thereby indicating that both men and women are part of that God.

Although women are considered the custodians of culture in the majority of our societies, most religious, cultural and traditional practices are defined on the basis of patriarchal norms that limit women's human rights. The growing power of religious fundamentalism, which emphasizes the role of culture, religion and the family, reinforces patriarchal notions about women's roles within and outside the family and deny women their rights.

In patriarchal religions and cultures, including modernized societies, women are frequently unaware that they can view experiences, especially those affecting their bodies, in ways other than the ones into which they have been socialized. This constructed ignorance has serious ramifications for the exercise of choice in sexual and reproductive matters.

If I say that women have been long denied their birth-right to be in charge of their individual lives and as such have been deprived of their decision-making power even on such vital issues as their own health care and care of their infants and young children as well as education and socio-economic well-being of their families and communities and gender inequality is perpetuated, it will not be an exaggeration.

Her status is influenced by attitudes of society, societal norms, interpretation of religion (which is very often in conflict with the core religious texts and teachings), work situations and wage discrimination, inequitable investments in human development especially for women and children, and denial of economic rights such as ownership of property and equitable distribution of wealth in a family and in a society. Hence women around the world continue to be victims of injustice, leading to oppression, exploitation and violence and when denied love and affection, wholesome food, shelter, opportunities for development, education and gainful employment, they are forced into a hopeless situation for generations.

Why are we after 56 years of independence still facing such obstacles? aren't dignity and love absolute elements of life for every woman, man and child? Isn't a woman born into this world with the same rights as the man, without the woman could there be any harmony with in the family, community and environment? No nation can develop without the woman's well-being.

The nation's health, education, economy depend on the well-being of the woman and violation of the rights of women is a serious obstacle in the development of the nation.

I strongly feel that religious institutions and religious leaders should now speak up against such rituals and traditions, which are adverse to women's development. Is widowhood in the hands of the woman? Can she have any control on the death of her husband? When I tried to question this I was given the story of Savitri who fought with Yam and brought back her husband. Is it possible to be a Savitri?

First of all it is imperative today that religious leaders start talking about what is really in the Bible, Quran and Bhagawat Gita. The ordinary men and women on the street are greatly influenced by the discourses delivered by religious leaders. The only religious leader in the present who has spoken up against dowry, child marriage, bonded labour etc. is the Arya Samaj leader Swami Agnivesh.

Health

It is imperative that the Government and NGOs and religious leaders involve themselves in primary health care to promote activities, which empower women and thereby communities.

Religious Ashrams and Saints should now network with NGOs involved with child development and women's empowerment to promote the elimination and exploitation of children and women through unacceptable, unfair practices such as child labour, negligence of street children, genital mutilation, child pornography and sex trade.

- Working with adolescent girls, especially among marginalized ethnic groups, who bear the brunt of harmful practices, who are frequent victims of sex trade, and to whom health care services are especially unavailable, thus helping them to improve their situation through better nutrition, health care and acquisition of skills.

- Strengthening health programmes aimed at women and the girl-child, especially in the field of nutrition and essential health services.
- Working with health care institutions to develop women-friendly and, child-friendly services which meet the special needs especially reproductive health needs of women and promote and operationalise her reproductive rights by helping her to have informed choices including family planning with dignity.
- Ensure women's rights on reproductive health to take all precautions in preventing the HIV infection.

Ensure that the scientific and technological advances are not used to exploit or harm the women and children.

We all recognize that health in all its dimensions is an essential component of development, is a process which is dependent on food security, access to safe drinking water and essential health care services, all of which are ultimately dependent on political, social, cultural and spiritual ideologies.

Education

Needless to say that even today girls are deprived of education. In a developing society like ours resources are few and choices are difficult. But the question is long-term investments in education can only create the best future for everyone. According to the UNICEF's latest report for 2004 some 121 million children have no schooling. Education is not only a fundamental right but it also underpins the exercise of all other human rights? Without literacy and basic education how can someone even be aware of their rights. The gap between the education of boys and girls is tremendous. According to the UNICEF's report out of those 121 million illiterates 65 million are girls.

Yet it is through the education of girls that society's "enlightened self-interest" really comes through. For when the investment is made to educate girls, a number of significant benefits emerge. It is said that when girls are educated, they are themselves as mothers more likely to send their own children to school. When girls are educated, their families are healthier and less likely to be poor. And when girls are educated, they are less likely to be drawn into exploitive work outside the home or face sexual abuse or violence. The religious temples can open up schools of learning which would teach secular, moral, ethical education for nation building.

It is interesting to note that the Bahai religion has recognized the fact of women's education and some 90 years ago, Abdul-Baha said, "The education of women is of greater importance than the education of men, for they are the mothers of the race, and mothers rear the children. The first teachers of children are mothers. Therefore, they must be capably trained in order to educate both sons and daughters."

Religious leaders could influence the several lakhs of rural population for quality education and also provide quality education. In addition to basic literacy and arithmetic, daily instruction should include ethics education, respect for diversity, education for peace and security and global citizenship, community development and basic life skills. Quality of education is particularly important in the challenge of closing the gender gap in basic education. Girls in particular face discrimination and challenging circumstances that keep them out of school and hinder their learning effectively. It is a strange coincidence that woman is worshipped but she is not the wealth of the nation. Out of 10 illiterate people 7 are always girls.

While writing all this my mind constantly questions why is there such a large gap between women's education and men's? Why no school for girls? And why this mindset?

At this point we must look deep inside ourselves and ask what are the real barriers that prevent the advancement of women and we must examine those thousands of social, cultural issues in all religions that have traditionally and historically subjugated women and valued contributions of men the over women.

I must emphasize here that a girl merely going to school is not good enough. What girls can do with their schooling determines the attractiveness of schooling. If women cannot be employed or self-employed, own land, open a bank account, get a bank loan, if they are denied freedom to marry or not to marry, if they are deprived of political representation, education alone will have little effect on their plight. The principle of indivisibility of human rights necessitates looking at education in relation to all other rights and freedoms. Indeed it is the recognition of all other rights, or the lack thereof, that affects education.

While we talk about health and education we must also talk about property rights of women and ensuring economic rights for women especially rights in share of the capital and ensuring adequate laws are enacted and enforced. Ensuring the control of property does not cease even after the death of the husband or after separation and divorce.

Religious leaders must prevail upon the government to remove lacunae in legislations regarding issues of gender justice and to ensure that women have equal rights. They should also talk about the existing economic system where there is total control and utilization of the wealth by men.

I was very happy to read the Supreme Court's direction that upheld that a Hindu woman has a share in the agricultural ancestral property. Such judgements are indeed a ray of hope.

Discussions by religious leaders will go a long way in changing the mindset of men.

Increasingly, women are coming forward to challenge the ways in which they have been, and are being, defined by religion, culture and tradition, and to claim their right to define and interpret religious, cultural and traditional norms and practices according to their own needs and experiences. It is imperative that women play an active role in the transformation of culture, calling attention to oppressive practices and interpretations that violate their human rights.

Today, we have came a long way from the past when apart from isolated exceptions, women were regarded as an inferior breed, their nature hedged about by superstitions, denied the opportunity to express the potentialities of the human spirit and relegated to the role of serving the needs of men. Clearly, there are many societies where such conditions persist and are even fanatically defended. At the level of global discourse, however, the concept of the equality of the sexes has, for all practical purposes, now assumed the force of universally accepted principle. It enjoys similar authority in most of the academic community and information media. So basic has been the revisioning that exponents of male supremacy must look for support on the margins of responsible opinion. We must remember that still vast numbers of people continue to endure the effects of ingrained prejudices of ethnicity, gender, nation, caste and class.

2
Caste and Women

Introduction

Mahatma Gandhiji said "I cannot even conceive how one human being can feel superior by the humiliation of another". His insight into values expressed then still echoes into the 21st century.

In India the Dalit woman is humiliated and insulted everyday–every-minute—as a poor woman—as a Dalit woman and as a woman. Oppressed, discriminated and tyrannized–she is reduced to sub-human level.

The 20th century has witnessed both positive as well as negative landmarks in human society. While we have developed means to cure diseases and eliminate poverty–we have not been able to cure the mindsets of certain sections of the society. One of these negative consequences have been identified in terms of genocide, brutal attacks and denial of human rights to the indigenous population of India, the Dalits.

Many people are becoming apathetic about discrimination along caste lines–especially against the 25 per cent of Dalits of India. To be a Dalit means living in a sub-human, degraded and insecure way. Every hour two dalits are assaulted, every day three Dalit women are raped and two-dalits are killed. The period between 1990 and 1999 witnessed 35 instances of Dalit massacres in which the total number of victims were 400 and 350 being dalits.

Dalits are not only socio-cultrural group but often represent an economic class as well. Dalit women make up a large number of professional sex workers. 90 per cent of those who die of starvation and attendant diseases are dalits. Untouchability and poverty feed each other–untouchable status accentuates economic exploitation and poverty strengthens low polluting social status.

Discrimination Against Dalit Women

Factors like class, caste, religion and ethnicity affect men and women's mindset to the extent that social and cultural inequalities are accepted as a part of social ethos. It is the same mindset that accepts the misconception that gender inequality is something sanctioned by religion, tradition and social practices.

Hence when women in general face discrimination on the basis of gender, dalit women face a complex web of discrimination- the "Triple Burden" of oppression–Class, Caste and Gender-Worker, Dalit and Woman. The list of work she does is endless–midwife, bonded labourer, agricultural worker, scavenger, sweeper and she is also the untouchable who becomes touchable when she is assaulted and raped. Dalit women comprise 16 per cent of the female population in the country. Whereas women face discrimination on the *basis of gender.* Dalit women are burdened thrice over being discriminated as women, marginalized as dalits and economically deprived due to poverty. So the dalit woman faces a triple burden of oppression. Ironically she who gives birth to men is victimized by gender oppression.

Literacy Level of Dalit Women

The most effective weapon, which helped in the perpetuation of untouchability, was the institutionalized bias and denial of access to educational resources. Within dalit community the literacy, levels amongst dalit women is the lowest in the country. The national average for female and male dalit literacy is 27 per cent and 49.9 per cent respectively while the national average for non-dalits literacy is reported to be 38 per cent and 66 per cent respectively (taking an example of a state in India, Rajasthan 8.3 per cent dalit women are literate. This rate drops to 4.73 per cent in the rural areas).

Kamla entered the school with dreams in her eyes and lilt in her gait. But the lotus flower wilted under the pressure of socially sanctioned discrimination. The teacher was blind to the stars in her eyes. He could only see her as an untouchable to be shooed away from the portals of education.

Even when education is available, a child burdened by nutritional inadequacy and a domestic framework totally unfriendly for education, goes to school only as a matter of routine without imbibing or assimilating anything. Educational principals are at total variance with social reality. These children are caught in the dilemma of theory and harsh reality.

Political and Capitalistic Oppression of Dalit Women

The Constitution of India enshrines equal rights to every Indian citizen in our country. Yet untouchability continues, due to misuse of political institutions by vested interests which divides and sub-divides caste to ensure a captive vote bank.

Democratic franchise is exercised not on the basis of political ideology, not on the basis of party performance, not on the basis of individual candidates commitment to development but purely on the basis of caste. Caste overrides personal merit.

In this web of caste and politics where the instruments of power position and wealth are concentrated in the hands of socially upward castes, the dalits find it difficult to assert their political identity. This voicelessness is further emphasized when it comes to the dalit women. So the dalit women are politically marginalized both at the grassroot level and in the highest echelons of power. The relentless process of caste and economic power mows down those who do try to make a difference.

Leelavati in Madurai as the president of the lowest elected body tried to make a difference to the villagers who paid an exorbitant price to the local mafia for nature's gift–water. Can you imagine having to pay out of your meagre resources for a bucket of water everyday, every month?

Leelavati dared to dream and dared to endeavour. She strived to bring piped water to her village. There was jubilation at the gush of water in the village. Next day, Leelavati's blood gushed out-slain by the mafia-trampled for daring to make a small difference to the village life. Leelavati's murderers are still free–because they are powerful–they are wealthy–they are of a better caste.

Globalisation and liberalisation have hit the dalit women the hardest as not only are the work opportunities getting limited further, but also land reform is off the agenda. In India over 66 per cent of all female agricultural workers are dalits. Most of them are landless workers. In many areas dalit owned land has been snatched away, despite the existence of land reforms. Landless agricultural labourers work for a few kilograms of rice or Rs.15 to Rs.35 a day, well below the minimum wage prescribed in the State. In this deal the sufferers are the dalit women. There have been innumerable cases where dalit women workers have faced brutal and savage oppression in the name of caste whenever they have demanded land or wages.

No ownership of land, bonded labourers, unequal wages, caught in the web of perpetual debt, the dalit woman is never in a position to change her social and economic status. Globalisation and a patently consumeristic society have taken its toll with social consideration being pushed to the back burner due to the all-important emphasis on profitability.

Example: Dalits living in Munni Khera, village in U.P., live in an area separated from the rest of the village. 35 per cent of the villagers are upper-caste, 25 per cent are backward caste. 12 per cent are Muslims and the rest are dalits. Ramchandra, a dalit from the village was married to Ramvathi and they owned a piece of land on which they had a house. Upper caste villagers were trying to take the land from them and Ramchandra and Ramvathi had objected to this. In September 1998 Ramvathi was gang raped by five men. Rape here was a tool of tyranny–as a means of isolating her from the rest of their community as the stigma of rape can never be wiped out. The police did not lodge an FIR or help them when they returned to the village on 30th January 1999 to reclaim their property. Then seventeen men beat Ramchandra and Ramvathi with sticks and she was raped again and killed. Till date Ramchandra has not received any compensation. No justice because justice itself is blinded by caste consideration.

Many labourers owe debts to their employers or other money-lenders due to which they are in danger of becoming bonded labourers. *Statistics* reveals that 90 per cent of bonded labourers are dalits and there are innumerable cases of sexual harassment by land owners, money lenders and their hired thugs. Caste oppression is a part of present day capitalism, which relies heavily on bondage and violence, and includes non-payment of wages, sexual abuse of women, physical harassment, public humiliation and outright killing.

Dalit Women are Triply Burdened and Doubly Victimized

They are victimized by the socio-economic oppression and victimized further as they have no access to legal resources.

A case that had come to the NCW, Kali Bai and her husband had been working for 10 years and were earning Rs. 300/- for every trolley of small stones filled. Several days' toil. They were bonded to the contractor from whom they had borrowed Rs. 3,500/-.

In 1998, Kali Bai and her husband heard that another contractor in another village was offering Rs. 600/- per every trolley filled, so they went to the contractor, they were working for and asked him what they owed as they didn't want to work for him any more. The contractor alongwith three other men started beating them up. He took Rs. 9,000/- from Kali Bai's husband and started pulling at her hair and clothes. Her whole sari was removed and she was left in a blouse and a petticoat. She was dragged around the outside of her house. She ran away, embarassed at her nakedness. She ran to her sister-in-law's house and borrowed a sari. She tried to file a complaint with the police but they reflised saying that her quarrel was with the contractor not with them. The station house officer reportedly advised her to leave the village–leave her home and wealth for daring to want-daring to wish to change their economic status.

Sexual Abuse of Dalit Women

It seems there is only one democratic institution that is the institution of sex. She is untouchable as a dalit. As a sexual object she is highly touchable!!

No one practices untouchability when it comes to sex. Rape is a common phenomenon in rural areas, as a part of caste custom or village tradition. The dalit girls are forced to have sex with the village landlords. Attacks on dalit women during massacres, police raids and caste clashes are common. Dalit women are easy targets for any perpetrator because the upper caste considers them to be "sexually available" and because they are largely unprotected by the state machinery.

It was in 1996 when in Bihar (Bathanin Tola massacres) the landlords wanted to reassert thir feudal tyranny over the poor Dalits who had started becoming more vocal, by attacking the most vulnerable women and children. They sent a clear message that they would not allow any one to disturb the social structure...women were raped and hacked. The huts and small houses in which the victims took shelter were burnt down. The shrill cries failed to draw the attention of the police posted a kilometre and half away because their food came from the landlords houses. Social systems are deafened by caste considerations, the National Commission a womer had to intervene to get justice.

One survey showed that the prevalence of rape in villages contributes to the greater incidence of child marriage in those areas. Early marriages between the ages of 10 years and 16 years persists in large part because of dalits girls vulnerability to sexual assault by upper caste men, once a girl is raped she becomes untouchable in the marriage market. This also leads to high maternal and infant mortality rates in dalits. In the rural areas infant mortality is 86.7 per cent for the global population and it rises to 104.2 per cent for dalit community.

Prostitution in Dalit Women

It was our great frustration to find that in rural areas women are forced into prostitution (Devdasi system), in the name of religion. The "servants of God" as they are called can be recognized by the jewellery (in most of the places) they wear red beaded necklaces with silver and gold medallion. The *necklace* symbolizes the bondage that defines dalit *devdasi* girls whose parents have given them to local Goddesses or temples as human *offerings.* These dalit girls become sexual servants to the upper caste men in the village and priests of the temple. They become public chattel, who can be used by men free of charge. Only in this aspect do untouchables suddenly become touchable. The upper caste men would not drink from the same glass as the devdasi, but they make use of her body.

During our visit to Hubli Yellama told us that she was nine years old when her parents sold her for Rs. 200/- to an upper caste man. He gave her a saree and a blouse and paid for the alcohol at the initiation celebration. After that, she became his unpaid concubine, begging for money and breaking stones for construction sites to support herself.

Religious duty often ends up as prostitution. Many dalit women leave the village to earn money in the filthy brothels.

A new form of bonded labour is prostitution. In order to pay up their debts dalit women sell their bodies and above all the human right of choice. When in debt the dalit woman is forced to sell her only asset her body. So she leaves her home for a brothel.

Reservation for Dalits

The Constitution of India provides for "reservation" in state legislature and union legislature or Parliament, in services under the states and educational institution for dalits. But reservation is just a "bandaid" on the wound. It does not cure the wound. Dalit women have hardly benefited from the rights of reservation. Even where educated dalit women have found employment, they are insulted and demeaned in a myriad ways. Among employees, social interaction is limited. For the majority the main employment is as casual workers in the class four category of sweepers. Or they work as unskilled workers on a daily basis, construction workers, bidi workers or in the unorganised sector. Dalit women who have skills as artisans rarely benefit from government schemes, which are normally monopolized by the socially *acceptable* castes. There are no schemes for their training and upgradation and thus they are condemned to live from generation to generation within the same hated framework.

Conclusion

The Hindu religious philosophy though based on human equality is practiced in a series of inequalities. This social sanction deeply entrenched in the psyche of the upper caste Hindus, leads them to see themselves as a superior race destined to rule and the dalits as inferior race born only to serve, hence this clearly depicts that "Casteism is Racism". The basic survival of the dalits is at stake because of the Hindu's complete lack of respect for the dalit's human dignity and equality. Indeed, the violation of the dalits fundamental human rights is a daily occurrence–social cultural, economic and political.

The social structure of India is stratified with inbuilt inequalities and injustices based on the caste system sanctified by Hinduism. The dalits form the inner core of poverty, which is birth ascribed. They have been excluded from the caste system (social hierarchy) hence *out-castes* declared ritually unclean, hence *untouchables* and pushed out for fear of pollution to live on the outskirts of villages hence "segregated". The worst affected in this discrimination are the dalit women as they face discrimination at every step. The dalits had only one medicine and that was "Hope" for a better living but hope is a good breakfast but a bad supper and the stage has been reached where the light of hope they had, is dying out. They have been oppressed to the level where they now need a ray of hope and I think, we can kindle that hope and help the dalit women to search for the solution of their difficulties.

The mission statement of the NGO forum of the Durban Conference on Racism in August 2001 were as follows:

- *Expectation:* We aspire to a world in which every human being can live safely and with full human dignity, a world in which we can see happiness in the face of every child.
- *Respect:* Transformation within ourselves will enable us to positively influence communities we live in, in order to bring about tolerance, respect and appreciation.
- *Discrimination:* We commit ourselves to the universal struggle against racism and all forms of discrimination.
- *Oppression:* We will struggle for mechanisms to address historical injustices such as slavery and colonialism, and strive for a world in which relations between nations and peoples are based on equality and justice.

At the Durban Conference there were about five thousand delegates at the NGO Conference. The dalit caucus was very very active and highlighted their plight on every occasion. Activists representing the dalits had won the first battle of a war against the social system which affects nearly 240 million people in India and the SAARC region when they were able to place the issue of caste on the agenda of the third day NGO Conference. It was shocking and shameful to hear the Indian government represented by Mr. Omar Abdullah, Minister of State for External Affairs say, "In the run up to the World Conference, there has been propaganda, highly exaggerated and misleading, often based on anecdotal evidence, regarding caste based discrimination in India".

Having worked in the field of grassroot empowerment of women, I have been witness to atrocities against dalits and caste based discrimination all over India. How can it be "anecdotal evidence" when I as chairperson of the National Commission for Women saw several incidents each day throughout my three years tenure.

Although the Bhopal Declaration has spelt out a 21-point agenda we wonder how many of these would really get implemented.

- Is it possible to implement free compulsory education for all dalits?
- Recognize the SC/ST women as a distinct category and accordingly make segregated data available in the census.

Let us just take the basic question. Is it possible to stop discrimination? Only then we can truthfully answer these questions. Will we be able to wipe out the power and prejudice scenario in the country.

3

Dalits: Slavery in the 21st Century

Even after five decades of promises and provisions in the constitution, discrimination and disassociation with the dalits has not been curbed. Where have we gone wrong? In the 21st century we still hear of cases of atrocities faced by dalits, for example, in the pioneer recently there was a article where a dalit women's hand had been cut-off after she refused to withdraw a rape complaint filed by her. Thus, a lot needs to be done to improve the condition of Dalits in India. The following are the key areas, which we need to focus on:

1. Education

When I say education, I mean educating the upper class. I do not want to throw the onus of getting educated to the discriminated class. I personally feel that the moment the higher caste gets educated, things will automatically improve.

How is it that is these 57 years the literacy rate amongst dalit women is just 23 per cent whereas the literacy rate among the upper class in nearly 46 per cent . This illiteracy rate has far reaching consequences because it makes them susceptible to superstitious beliefs and misinformation. Their fertility rate is also higher than non-scheduled caste women.

2. Livelihood and Basic Amenities

Secondly, till today dalit is deprived of land rights and right to livelihood. They are deprived of knowledge, by way of science and technology. They do not have adequate infrastructure and have very little say in industry and science. Even today they live in secluded areas, deprived of basic amenities such as electricity, sanitation and safe drinking water. The statistic go to show that only 31 per cent of Dalit households are equipped with electricity, as compared to 61 per cent of non-dalit households. It is ironical, but only 10 per cent of SC households and 27 per cent of non-scheduled caste households have sanitation. Dalits are deliberately excluded from such basic amenities. The very fact that we wanted dalits to be elected in the panchayats was to see that all dalits are included in those basic facilities, as it has been seen that the upper caste section of a village has electricity, sanitation and safe drinking water but the neighbouring dailt colony is neglected. The global economic forces had not helped to improve the situation of the large number of dalits living below the poverty line. This globalization has pushed the percentage of dalits even further down in the last few years.

3. Gender Equality

During my tour of the length and breadth of India and the many public hearings, I came face to face with thousands of dalit women who were twice discriminated. One, because they were dalits and two because they were dalit women. Most cases that came to us at the National Commission for Women were extreme forms of violence, discrimination and exploitation at the hands of the upper class. The victims who came with incidence of rape appalled me and of course Bhawri Devi's case is well-known all over.

It is women who bear the brunt of violence and brutality, mutilation and molestation and I need not go into the several incidents of disrobing. The coal community of Chitrakut work as bonded labour to the thakurs for a meager fist-full of rise. In spite of our several protests and public hearings this still goes on. An average of two women are raped per day and this figure does not indicate the thousands of other cases that go unreported either due to fear, intimidation by police and ignorance of the procedure.

In the unorganized sector, 90 per cent of dailt women participate in some sort of productive activity outside their home. 82 per cent of all women work in agriculture where they get low wages, irregular work and no social security. Their children grow up on the streets, as there is no maternity leave, no support services by way of crèches and untold sexual harassment.

I am happy that UPA government is planning to introduce the unorganized sector workers social security bill, which at least in law would take care of the discrimination, After the law is passed, I hope adequate measures will be taken to implement it. It is a sad reflection that there is a identity crisis for a dalit women, as she is a victim of caste and gender. Hnece the cause of discrimination needs immediate attention and I will even so far suggest a separate wing of the National Commission for Women just to look into the grievances of the dalit women.

4. Right to Employment

Since centuries the dalits have continued in the same profession as their forefathers, thus perpetuating the discrimination against them. No human being in the 21st century with globalization and nuclearization should be doing manual scavenging. It is a shame on our national pride that even today 8 lakh dalits carry human excreta for a mere Rs. 50 a month. Untouchability exists in various forms all over India. In such a scenario, what is the use of reservation in employment? The elite are still in control of appointments and half the reserved seats remain vacant. Of the total SC reservation quota in the Central Government 54 per cent remain unfilled, and more than 88 per cent in public sector, and 45 per cent in banks remains unfilled

Now what are the solutions? I hope that future meetings throw some light on the solutions with respect to right of education, right of livelihood, right of gender equality and right to employment.

4
Reinterpretation of Tradition

We have been working in a small way with the trials and tribulations of the sisters from the Muslim tradition in the militancy affected areas of Kashmir, riot affected areas of Gujarat and various states where the status of Muslim women is equal to non-existence. Deprived of education, health, nutrition and access to information and technology they are last to be recognized or participate in any of the activities.

India is not a theoretical country. It is a secular country, it is a secular state where every tradition has ample chance of expression, growth through personal laws pertaining to all religions is allowed. However there cannot be a separate judicial system, a separate court and verdict in isolation to the law of the land.

I still remember that is my college Isabella Thoburn College, at the Lucknow University, I had a large percentage of fellow students from the Muslim community who have made a mark as writers, scholars, authors and even bureaucrats. Today after 40 year when I ask my granddaughter how many of her classmates are of the Muslim tradition the numbers seem to be dwindling. If that be the case and girls are not sent to schools how can we dream of a just and gender sensitive society?

Since the past few years we have heard of their deprivation through such pronouncements like "Imrana who is raped should become her husband's mother by marrying her father-in-law". Then there was a case of Gudia who had assumed that her husband was killed or missing in the war. A young bride Gudia got remarried only to be surprised one fine day after a few years when her child was two years old, when her first husband who was supposed to be dead or missing appears suddenly. And imagine what was the clerical decision? She should give up the husband with whom she had a baby and return to the missing husband! Then there is a case of a brave Muslim woman whose husband died in the Kargil operation. Her pension, compensation, etc., I was claimed by her in-laws in the name of the Shariat and since the past four years she is in abject penury and there are many more incidents like this.

Now the latest Fatwa from Darululum a place from where freedom fighters came including Maulana Madni, once upon a time a progressive school again wanting to push back women in the 13th century! All women in India should unite and seek justice wherever, whenever they face such gender discrimination.

And what does Darululum Say?

1. That Muslim women should not participate in democracy. How will they ever raise issues if they never enter the policy-making body?
2. That Purdah would be mandatory for them.

How are they going to face the electorate? What is the meaning of our Constitution, which gives equal rights to men and women?

However, I am happy to note that there are progressive groups. Also women who have for the first time in Indian History constructed a mosque exclusively for Muslim women. Then there are groups of women who are becoming Maulvis and progressive women who are participating in our democracy even at the highest level. It will a shame if we let the Muslim women lag behind and not be equal citizens along with the rest of the country.

A time has come when we really need to sit down and think of the all round development, empowerment of women, irrespective of their colour, caste and religion.

We need debates and deliberations on the status of Muslim women and awareness building programme of what the Quran actually says.

5
The Sacred Fire

Fire, Fire, Fire... the most sacred witness to marriage vows, the radiance of fire, on the brides face beaming with happiness for a long happy married life. A few days or months from the date of going around the fire the bride is engulfed in the same fire. Why, why, why? Fire the very witness of the marriage vows takes away her life and a home meant for peace and happiness becomes the most dangerous place for her to live in.

Is marriage a dangerous institution? It is the most celebrated event of one's life. Is it too much to ask from a marriage a piece of paper, that is a marriage certificate?

In India any amount of laws will be meaningless if the social attitude for subjugation of the girl is not removed. Recently Mr. Rajeev Dhavan wrote in the *Hindu* "Nisha's case reflects the unreal existence of laws in our society. Laws exist only on paper, and have little meaning for those for whom they are made. They are as fickle as society wants them to be. Laws are mobilized by people. Only the organised well off can play the legal game. But for the rest, "law" is a chimera and litigation a devious evil which corrupts the soul, batters the mind, empties the pocket and destroys the married life of ordinary people. This is why Anuparna's father ran away from the law to the panchayat".

What he says is most apt because till such time that we change the social fabric of the society the evil of dowry would survive in a greedy consumer and commoditised society where girls are battered and harassed and even killed for a motor cycle or a car.

Neeta, Sunita, Rita, Fauzia each day there would be innumerable young girls who would walk into my office, two months, three months or years and years after marriage. Crying over the bigamous nature of man, dowry demand, maintenance, property rights and innumerable such cases which disturb the family equilibrium.

I would like to relate the tragic incidents of four minor girls who were married to much older men only to be sold to the brothel keeper later. If only there was compulsory registration of marriages these little girls would not have been married before 18 years and also would have had a legal marriage certificate and thereby not been sold.

Matrimonial relations are part of the way society organizes and regulates itself. This is true for all civil society regardless of the religion of the parties. Therefore, there should be one law to govern the status of matrimony.

Most of the problems that arise in matrimonial relationship are universal. They may additionally be culture specific, which is not necessarily specific to the religion of the parties. It is important to find the common thread running through this most universal legal relationship and deal with it within the Civil Law.

It is necessary to give emphasis to the fact that rights and duties within matrimony are part of one's civil rights and duties and subject to the overall law of the land, especially the Constitution of India. It is therefore necessary to have one law of marriage for all of India.

It is necessary to avoid confusion about the basic prerequisites of a legally valid marriage and its consequent status, regardless of the religion, caste and customs of the two parties.

In order to avoid confusion amongst administrators of law and justice about the prerequisites of marriage and divorce. It is important to have one marriage law.

Ms. Devi was married to Selvam 18 years ago. Her husband works in the Airways. In these 18 years she has had three children. Daughter 12 years who lives with her aunt in Tamil Nadu, Son 16 years who lives with her and Devi works as a domestic servant and lives in a servant quarter. Each day was a day of agony for Devi. Her husband who was a severe drug addict would waste all his money on liquor and torture Devi day in and day out for bringing in material wealth. Devi's sister-in-law who was also living in Delhi would also torture, abuse Devi on a regular basis. She knew that being a Catholic she could not ask for divorce. Is the girl to undergo torture day in and day out and not to be in a position to divorce her husband? If the Church could protect Devi, it was a different matter. Devi tolerated it for 18 long years just to maintain peace for herself and her parents and to be within the limits of community norm. But enough was enough. She came one day to our Family Counselling Centre in Guild of Service and made an official complaint about the dowry demand.

It is therefore necessary to have one clear law on marriage and divorce.

After hearing these thousands of cases we at the National Commission for Women recommended compulsory registration of Marriage Bill 1994. This was a result of wide consultation and deliberation. We were hoping that this bill and our recommendations would change many lacunas in the laws that existed and would get the immediate attention of the government to place them in the Parliament as bills. The National Commission for Women constituted a number of expert committees to review laws and also had countrywide discussions for several problems that needed urgent attention. One such important recommendation that emerged was the compulsory registration of marriages. It is sad that these recommendations are buried in the shelves of the ministry and getting cobwebs.

After a great deal of debate and discussions we identified certain concrete advantages for the compulsory registration of marriages.

(i) Certificate of marriage is a Government document, which provides valuable evidence of marriage;

(ii) Certificate of marriage is a government document providing social security, self-confidence particularly among married women;

(iii) Certificate of marriage is useful while accompanying wife/husband to foreign country;

(iv) If a person dies without nomination for bank deposit or life insurance policy etc. It will be useful to get such money in the name of husband/wife.

(v) Registration would prevent child marriages and thereby prevent sale of girls and trafficking.

(vi) Men would be afraid to have bigamous relationships as a certificate would safeguard the girl.

What is compulsory registration of marriage? It is ironic that in our country we register births, we register deaths but we seldom see the necessity of registering marriages. A very important event of ones life. Marriages must be registered and

- Provision to extend it for the entire country.
- It applies to all marriages performed in India and to all persons irrespective of race, religion, caste or creed of the parties.
- It shall come into force immediately on the expiry of three months from the date of assent of the bill by the President.
- That if these recommendations become an Act it shall have overriding effect on all other laws in force and all such laws shall cease to have effect insofar as they are inconsistent with the provisions contained in this Act.
- Laws in force would mean "to include all customs or usages having the force of law".

Then we went ahead to stipulate certain conditions for such marriages:

A marriage may be performed between any person of the male sex and any person of the female sex, if the following conditions are fulfilled at the time of marriage, namely:

(a) Such person, in the case of a male, has completed the age of 21 years, and in the case of female, has completed the age of 18 years.

(b) Neither party has a spouse living.

(c) The parties to the marriage do not fall within the degrees of prohibited relationship.

(d) Both the parties have consented to the marriage:

Registration of marriage could be before or after a marriage that is solemnized provided that they fulfilled the following conditions:

- a ceremony of marriage has been performed between the parties and they have been living together as husband and wife ever since;
- neither party has at the time of registration more than one spouse living;

- neither party is an idiot or a lunatic at the time of registration;
- the parties have completed the age of twenty-one years at the time of registration;
- the parties are not within the degrees of prohibited relationship.

Registration of marriages makes it very easy for the couples to go to a court without incurring any expenses, which are usually involved in marriages in India. Some of the provisions that we brought about in the bill were as follows:

(1) The Marriage Officer for any geographical area, for the purpose of this Act, shall be the person competent to make entries in the Register of Births and Deaths for that area or such other person as may be designated as Marriage Officer for that area by the State Government.

(2) There shall be a District Registrar of Marriages for every district who may be such officer as may be appointed by the State Government or, in the absence of such appointment, the District Registrar of Assurances.

(3) The duties of a Marriage Officer shall be those which he is required to perform under this Act and the rules made thereunder.

(4) The Marriage Officer shall forward to the District Registrar of Marriages copies of the entries in the Marriage Register, in duplicate and one set of all such returns arranged area-wise shall be kept as permanent record in the custody of the District Registrar of Marriage.

(5) The Marriage Officer may within two months of the making of any entry in the Marriage Register correct any error, which may have crept into such entry provided that no such correction shall be made unless the parties to the marriage or their legal representatives have been given a reasonable opportunity of being heard. Copies of the corrected entry shall be communicated to the District Registrar of Marriage and dealt with in the manner specified in sub-section. We had hoped that at the village level the Panchayat Samiti would be a Registration Office to make is easy for the couples to have access to the Registration.

We found that through this process of registration it was easy to deal with the issues of maintenance, residents of spouses etc.

Is it not time that we in the civil society really think about getting our daughters, sisters married under the compulsory registration? The time has now come to have this very important event in one's life, which affects each and every family in the country registered and thereby save a lot of problems.

The Hindu Marriage Act of 1954 makes a provision for registration of marriages, but it also makes the provision that the validity of marriage is in no way affected by non-registration. Non-registration of marriages affect women the most because they are the victims of bigamous, polygamous relationships, and property disputes. Moreover marriages involving under-aged girls are rampant in those states where registration of marriages is not compulsory.

Some of the broad recommendations to prevent atrocities of women and to curb the evil of dowry were:

Recommendations

- One of the main recommendations was to have a dowry prohibition officer in every district and also to link up the sarpanch of a panchayat to see and bring about a change in society. (However, these recommendations although are on paper, in reality there were no dowry prohibition officers).
- We had asked for compulsory registration of marriages, which would automatically while registering the marriages, also register the articles that are given as gifts to the daughter. This would also make it possible at a later stage if there were a divorce to retrieve those articles. This registration of "Streedhan" was a safeguard.
- We recommended equal property rights in the natal home. Needless to say that equal property rights to women would go a long way in bringing down the crime of dowry. If the girl inherits property then violence against women will come down, dowry demand will be lessened and the girl would have more safety.
- Sections 2, 3, 4, 7, 8 and 8A of the Dowry Prohibition Act may be suitably brought into the Indian Penal Code, Criminal Procedure Code and the India Evidence Act.

- Under the Indian Penal Code a new Section 498B shall be inserted providing for a stringent punishment of not less than 5 years and which may extend to 10 years for those whoever takes directly or indirectly or participates in the negotiation or otherwise the taking of dowry.
- Dowry Prohibition Offiers (Section 8B) —The Commission has recommended for the appointment of Dowry Prohibition Officers in every district/village with suitable powers. Have special cells of women police officers as heads for investigations on dowry murder.
- It is also proposed that marriage expenses in no cases should exceed 20 per cent of the annual income of bride's parents or guardians.
- Publicity to be given to the provisions of the Dowry Prohibition Act.
- The Dowry Prohibition Officers so appointed will conduct periodically discussions with various groups like NGO's, police officials etc. within their jurisdiction.
- Arrange for audio visual presentation about the evils of dowry system and the benefits flowing from the complete eradication of the dowry.
- Every Prohibition Officer shall maintain a list of marriages held or to be held within his jurisdiction and shall ascertain and confirm by suitable means whether the provisions of the Act are or are not being contravened.
- The giver of dowry should be exempted from punishment.
- Advisory boards to be appointed to supervise and guide the prohibition officers and other officials.
- Involve panchayat head for premarriage settlements.
- Have jail adalats to dispose of cases registered under Section 498A so that speedy justice is given and families languishing in prison can be settled.

The High Court of Delhi has come out with the judgement that dowry law needs to be reviewed. We have to take a holistic approach when we talk about crimes against women. The marriage law, dowry law, divorce law, property rights, maintenance and child custody have to be looked at with an integrated approach.

After 50 years of independence we are still struggling with gender equality. I am glad a few girls have taken at least courage to call off their marriages in protest against dowry. It is Nisha, Vidya, Farzana of today who are going to change the patriarchal social order, which constitutes the mainstream of the model family of India. Today, it is not surprising that much of the violence women suffer are executed within the framework of marriage. The crime statistics of India show that within the family the primary unit responsible for maintaining the social order, crimes have increased so much that there is a bill pending in the Parliament to curb domestic violence.

In the process of socialization, violence is a means by which discipline is enforced and values instilled. In addition to this, self-effecting subservient attitudes are enforced through strictly prescribed norms and moral prescripts of 'good' behaviour. For the Hindus, it is best summed up within the parameters of Manu's Code, which continues to form the basis for laws governing Hindu women. Ironically the upper-caste norms are being emulated by others. These notions of subservience and seclusion prepare the ground for acceptance of subordination, within the family and outside. Thus, non-acceptance of these norms by a daughter-in-law would itself be seen as an act of 'defiance' by a society which has for decades now put up with bride-burning on account of a daughter-in-law bringing insufficient dowry. Wife-beating and abuse are imbibed by young males as inherited forms of consciousness/behaviour, along with other notions of macho image. Internalisation of such forms of consciousness are a major factor for a large mass of women still accepting these without any complaints and for crimes executed within the family still largely unreported.

In order to get this malignant disease out from within the society, we have to work together—the judiciary, the NGOs, the police, lawyers and National Commission for Women. Attitudinal change has to be brought out and last but not the least gender disparities removed from the cradle itself. Let us hope that we will find the prescription for this cancer.

6

Marital Counselling

Summer, winter, spring or the monsoons throughout the quest for happiness goes on and on. Love radiates through all seasons and comes to a standstill when we suddenly hear "Maam I love my husband but I am not happy". "Life seems a burden", we hear this time and again from couples struggling to fix up a marriage that has taken a wrong turn. In the days gone by the support structure by way of aunts, uncles, sister, sister-in-law were very strong. Today those structures are weakening and being replaced partially by counselling centres.

Of course marriage has been and will always be a partnership of compromise, give and take, and adjustments. Fortunately the majority of the couples who come to us, we find that their marriages are repairable even when they have become very uncomfortable for one or both partners.

Marriage counselling is an educational experience that emphasizes self-exploration, self-revelation, and the acquisition of interactive skills, which promote mutual understanding, recognition, and appreciation of your partner. Other goals include learning, developing, and practicing techniques for constructive communication and conflict-resolution for long-term marital harmony. This approach equips you and your partner with lifetime tools that will enable you to honestly and effectively confront and resolve whatever problems may arise in the future.

What is counselling? I find that counselling is a series of solutions oriented conversation based on clear rational psychological principles and methods.

Our goal is to help you recapture the love, romance, and mutual goodwill that characterized your relationship at its height — at a mature and sophisticated level. Apart from the above interaction with us to facilitate a change in the behaviour of the client to enhance the coping skills and to improve the relationships.

It often happens that people choose partners with whom they are generally compatible. However, as the marriage matures and children and other life cycle events interrupt the relationship and problems arise. When couples come to our Family Counselling Centre we always assume that the marriage is viable and counsel both the partners regarding their problems and relationship.

A Counsellor should have the ability of forming an instant rapport with the client, must have some personal warmth and good sense of humour. Counsellor should understand the client and develop the healthy relationship without getting entangled emotionally with the client.

The Counsellor's listening skills are most important. She has to make suggestions and draw out the person to talk and lessen the anxiety of the client.

In relationship counselling, for married and premarital couples, we help people who chronically fight or argue futility, withdraw during arguments, or have stopped communicating altogether. We deal with a wide variety of problems including alienation, diminished affection, loss of intimacy, and lack of togetherness. We help couples tackle longstanding nagging problems, including in-laws, sex, roles, responsibility, commitment, and money, as well as crisis situations such as infidelity or threat of separation or divorce. We are also very experienced with, and sensitive to, issues that involve differences in religion, race, ethnicity, culture, values, lack of respect, and anger management.

Marital therapy can take a variety of forms. Frequently, one partner comes to us seeking help with depression or anxiety and eventually it comes up in therapy that one of the reasons for the emotional distress is an uneasy marital situation. Other times, one partner phones the office, hoping we can help to convince the spouse to enter marital therapy. Thankfully, there are also those situations when both partners realize that there is a problem and agree to enter treatment together from the start. Either way, once treatment with both partners has begun, most of the couples, we see are able to resolve their problems and create a strong relationship, often better than it has ever been.

People often ask whether we believe their marriage can be fixed. There is obviously no easy answer, but we have found that as long as both partners are willing to work at the relationship, the vast majority of the couples we see stay together and report that the relationship is still healthy at follow-up visits. Another frequently asked question is how long treatment will take. Again, there is no easy answer, but with two people involved, the modal length of treatment is six months. Few couples take longer to complete treatment, but many need less time. Yet another question we hear is "Can you help me to fix my marriage if my partner refuses to come to treatment?" While technically this is possible, our observation has been that when only one partner enters treatment, even though he or she is working hard to change destructive or dysfunctional behaviours, the relationship may improve, but most often does not stabilize. It takes two to create a good relationship. There is one question that is easy to answer. "Is it all my fault?" No. Just as it takes two people to create a good marriage, it takes two people to create a bad one. While one person may have a more obvious problem, such as an affair or anger or depression, there are issues involving each partner that will be dealt with in therapy to ensure that the new, improved relationship avoids the pitfalls the old one fell into. And finally, the question, "Do you deal with affairs?" One of the guiding philosophies of the centre in doing marital work is that problems are relationship problems. While an affair is a significant breach of trust within the relationship, there are most often other problems within the marriage which also need to be explored. Given time and effort by both partners, even the affair can be overcome. We have seen couples get over an affair and leave treatment with a healthy relationship.

There are many types of counselling. We deal with personal counselling where we talk to the individual who is having several emotional difficulties like grief, depression, anger, anxiety, low self-esteem, social skill deficiencies. Personal counselling is generally conducted in one-to-one relationship with the counsellor.

Then, we have Marital Counselling where we give help to couples dealing with such issues as role definition; communications breakdowns; loss of significance, motivation or trust; poor sexual adjustment or dysfunction; traumatic events or marriage breakup. A husband and wife counselling team is available for marital counselling, if desired.

Family Counselling Centre: We also counsel the whole family to restore confidence and bring out the harmony in the family itself. We focus on all the family members for an interaction.

***Religious Counselling*:** It focuses on any or all of the above areas, with emphasis on and sensitivity to issues related specifically to the mission field (e.g., cultural, social and interpersonal areas). Religious counselling may be conducted on a personal basis or in a group, and is an appropriate tool for pre-field assessment as well as post-field debriefing.

7

Threat to Women

The Times of India on 26th December 2003 once again brought out the vulnerability of women. I quote "Shocked at the acquittal of rape accused by a high court on the grounds that the victim had already lost her virginity and that she did not have any injury marks, the Supreme Court has asked the judiciary to be conscious of the fact the rapist is on trial and not the victim.

An unmerited acquittal encourages wolves in the society, more so when the victims are helpless females or minor children. A Bench of Justice Doraiswamy Raju and Arijit Pasayat said while, sentencing one Ram Dev Singh to seven years imprisonment for raping his maid servant 18 years ago."

It is heartening to note that the apex court said a rape victim stands on a higher pedestal than other victims as she is injured both psychologically and emotionally. The apex court also categorically mentioned that the case of rape does not depend on the victim's sexual behaviour but on the plea that license cannot be given to any man to commit rape whatever her character be.

Cases of goondaism, eve-teasing, molestation and sexual harassment against women are increasing every day. Public transport, cinema houses, markets, railway stations, bus stops, places around schools, Colleges and places of worship are no longer safe and have become dens of anti-social elements. Although policemen are posted in the vicinity of all these places, yet they choose to be silent spectators and shy away from facing the anti-social elements. People, in general are also afraid of coming forward to help women victims.

Even if the matter is reported to the police, they are not helpful and harass the women victims. The police after all come from the same society and their mindset is attuned to societal norms.

On the other hand working conditions of women have undergone many changes in the recent past. They have to move at odd hours for the discharge of their official, social and domestic chores. Public transport, auto rickshaws and taxis are not at all safe. Women are harassed, raped and murdered within their homes and outside.

What is Sexual Abuse?

Sexual abuse is verbal or physical behaviour by one person (perpetrator) towards another person, which is considered in their culture to be quite significantly upsetting, demeaning, harmful and/or traumatic. The abuse can be verbal abuse, psychological abuse, physical abuse, spouse abuse, elder abuse, child abuse or baby battering. Generally the perpetrators are men and the victims are women or children.

Sexual Abuse of Girls—1. Winking or whistling at a girl or eve teasing. 2. Talking in obscene language to a girl on the phone. 3. Exposing genitals in the presence of a girl (exhibitionism). 4. Writing obscene letters to a girl. 5. To show naked pictures or to make gestures suggestive of sexual intercourse. 6. Pinching the cheeks or breasts, pinching her buttocks or genitals, pressing his penis to her body in a crowded situation. 7. Keeping his hand on the shoulder of a woman, or trying to observe her breasts. 8. Kissing or embracing her against her will. 9 Female circumcision. 10. Rape. 11. Any act of gender based sexual violence.

Sexual Abuse of Children—The perpetrator is generally an adult or a significantly older child. 1. Touching or fondling the genitals of a child. 2. Asking the child to fondle the genitals of an adult. 3. Exposure of genitals in the presence of a child. 4. Showing pornographic pictures to a child or using a child for making such pictures. 5. Having sexual act with a child (anal, genital or oral sex).

Sexual abuse is not uncommon. Many such instances are not reported for the sake of preserving the honour of the family and preventing shame. Therefore, they do not come to the surface. Over 15 to 30 per cent of girls are seriously abused or raped. Over 85 per cent of perpetrators are from amongst the family members, neighbours or acquaintances.

- Total rape cases registered in Delhi till November 30, 2003: 448.

- Conviction rate in 2003: 24 per cent—A study conducted by the Delhi Police reveals that most rapist in the Capital belong to the 18-35 age group and are from the lower socio-economic strata.
- 87 per cent of assailants are class 10 dropouts.
- 95 per cent of assailants are known to the victims.
- Effects of Sexual Abuse Apart from the preponderant effects of sadness, anger, helplessness and distrust of men, sexually abused girls have been found to be prone to a variety of psychological and behavioural disturbances caused by the trauma of abuse. These could be bed wetting, nightmares, sleep disorders, depression, anxiety, extreme inhibition, low self-esteem caused by a sense of guilt and shame, and other multiple personality disorders. The situation worsens if the girl becomes pregnant or gets STD/HIV infection. When she grows into a woman, she may show adult sexual dysfunctions like frigidity, vaginismus or absence of orgasm. The victims invariably tend to hide the sexual abuse from their parents thinking it to be their own fault for which their parents would get angry. On the other hand, whenever the children or the adolescents boldly tell such instances to their parents, they (parents) do not believe them, especially when the perpetrators are close relatives. In fact, many parents and teachers do not believe that the sexual abuse exists. Parents also feel that it cannot happen to their daughter(s).

Studies indicate that one in every four girls is sexually abused before the age of 18 years. Children even 11 months old are known to have been sexually assaulted. From the police records of 1992, it has been found in Delhi that 54 per cent of rape victims were found to be below 15 years of age, and in 80 per cent of these cases, the rapist was known to the victim (now, called the survivor). In several sex scandals in Maharashtra, the girls were raped, photographed and blackmailed. The girls feared to disclose the sexual abuse to their parents and therefore underwent further sexual abuse. Sexual abuse of any form is an offence. There is provision for punishment and or fine under several sections of Criminal Procedure Code. Hence such instances should be promptly reported to the police.

How to Avoid Sexual Abuse? This is a difficult question to answer though several suggestions have been made by the experts.

This can never be foolproof. Safety tips: (a) "Your body is yours" (the right to privacy).–Nobody has got the right to touch you if you don't want to be touched. If somebody is bothering you, no matter who that person is, you have the right to stop him and tell the trusted adult (e.g., mother), (b) Do not talk to strangers or go out with them. You have the right to say 'No' to adults, not answer their questions, and scream for help if you feel you are in danger, (c) "Find a grown up who listens to you." If some one bothers you, hurts you, or scares you, find a grown up who will listen to you, and tell him/her what happened, (d) "Trust your instincts." —If you get a feeling that something is wrong, you have the right to get away.—Be alert to your surroundings. If you think some one is following you, you can cross the street, change your route, run away, or go to a store or a restaurant, (e) "Know your neighbourhood."—Know where the police department is located or the stores and restaurants where you could go for help, when necessary, (f) "You have the right to get help." - Think about the adults who can help and the adults who will listen to you. (1) At home, at college or, at workplace if any man tries to make sexual advances, be strict right from the beginning and tell him that you do not like it. Run away from him or, at once, shout for help. (2) Anonymous obscene telephone calls fall under non-cognizable offence under the Section 115(2) of Criminal Procedure Code. When such calls are received regularly, a written complaint may be lodged with the police who will inform MTNL to trace the call. You can also complain in writing to Divisional Engineer in charge of your exchange, who can trace the caller and take the necessary action. If the perpetrator continues to make obscene calls, his telephone will be disconnected under Rule 427 of Indian Telegraphic Act. (3) The mother should not leave the custody of the girl to a single man. The person may be trustworthy, but his sexuality may not be. (4) The mother should establish a good communication and friendly relations with her daughter, so that she is free enough to disclose her love affair, or sexual abuse. The parents should make her feel that she will be loved and supported in any circumstances. Many girls do not inform their mother sexual abuse of because they feel that it is their fault too, and that the mother would scold them for the same. (5) Boys and girls should be given sexuality education so that the girls will be able to protect themselves against the possibility of rape by learning self-defence, by assessing the situation that may be dangerous and by assertiveness skills. The boys too will learn that sexual abuse is a punishable crime, and will realize their responsibilities and will refrain from sexually abusing the girls.

Rape is a forced sexual intercourse with any woman against her will, without her consent, or with her consent when the consent has been obtained by putting her in fear of death or hurt or under the influence of drugs.

Rape is a serious crime and any woman is at risk of getting raped whether young or old. The effects of rape are very many and severely traumatic. Nightmares, insomnia, loss of appetite, extreme fear, anxiety, anger, loss of trust, phobias, sexual problems, feeling of worthlessness, feeling unsafe are some of the common reactions of rape. In society, there is a tendency to blame the survivor (victim) rather than the perpetrator. The survivors of sexual assault need reassurance and encouragement from someone close; assurance that she is still loved and accepted and that she is not a criminal. It is the rapist who has committed a crime and not she. In many circumstances, it is hard to prevent rape.

Again I quote from the *Times of India* on 26th December 2003 regarding setting up of special courts where women judges will try rape cases. This brings a new dimension to the whole legal system.

Little Tinku was raped by the bus conductor after the other children were dropped by the school bus. It was a trauma for the 4 year old girl to recount minute details of the incident in front of a male Judge. A motherly female Judge could have understood the trauma. With the setting up of special courts a very humane system could be expected. Only a woman understands what another woman suffers.

We are all aware that the conviction rate is very low and if we have women Judges one can hope that enquiry into rape cases and the conviction rate will improve.

Some guidelines of rape prevention adopted from "New York City Advisory Task Force on Rape" are mentioned below:

1. Be aware of your environment at all times.
2. Trust your instincts when they tell you, danger is here.
3. Don't even be afraid or embarrassed to make a scene or draw attention to yourself if someone is threatening you.

4. Be especially alert when you are sick or tired or have taken alcohol.
5. Have a positive mental attitude, "I can succeed, I am strong and powerful."
6. Be aware of your rights: "I have a right to say 'No'. I do not have to follow another person's orders. I have a right to be where I want with to be without harassment."
7. Be aware of the dangerous places in your life. Think about your options at home, on the street, at work, at play. Where could you go for help? Would some one be near enough to hear your scream?
8. Be alert in badly lit areas, in elevators, with groups of people you don't know well. Don't be afraid to change your plans or your directions if you sense danger. Being rude is better than getting raped.
9. Public restrooms should be used with caution. It is best to have someone to accompany you.
10. Never accept a ride from a stranger.
11. Young people should tell their parents where they are going, with whom they will be and when, they will return getting home, they should call and let parents know that they bn detained.
12. Shortcuts through deserted areas, vacant lots or abandoned buildings should be avoided. Walk to and from the school/ college with friends if possible.
13. Discuss with parents any incident, which is disturbing or confusing, even if it seems embarrassing.
14. Parents should exercise care in selection of baby-sitters. Baby-sitters should also know something about the families for whom they baby-sit.

Women particularly need to be aware of situations that may lead to violent sex and of people who may put them in those situations. They also need to learn ways of avoiding or dealing with pressures and threats to have sex. Here are certain tips given in the "School Health Education Programme" prepared by WHO and UNESCO in 1994. — SBE assertive. — Avoid lonely spots. — Do not go to any person's room if no one is at home. — Do not accept money or presents from people not known to you. — When someone suggests having sex and you don't want to, leave with a friend, move to where there are other people or phone someone if phones are available. When someone becomes physical and tries to force you to have sex, scream; fight; kick in the testicles if you can; get away quickly; delay; bargain depending on the situation (if your life is threatened or a weapon is used).

Self-Defence Education is a Must for Women

Self-defence education addresses the pervasiveness of sexual violence in at least two ways: through awareness and fighting back. The first step in defending yourself is becoming aware of your surroundings, both physically and politically. One of the first things taught is how to present yourself as a "hard target" —making yourself appear confident and aware, in spite of how you may actually be feeling. This education signifies confidence in several ways, such as looking straight ahead rather than at the ground, standing up straight rather than letting your body collapse in on itself, and walking with purpose. Confidence means you project yourself in that way to people. You look confident, yet you may feel everything but confident. Making yourself look confident often makes you more aware of the space you inhabit, and the people inhabiting it with you.

Being politically aware of sexual violence means taking a critical look at the responses to such violence. We are constantly presented with images and narratives of sexual violence that portray women as passive victims. Rarely are we presented with images of women fighting back. The threat of sexual violence has created a climate of fear. Even my highly-educated women friends, whom you would expect to be critical of popular representations of sexual violence, question women's ability to fight back in assault situations. These women know what violence is, and they are aware of its systemic nature. Despite their understandings of the pervasivenes of vidence they refuse to believe that self-defence offers a way to respond to violence, physically and politically. Many women still don't believe they have options in dealing with violence. To the contrary, it is every woman's responsibility to take a feminist self-defence class —one which specifically addresses violence perpetrated against women. If women refuse to take care of violence on the personal level at which it's perpetrated, who will? No one.

Teaching and learning self-defence is political because it challenges the ways we perceive women responding to violence. Women need to take action for themselves. According to Debbie Leung, self-defence instructor, writer and activist, police respond to only 1/2 of the calls they receive regarding domestic violence. In addition, court cases against rapists and domestic violence perpetrators often put the survivor, rather than the attacker, on trial, analyzing her behaviour, dress and occupation (especially if she works in the sex industry or certain service industries). Social responses compound the lack of institutional response. A survivor's friends and family may not even believe she's been assaulted, especially when the assailant is an acquaintance, friend, lover or family member.

Becoming aware of sexual violence and its socio-political context is only the first step to defending oneself. Women need to learn physical techniques to stop physical attacks. Fighting back depends upon women's ability to act for themselves. Fighting techniques can range from yelling, running from an attacker, striking vulnerable body parts (e.g., knees, throat, eyes, nose), to crippling an attacker. Again, resorting to more individualized responses to systemic violence may seem counter-productive, but this is not the case. According to Brooklyn Women's Anti-Violence Education Center, eighty percent of women who yelled and ran from an attacker were able to get away without physical harm. Sixty per cent who either yelled *or* ran got away. These are examples of women, acting by themselves, warding off attackers.

The key to fighting back lies in the transformation of fear into anger into power. To move from fear to anger, women have to believe that they are worth defending. When you realize that you have worth, an attack on your person becomes unacceptable. In attack situations, a defender's first impulse may be to freeze up —this is a normal, but crippling reaction to fear. Becoming angry allows a defender to relax and use adrenaline to demand that an attack stop and to follow-up with physical strikes. Most women shy away from yelling and using their full power at the beginning of our self-defence courses. They tend to keep their power inside, almost as if their strength is something to hide or keep secret. These students look surprised when they yell "No!" and hit a padded target with exceptional force, throwing the pad holder backwards by a foot (padded targets are foam-filled rectangular devices that you can hit without getting hurt). Self-defence as physical education means developing the strength that comes from combining physical techniques. In our self-defence classes conducted by Ms. Vimla Mehra, Jt. Commissioner of Police, Crime (Women) Cell, Delhi, we educate women to do whatever is necessary to get away from an attacker, while ensuring that the attacker cannot continue the attack.

Recently we conducted a Self-Defence course for the village girls of Najafgarh. It was interesting to note that the men of the village supported the whole endeavour and came to watch with pride the Certificate giving ceremony. There were two girls who had come in sarees and veils and it was amazing to find these women taking the fighting stance as an expression of their self-confidence. They kept their shoulders back, knees slightly bent, one foot staggered in front of the other about shoulder width apart and bent both arms till elbow at 90 degree and attacked the opponent.

Combining verbal and physical techniques increase women's strength. In an attack situation, using your voice transforms fear into anger into power by pushing energy out at an attacker, just as hitting a padded target and yelling will be much more powerful than if you just hit the target. When we discuss using your voice in our self-defence classes, I always like to tell a story of how one woman verbally demanded that her attacker stop his attack, while using only one other physical technique. Here's the story. An elderly woman awoke one night to find an armed young man standing over her, wanting to rape her. He was undressed. As he climbed over her, she grabbed him by the testicles, refusing to let them go despite the man's requests and called the police. She held him by the testicles until the police arrived. We can safely assume that this woman was not as physically strong as her young attacker, but she combined verbal demands that he stop attacking her with one physical technique. In this way, she was able to stop an attack, and ensured that he could not continue the attack. Fighting necessarily requires a combination of techniques: verbally demanding that an attacker stop attacking, yelling loudly to attract the attention of other people in the area, striking the attacker to make him/her stop, and running to get away. All these techniques combined increase a woman's ability to become a hard target and to stop an attack.

Teaching self-defence must be part of a larger political project. Self-defence cannot eradicate violence. Ending sexual violence requires a systemic response—one which dismantles the very foundations of patriarchy and its interconnections with other forms of domination. Self-defence cannot do this, in part, because it criticizes patriarchy on an everyday level, not in its constitution of the social order. Self-defence does, however, prepare women for violent situations, which threaten them until patriarchy is permanently dismantled.

Self-defence education helps women demystify myths about sexual violence and to act against violence. How many times have we heard that a woman was asking for it, or that a woman was lucky that she survived an assault? When a woman survives an assault, she wasn't lucky, she was strong. Self-defence teaches women to say "No!" to sexual violence in ways that cannot be ignored.

It is interesting to note that the person who is involved in the confrontation will have the opportunity to decide as to what has to be done to defend herself.

By observing the above tactics for self-defence, we could prepare our young girls for a future free of fear and violence.

8

Changing Mindset's

With great expectations and eagerness I was looking forward to the much awaited marriage of my niece. For days we discussed the sarees we were wear going to wear at the different functions. I thought that as an elderly aunt my presence would be welcome and it would be a good opportunity of meeting relations and interacting with nieces', nephews etc. I wore a bright colour sarce with matching jewellery and there was no difference between my attire and that of other relations and guests. Jingling of the bangles, soft music being chanted and the general atmosphere was full of fun and gaiety. Everyone was most enthusiastic in greeting me and meeting me and I was the most sought after person. Suddenly the Purohit (Priest) said that it was time for blessing the *Mangalsutra* and all Simangalis should bless the Mangalsutra.There was *turmeric powder*and *Akshai* being offered on the Mangalsutra. Suddenly I saw my relations look at me with a guilty look and one of them old me that I should go away from the room as it was not auspicious for a widow to be present at the time of muhutham auspicious occasion). There was pin drop silence suddenly and I was totally taken aback. Of course I knew. The discrimination against widows does exist but I did not think that close relations and ones own family would look upon me as an inauspicious woman.

Throughout the history of Indian womanhood a single woman (widow) has always faced subjugation in one form or the other. Prejudices against her, seen and felt in the language, attitude and practices are prevalent in the society. Even when women are empowered "like me" or our leaders they are still seenasabnormal and not real women.Of course, we face further humiliation as we are forced to carry on certain trites and traditions not only at the demise of (the husband but throughout remaining period of our life (like Shraddh ceremonies and Pind Dan). It is interesting to note the moment you say that some one is a widow there is a general misconception that she is elderly, ugly, not smart and dressed badly. These are the very misconceptions perpetuated by society that need to be addressed and rectified. Today there is an urgent need to pay attention to their status as wars, poverty, earthquakes, terrorism and man-made calamities (like Bhopal gas tragedy) and more recently AIDS has created countless young widows. I am even referring to the countless child marriages that iake place to elderly men who naturally leave behind voting widows.

One of the major problems of South Asia is that of missing women, but even more pathetic is the position of those women who are discriminated against socially, culturally and religiously. Even though the Constitution of every country guarantees equality to men and women, the discrimination against widows, even now in the 21st century makes one feel that they belong to no human category. Her human dignity is trampled upon and the human right of freedom of expression is snatched away. Her physical security is at stake and she is tortured both physically and mentally. This state of affairs is present in almost all South Asian countries. The main focus of deprivation is:

- Social Discrimination—this discrimination is given the approval of traditions and religious sanctions.
- Economic Deprivation—the traditional breadwinner is no longer alive and she herself is not equipped to earn.
- Legally Marginalized—Unaware of her rights and incapable of asserting herself—she has no judicial recourse.
- Lack of Support—very few governments and NGOs view widows as a special category with individual problems and a specialized status.

I was recently at a conference on Widows Without Rights and was shocked at the simioarity of the situation in India and Africa. In Africa also myths are often shrouded in mystery and has great repercussions for anyone who dares to ply into them. In Africa one such myth is that the widow is accused of being her husbands murderer. She is punished and certain harmful widowhood rites are imposed on her. I would like to show the similarity of the situation when I have met several widows in India whose family members have said that the recent widow had brought bad luck to the man and was instrumental in his death. Can you imagine a similar situation when a man loses his wife people tend to pamper him that he is alone, lonely and in need of urgent company and should get married. He is given a list of names for remarriage even before his wife is cremated. Margaret Owen in her book "A World of Widows" explains that in South Africa there is no word in the vernacular for widower because they remarry so fast they simply do not exist. Another such myth is that if these rites are not performed then the spirit of the deceased will haunt the widow. The practices have been in existence for so long, that no one has questioned or challenged them. People were also genuinely ignorant as to the actual dangers and effects of these rituals. They had no knowledge of their historical significance or meaning. There was disc fear of the, consequences" of not adhering to practices.

Dr. Eleanor Nwadinobi of Nigeria in her presentation talked about three D's Dethronement, Defacement, and Disinheritence. While I was listening to her presentation I thought how similar the situation is in India. In India a girl is always known as a daughter, wife or mother.

Dethronement. She has never got an identity of her own. It is only in her marriage that she finds dignity and honour and the moment her husband dies she immediately loses her position of power and recognition. Dr. Eleanor Nwadinobi says that a *similar* derecognition takes place in Nigeria and as part of her humiliation she is made to sit on the bare earth, straw mat and made to sleep on the floor.

Defacement. I remember the day that my relations came back after the cremation of my husband. They were afraid to approach me on the subject of rituals and wondered if they would dare to have the usual rituals associated with widowhood. I was wearing a coloured saree, bangles and the vermilion (*tika*) still adorned my forehead. I could hear the whispering campaign that was going on around me arid nobody was daring to tell me that I should wear a white saree brought from the brothers house and telling me to break the bangles. The belief is that the beauty of a woman is only for her husband and when a woman loses her husband she is supposed to look unattractive. The Igbos community of Africa have a similar tradition and they go even further by making the widow drink the water of the bath that is given to the dead body of her husband. "She is not allowed to have a bath and is expected to look dirty, unkempt and smell foul.

Needless to say in many parts of India a widow is also expected to shave her hair to deface her a little more and humiliate her. As if the death of one's husband is in our hands.

Disinheritance. In a society where women have hardly any property rights and even where there are rights prescribed by the law women ate afraid to demand it. One can imagine the plight of a widow who according to Indian custom has been given away in Kanyadaan and when she is widowed in the husband's house she has nowhere to go. Inheritance of an property is tied to customary laws of marriage and a married woman hardly has any claim or succession rights on either the property of her husband or the property of her father. Savitri a widow whom I met at Vrindavan gave up all her rights and came away to Vrindavan thinking that if she does not claim her property her children would be taken care of by the husband's family.

The Hindu Women's Right to Property Act, 1937 gave better right to Hindu women in respect of property, but gave a limited estate which is held by hei only during her life time and then reverts to her husband's heirs. But in view of the limited right becoming an absolute right by virtue of the Hindu Succession Act, 1956, the question of divesting the property on remarriage does not arise. Under Section 14(1) of the Act the widow's limited interest gets automatically converted into an absolute right.

It is now judicially settled that once a widow has succeeded to the property and acquired an absolute right under the Hindu Succession Act, 1956 she cannot be divested of this right on remarriage.

In India's traditional Daybhaya system people held the property, as tenants in common. When the father died the property was divided between the heirs and they could hold it together if they wanted but their shares ware defined. Whereas under the Mitakshara system a male member of the joint family had an interest by birth in the ancestral property. A man could ask for partition of his ancestral property but if he did not, when he died, his interest in the ancestral property was diverted to all male members of the coparcenary. It went to them by survivorship and not succession. Women were not coparceners and did not have any interest by birth on ancestral property. The Law commission of India in its 174th report has recommended that daughters also be made coparceners. They were only entitled to maintenance i.e. expenses or food, shelter, clothing, education and marriage. However, if partition took place between the male members then mother and wives were entitled to limited interest basically for the purposes of maintenance and on their death the share reverted to the husband or son's heirs. She was not entitled to sell, mortgage or will away that property.

The Hindu Succession Act, 1956 brought about some changes. The most important changes were (a) to give equal rights to sons and daughters in their father and mother's property and (b) abolish the concept of a widow's estate which gave her only a limited life estate. But it did not do away with the concept of copaercenery nor did it give the daughter a right by birth in ancestral property. However, a Hindu male is entitled to will away his interest in the ancestral property. If he died without making a will his share would be divided among his heirs. His four primary being his sons, daughters, widow and mother; the others are derivative heirs, i.e., children of pre-deceased son or pre-deceased daughter, widowed daughter-in-law and children of pre-deceased grandson and his widow.

Thus, if a Hindu widow is in possession of the property of her husband, she has a right to be maintained out of it and is entitled to retain the pussession of that property in lieu of her right to maintenance.

Similar is the case of disinheritance in Africa. Inheritance is tied to customary law marriage. Marriage under customary law requires the consent of the parents and the handing over of the bride after the payment of a bride price. It is sometimes polygamous. This means that the death of one man sometimes results in more than one widow.

An unmarried girl has no succession rights to her father's property. A married woman however has certain succession rights to her father's property but it eventually all belongs to her husband.

In his lifetime a woman cannot question her husband about his will. In case she wants to find out if she will be benefited by his will she is thought of as a bad woman. An uneducated rural widow faces even greater problems as she lias no means of livelihood and does not inherit land rights and is at the mercy of her husband's relations. The truth is that the widow belongs to no one and has to fend for herself against family, society and the community at large. The woman faces severe sufferings which result in her doing manual labour and deprive her children from going to schools as they have to earn also.

Islamic rules of succession are based on the provisions of the Quran. Where a husband dies without any surviving children, the wife inherits one quarter of the estate. Where the deceased husband left a surviving child, the wife or wives will inherit one-eighth of the estate.

Some of the African traditions and customs made me weep. It was so astounding that I cannot help recounting them:

Nakedness. The widows in Uzo Uwami , in the South of Nigeria sit naked for 3 months with their hands covering their breasts. In neighbouring Igbo Etiti the cloth which the widow wears for 28 days is washed at night and she has to stay naked while waiting for it to dry.

Sitting and Sleeping on the Floor. In the Uzo Uwani and Aninri areas in Nigeria, the widows are not allowed to bathe for 28 days, even if they have their monthly period.

Routinised Weeping. This orchestration of grief is forced on the widows where they are made to cry whether they want to or not.

Feeding by others. In some areas the widow is not allowed to feed herself. She is fed by her relations and this may lead to her feeding times being reduced.

Of course many of these in some way or the other are also followed in India. There are several health hazards, psychological and physical trauma that a widow has to face. Imagine a Nigerian widow who does not have a bath for 28 days would naturally be prone to scabies and other skin diseases.

All these stresses that a woman has to undergo leads to hypertension, stroke and heart attack.

It has come to my knowledge that many of the widows are forced into prostitution and are exposed to high incidence of HIV, AIDS and STD's. it is of course now time that we carry out some kind of research of all those widows whose husbands have died of AID's and how many of them are now forced into the practice of levirate. Isn't it an irony that young widows who are still sexually active are expected to be celibate arid thus deprived of the normal sexual activities.

I am told that Ghana, Zimbabwe, Uganda, Kenya are also not different from Nigeria. In Kenya in fact there are several polygamous unions which means the death of one man may bring about several widows!.

The very fact that widowhood has been described by writers in the following terms or quotes goes to show the horrors of widowhood

"The Exploitation of the Doubly Oppressed" Agozine, 1987.

"A Year in Darkness" title of article by Marie Claire Magazine, February 2000, UK Edition.

"Cruelty of Mourning" title of artcle by Elayne Chft for Freedom Magazine.

"The Tragedy of Neglect" title of BBC radio script in March 1999.

"The Rape of Human Dignity" Donna Snook.

We are hoping that similar to the African status quoted above we will be able to get inputs from the South Asian countries on the status of widows. The present state of affairs in almost all South Asian countries is social discrimination, economic discrimination, legal action marginalise and lack of support.

Hence, we feel that it is vital to raise the issue of discriminated widow as a case for international concern and use the sensitivity of the UN system to build the capacities of this section of society.

This year on the 1st of February, we will be having the International Conference in Delhi on Capacity Building of Marginalised Women: Widows where participants from all over the country and the SAARC countries would converge to deliberate upon the various aspects of capacity building for the marginalised widow. Our objectives at the conference would be:

- Vital gender bonding through networking in South Asian region.
- Research, to document the status of widows in the region emphasising the commonalities and diversities resulting from socio-economic, religious and cultural differences.
- Attempt to duplicate the best practices on empowerment of widows.

- Governmental intervention in the form of (a) social policy (b) legal remedies and safeguards.
- Creating awareness among UN systems so that the plight of widows becomes and international issue of concern.
- Making use of UN bodies and programme for effective implementation of empowerment projects.
- Analyzing the role of religion on the status of widows —traditional practices.
- Advocacy with policy-making bodies.
- Most countries have guaranteed equal status to both men and women in their constitutions. However in spite of this certain sections of society face discrimination, isolation and abuse. Widows belong to this category. It is irrelevant that widowhood is not voluntarily embraced by a woman it is thrust upon her either by circumstances beyond her control or as a result of conflict situations not of her making.
- Countries of South Asia practice social norms, which are very similar. The widow in all these countries faces the same social, economic and legal handicaps. Either by tradition or practice these widows have been denied their fundamental rights of equitable justice. The widows in-particular are singled out as victims of social abuse at the time of then husband's death, ostracism from social activities and denial of their established legal rights.

We have in the women's movement come a long way since the 1995 Beijing conference and the 1993 world conference on human rights where gender violence was defined as "violence which jeopardizes fundamental rights, individual rights and women's physical integrity." Again in March 1999 the UN Commission on the Status of Women adopted an optional protocol to CEDAW. According to this mechanism it allowed all complaints to be submitted by individuals or groups on their behalf before the community on the Elimination of Discrimination Against Women CEDAW[r] was signed by India also alongwith 160 other countries.

A time has come today when we have to challenge all traditions, customary laws male patriarchal attitudes and lobby with the governments, with the society for the human rights of widows.

9

Gender Equity

Gender equity is a fundamental human right. In a socially just world women's aspirations, life choices and achievements would not be constrained by the question of gender. But harmony and peace can only be maintained if Gender parity exists in society. There has been a growing tendency in the past two decades to foster gender equity and justice. An urgent need is felt for bridging the growing technological, cultural and political divide not only with the nations but also between men and women. Needless to say, the gender divide is serious.

Women have long borne the responsibility in several key areas of everyday life vital to the economy of the nation like farming, plantation, beading, harvesting, threshing, storage of agricultural products. Apart from this they are burdened with additional chores such as home keeping, child care, nursing care which have such a vital impact on the economy but still remain unaccounted for in the National Income. When we talk about gender equity the term is used to describe a set of qualities and behaviours expected from men and women by their societies. A person's social identity is formed by these expectations. These expectations stem from the idea that certain qualities, behaviour, characteristics, needs and roles are "natural" for men, while certain other qualities and roles are "natural" for women. Gender equality refers to a situation where both men and women have equal rights and opportunities at all times.

Where is the peace in the home—ironically called the haven of peace?

The major contributing factor in the traditional mindset is the result of centuries of gender prejudice. Why else would there be a dress code prescribed for widows—not for the widower? It is the basic streak of the human psyche to feed the ego by the humiliation of the other. It probably has got nothing to do with man or women. But because human society evolved broadly on patriarchal lines the male ego was always on the high. The violence of the home spills into the society or vice versa. We are all aware of the rising incidence of sexual crime, and gender based violence. Women are stoned to death, gangraped, paraded naked—everything to wound her body and, more horrifying, her psyche and soul. The even more telling social injustice is the thread of economic dependence that is visible throughout in all the SAARC countries. In India 62 per cent of all boys and men are in the workforce but only 19 per cent of women and girls. Bangladesh has shown a very heartening trend—from 5 per cent women in the workforce in 1965, 1995 shows 42 per cent . This has been important for the export growth since a large segment in the garment industry is composed of women. But the catch is that women put in 31 hours a week of unpaid work like cooking, collecting fuel, looking after children etc. On the other hand men put in 14 hours a week of unpaid labou.

How can peace survive as a companion to social and economic injustice?

Education, the major tool to progress, has permeated very slowly among the women. In India female adult literacy rate was 39.4 per cent in 1997, i.e., 39.4 point rise on the index of 1985. Nepal literacy rate is 20.7 per cent which is 104 point rise on the 1985 index. On the other hand, the rate in Mexico, a developing nation, the rate is 87.9 Venezuela is 91.6, Philippine is 94.3. The very slow permeation of education keeps the women in ignorance of legal, social and economic rights. Unfortunately in her case ignorance has not given any bliss—but only low self-esteem and made her a victim of socio-economic tyranny.

Globalization creates new opportunities. Paradoxically, it creates greater availability of the tools of crime. Gangsters use arms manufactured across the sea, terrorists use remote controlled bombs, women and girls are smuggled from South Asia and find their way to the sex shops of Europe. Chinese triads are in the restaurant trade in London and the Japanese Yakuza are financing pornography in Netherlands. Illicit trade in drugs, women, weapons and laundered money is contributing to the violence and crime that threaten all neighbourhoods. Organised crime estimated to gross 1.5 trillion dollars a year has the economic power to criminalise politics, business and police. Stop and think what this unbridled power can do to the most vulnerable sections of mankind today—women and children.

Closely related to this is the rampant commodification of the human body—rather the woman's body. Media stereotyping is probably the most visible culprit in reducing women to a commodity and a possession of man. Films perpetuating the image of woman as a weakling and a silent puppet with no control of her destiny is familiar to all my SAARC sisters. Compounding this is the advertising that uses the women's curves to sell everything.

The commercialization has snowballed to such an unwielding proportion that you need a woman's body to sell anything.

How can there be peace for an object to be played and dropped therewith? And finally in this broad term of peace is the lack of political identity and respect. The SAARC region has produced 4 Prime Minister's in the last 5 decades. But the percentage of women in the Indian Parliament's Rajya Sabha is 12 per cent and the Lok Sabha is 7 per cent . But only 5.8 per cent women are in the government. Of this only 3.2 per cent are at ministerial level. The corresponding figures of Pakistan are 2.6 per cent of women in the government—in Bangladesh only 1.9 per cent and 5.3 per cent in Bhutan. Clearly indicative facts that women have still to take to political avenues to lobby for non-gender discriminated programmes. The cry of the woman as a victim of socio and economic tyranny is searing and powerful—but it never reaches the echelons of the government.

Lobby power is the vital weight that tilts the balance in favour. How strong is the woman's lobbying power?

Where then would there be peace in the silence of victimization?.

In the larger concept of peace as linked to development and equality the index of the SAARC countries is abysmally low. Are we to remain as Gertrude Mongella voices victims or witnesses?- Can we not be more than that when peace comes under threat?. Yes of course women can and must be the ultimate initiators, builders and preservers of peace as linked to development and equality.

Empowerment begins first from within. The strength is within us, all we need is to unlock that vital force.

The narrow meaning of peace is the absence of war, armed conflict and terrorism. The SAARC region has been be set with them. Where must be the ultimate initiators, builders and preservers of peace liked so development and equality can begin? In peace that development and equality the index of the SAARC countries is abysmally low. Are we to remain caught in a debt trap? Money is borrowed to pay off more debts.

The socio-political framework gets fractured. The crack widens with every revolt that is fuelled by arms traders who make hay while guns boom. India, Pakistan and Sri Lanka have been witnesses to armed conflict.

In a region as closely knit as the SAARC every armed conflict will resound in the other countries either as cross-border terrorism or as low intensity wars. When the cause of absence of peace is to a great extent economical, the solution must correspond. It is vital to insulate inter country cooperation from political tensions. In this context the South Asian Preferential Trade Area and South Asian Free Trade Area assumes great significance. This is the kind of cooperative effort that is likely to benefit all and have a direct impact on the people to whom the benefits accrue. This will in turn dispel doubts on interactive cooperation. Surely patriotism must be fuelled by the war against non-development and inequitable distribution of resources.

While inequality and warped development exist through non-empowerment of the marginalised sections, peace can, at best, be an aim alone and not an environment. Mahatma Gandhi once stated that women have the power to kick the atom bomb out like a football. Along with you I see that power—half awake certainly but awake nevertheless.

"O lord why have you not given woman the right to conquer her destiny—why does she have to wait head bowed by the roadside waiting with tired patience hoping for a miracle in the morrow" Rabindranath Tagore said this in the beginning of this millennium. The millennium is over we are not waiting for a miracle, the miracle is within us. We have the means to shape our destiny and that of our region, the courage of endeavour to stop the world from a mad roller coaster ride on the tracks of a weapon arsenal.

10

Powerfully Empowered

"At last the twelve months (365) days of getting the women empowered conies to an end! Did we really go even a step towards the direction of empowering the weak, the widowed, wailing, weeping women"?

I had hoped that this year would see tremendous changes in the grassroot empowerment of women the 73rd Amendment would really bring a sea change in the villages of India, health situation of women would improve. Saws pertaining to women would be implemented and last, but not the least, the 33 per cent reservation for women that we have been demanding in the Parliament would become a reality.

We are citizens of a free and vibrant democracy and swear by the concept of equality; our Constitution abhors discrimination in the name of sex. If that is the constitutional creed which we desire to permeate in society, how can we tolerate behaviour and action opposed thereto? Theoretically we condemn it, but at the same time we practice it.

For gender justice to be really meaningful we have to respond to the several discriminatory practices towards women and specially girl child as our legal social and political system is inundated with discriminations and discriminatory laws. When we talk about gender justice we do not talk about a system where a woman is totally empowered but where she is in partnership with man and they work on issues side by side.

From the beginning and through the year we only heard promises and promises, seminars and seminars for improving the plight of women. There were recommendations after recommendations made by the National Commission for Women in 1987 that went to deaf ears and none of them were even put up to the women empowerment committee of the Parliament.

Today our courts are crowded with pending litigations and many a times justice does not see the light of day for years and years. Of course some may claim that women are now legally in a position of little discrimination but justice remains a far cry. Large sections of women are still spending their time in jails as under trials even when not guilty of the crime.

Trafficking among girls continues unabated and every day thousands of girls are sold in open markets through unscrupulous men. Our survey showed that young girls who have passed class 8 or 10 do not get jobs and are an easy prey to prostitution. They are trapped due to frustration of not getting employment by unscrupulous middlemen who offer them jobs and take them to brothels. Let us for a minute look at the mental asylum. Their plight is not better then the rest. Men find it so easy to get a doctor's fake certificate to prove the mental instability of his wife and get a divorce. How often do we have reviews of the mental conditions of these women?

Let me take a look at the Panchayati Raj. Has the 33 per cent reservation really helped the women?

With great difficulty and persuasion 60 articulate and vibrant women sat listening to the trainers wanting to imbibe as much as possible for their own capacity building. Suddenly Vimla Devi's little breast fed baby started screaming, she looked behind her and found her escort husband sitting and twiddling his moustache. She beckoned him with her eyes and asked him to take the baby out so that she could concentrate on the lecture on legal literacy that was going on. The husband Phool Singh looked daggers at Vimla and nudged his colleague another "Pati Pradhan" and said "If I take the child people will laugh at me and it is not the job of men to take care of the child I've to think of my *mardangi.* Some people around the room heard these comments and in low tones discussions were heard and people started saying "Was he not ashamed at the time of siring the child that today he feels shy to pick up the child". But all the men who had accompanied their wives to the workshop were supporting the husband and asking the women to take away the crying child from the room and get out. Needless to say that though we have a 5 per cent success rate during these workshops the most important thing is to change the mindset of the man and society. Women have been in many places elected as an avenue for the ambitions of their political savvy husbands. She has added a new role to herself, but without any realization of her responsibilities or any control over her authority. Was this the spirit with which the 73rd Amendment was passed? Was this the impact that was envisaged by the women's movement? These men the "Pati Pradhans" also create a fuss when women are served food before they are served. They expect the gender status quo to be maintained.

The major hurdle we face in most workshops is the very presence of men during the training period. Men at times become so articulate and abusive that the 5 per cent vibrant vocal women are mocked at and made fun of by the men. Hence apart from changing the mindset of men in society there is a need to see and train women to come to these workshops without the men. Suresh Kumari stood up during the workshop and said that if she could learn how to ride a motor bike then she would come without fear to these meetings. The very fact that women are wanting to learn cycling, bike driving etc. reflects their great desire to be independent and mobile. Many of these women tell their husbands to drop them and go back but they consider this a social stigma to keep their wives unescorted at any place. Look at the irony of society. These are the same men who do not think twice while raping or molesting any girl at any given time and yet are protective of a woman not that they care for her but because society dictates so, because the honour of the family reposes in the body of that woman—his wife.

Women have problems attending these workshops because they have the sole responsibility of looking after not only their children and family but also their cattle. Ishoo Devi a very vocal and sincere young 35 year old with lovely long hair said that the night before, after the workshop she reached home at about 8:00 p.m. Till then her cow Bindiya did not allow anyone to milch her. This is a problem we have faced several times during our interactions. In fact it was hilarious when one of the participants said that at the next workshop she would bring her along with her husband since one won't let her be on her own and the other can't do without her.

In order to make women's role meaningful in Panchayati Raj we should also have a training module for men and other family members to share household chores so that a woman could really become an effective instrument of change in society. It has often been realized that it is the men who won't allow the women to take their elected roles seriously. Nothing or no one in the home will make an of effort to allow her to perform her official functions. It suits many of the men to keep the women in a perpetual stage of ignorance. Astonishingly, in many of these workshops the women had to ask their husbands the name of the block of which they were the elected Pradhans. This is the tragic irony of grassroot democracy!

To conduct a residential training workshop for grassroot governance in backward states like U.P. and Bihar is very difficult and hence we will have to develop modules of shorter durations with emphasis on one topic at a time spread across a week which would make it easier for the women to come.

In all these workshops our response has been women wanting incentives to attend these workshops. To my mind this is an insult to education. When we asked Rajwati why she wanted this kind of incentive her answer was if she goes back empty handed to the village people in her village would laugh at her and tell her that she has been fooled by city dwellers who have not given her anything. As far as a conveyance reimbursement is concerned it may be a genuine need. But any incentive beyond this seems like a bribe for education. We must find out ways and means of getting the women motivated for the sake of knowledge as a means to better their performance as elected leaders.

If this is the result of reservation then what is the solution for the many other ills?

I would like to now talk about the girl child who is most unwelcome

It is really increasingly evident that women have been invisible in all aspects of social existence. The 1961 census recorded bride price not dowry as being practiced by more than 60 per cent of Indian population. Dowry they said was the main reason for killing women before birth, after birth, or after marriage. Female foeticide and infanticide has become the major area of concern. For the lot of women suffering from harassment at workplace, the Supreme Court has issued guidelines, however, deep rooted patriarchal set ups in various offices prevents any case of sexual harassment being solved.

I believe that there are 13 lakhs complaints of sexual harassment in private sector in the Department of Company Affairs and if this is happening to educated, economically independent women then one can imagine the lot of those who have not even registered their cases for fear of stigma.

The recent bill proposed by Justice Leila Seth on Property Rights of Women has to some extent given a hope to the woman of this country in matters relating to inherited property. Yet very often justice is denied to women by their families. In many instances the women concerned are illiterate and therefore are duped into signing away their legal rights to property. If they are aware of their rights, they are either coerced or emotionally blackmailed into giving up their share in the interests of maintaining harmonious relations with their families. Women are hampered in their quest for justice by the fact that the necessary documents relating to inherited land are often not available or withheld from them by local administrations or village panchayats, weakening their case in the lower courts.

I would like to focus on crimes against women which are mounting and unabated day after day. It is not as if we have no Manila Police Stations and Crimes Against Women's Cells but creating them and then dragging the cases for years and years is not really the answer. If we really go deep down into the reason for this kind of a crime, needless to say drinking comes foremost.

The anti-arrack agitation of Nellore district has been one of the most significant women's agitation in the last decade in India. Liquor emerged as a central issue that pushed household economies to the brink, in the light of the deteriorating economic situation of the poor, consequent to the new economic reforms. However many more elements of change have taken place in these villages. An effective thrift programme which is self-managed has followed the arrack struggle. It has also been followed by effective social action by women in groups against social crimes such as the use of female child labour, child marriage, rape and other forms of violence against women, revealing that women's collective struggle against arrack has a greater value and wider value than the elimination of liquor from households. Women's struggles have tended to be against policy, sometimes against development, but women have rarely been able to translate their struggles into a political platform. The anti-arrack struggle proved that it can be done under certain conditions.

Women in the hilly regions of Uttar Pradesh have been agitating against men's drinking habits for several decades. They also agitate against DABUR and other Ayurveda tonics, as they contained high percentage of alcohol and men took these for their 'ride'—the hilly districts have been agitating for a separate state, Uttarakhand, where again women have been in the forefront. These women reveal extraordinary clarity in defining the kind of laws, economic policy and political arrangements they demand. They want full rights guaranteed on them over village trees, land and water. These women want 50 per cent of the places on the agencies that control forest land (van panchayats). They want charge of developing the tourist industry as tourism today threatens women's security-—it brings with it liquor and prostitution.

A large sector of our population is in the field of agriculture. According to Dr. M.S. Swaminathan the renowned agriculture scientist, in many hill and remote areas of developing countries, such as the Himalayan region agriculture is largely in the hands of women, since men tend to go to towns and cities in search of salaried jobs which can augment family income. Therefore without the total intellectual and physical participation of women, it will not be possible to popularise alternative systems of land management to shifting cultivation, arrest gene and soil erosion and promote the care of the soil and the health of economic plants and farm animals. Scientific and technological empowerment of rural women alone can usher in prosperity to them as well as the rural society. In the past the research and development institutions have unwittingly ignored this angle. The contributions of farm women have been quantified, recorded and recognised with the result they have been neglected from the mainstream of development, may it be research, education or extension. If we have a good grassroot networking with institutions of agriculture we could change the lives of many women as 80 per cent of our women live in rural areas.

Last but not the least we had planned that the National Policy for Women would be adopted this year like the several amendments to laws that were recommended by the National Commission for Women way back in 1997. These are also postponed everyday and today the empowerment year has gone by without the National Policy on Women.

My friend Indira Jaisingh had helped to draft the Domestic Violence Bill which has now become an Act but violence continues on daughters, sisters, domestic maids but none of these have found solutions.

At the end of the year I really wonder whether one year is sufficient for changing mindsets of centuries of patriarchy and isn't it time that we think of empowering men towards gender justice and become the agents of change for society. I strongly feel that we should dedicate at least a decade to change attitudes among men and communities and societies.

11
Federation of Panchayati Women

The 73rd Constitutional Amendment introduced by Shri Rajiv Gandhi is a major step forward in strengthening and revitalising of Panchayats, the third tier of governance. The important provisions of the 73rd Amendment are regular elections at village, intermediate and district levels, reservation of one-third seats for women and reservation for SC's and ST's including for the office of the chairpersons, Constitution of Finance Commission, powers to raise resources.

What is sought to be achieved by the 73rd Amendment is to make Panchayati Raj institutions instruments through which people could fully participate in the development process and it would promote genuine devolution of powers, functions and resources to local bodies at the state level.

A significant feature of the 73rd Amendment to my mind is the provision for one-third representation to women in the elected bodies as well as reserving one-third of the offices of chairpersons for them. This provision has had far reaching consequences in India's social and political life. In a traditional society like ours, women, particularly in rural areas, are often prevented by cultural barriers from interacting or participating with menfolk and ousiders in matters of common interest. Further, there is ample testimony to the male bias in our society.

Traditionally, rural women are confined to child bearing, child rearing and household duties and work outside only to the extent assigned to them. Their participation in public life is minimal. As a result, women suffer from an innate sense of bondage and dependence. They have a low self-esteem and start with the premise of that they cannot do too many things which the menfolk can do and further they are not designed to do several things which lie exclusively within the domain of men. This myth - foolish myth has been perpetrated by a patriarchal society to ensure the exclusive dominance of the patriarchs. The 73rd Amendment has for the first time in our country paved the way for rural women's participation in social, political and economic fields. In order that the rural women prepare themselves for this role it is essential that they are first convinced about their separate individual identity. They have to be made aware of their immense potential and capability. They must be inspired and activated to have their own aspirations, ambitions and social role. The quality of leadership amongst rural women has to be encouraged and allowed to grow so that women can develop confidence in decision-making, can identify their own problems, priorities and preferences and use their own wisdom, knowledge and judgement to suggest ways and means to resolve them.

Governance is a very broad based concept while democracy has many shades. As somebody put it, democracy is like a hat which has almost entirely lost its original shape in the process of having been worn by many. It has to be acknowledged that a working definition of democracy has to be that of a participatory system which provides adequate, unhindered, universal opportunity for all, the promotion of an equitable and sustainable social and economic order. For achieving optimum results in a democracy, there has to be a partnership accord between women and governance, ensuring as also safeguarding individual liberty and dignity and common interests. In almost all cases, the failure of democracy happens because of the failure of Government. In the words of Subhash C. Kashyap, "governance has become a casualty of Government" with Government themselves more concerned with survival rather than attending to the needs of the people.

Panchayati Raj thus gives a great deal of importance where people themselves articulate for the first time. Because of women in Panchayati Raj women come to the centre stage thus bringing about peoples participation. Women's participation in the political process is the giant leap that will take us towards a truly gender bias free society. Once involved in political decision-making, her face is to be reckoned with both within society and the family. The sense of achievement in actually helping to make things change is the greatest filip to self-esteem. And as I always say–you respect yourself and the world respects you.

Since democracy thrives through democratic institutions, it is not an isolated and insulated phenomenon. The effectiveness or usefulness of democracy would depend upon the structures supporting it. Panchayati Raj can really be effective if the quality of that democracy means that everyone, and especially the poor and the marginalised like backward social groups and women, have access to decision-making levels through inbuilt appropriate strategies so that their voices are heard and heeded. Further, as is the present case in our national government, democracy based on the principle of "consent" is more beneficial. The success of democracy, in so far as it concerns women would definitely be tested on the question of sensibility, sensitivity and suitability to answer to the needs of feminist concerns, though not divorced from society, nation and international interest.

Prof. Sushila Kaushik conducted a study on Stock Taking of Participation of Women in Panchayati Raj in 6 States in India under the aegis of the National Commission for Women. This study aimed to examine the patriarchal and myopic, critique of women's functioning in Panchayati Raj (rural local self-government), and to find out the problems faced by them in the course of their work, and the ways in which they cope and seek to overcome the same.

The working of Panchayati Raj and the participation of women in the same, has to be understood at the local level and in the local context. The present study, hence, deals with the experiences of panchayat women in six states of India —Haryana, Madhya Pradesh, Orissa, Rajasthan, Tamil Nadu and Uttar Pradesh.

Most of them faced opposition from political parties. The patriarchal view of men and even women considered that women were not capable and they were not fit for politics. Some women candidates also found illiteracy and lack of economic resources to be handicaps. Quite a few women also found social environment to be unfriendly and the purdah system disabling them. Domestic work, child care duties, lack of mobility partly due to social reasons, were also handicaps.

Many women were also subjected to votes of no-confidence in Uttar Pradesh as their resignations will either enable the Sarpanch (often a male) to succeed or lead to a suspension of the panchayat and a new election. It will either way lead to a dereservation of the post. It is now believed that this sort of vote of no-confidence motion is being brought up repeatedly against women chairpersons who feel victimised.

Since independence, India's people have viewed their democracy with a sense of pride, and an appreciation that democratic governance is the key to a strong nation, a viable economy and a sense of social stability. A recent public opinion survey conducted in India revealed that two-thirds of Indians have confidence in the political system, a figure which is as low as 25 per cent in other parts of South Asia. A remarkable 93 per cent of those polled asserted that they vote in elections, displaying a high regard for the democratic system and its potential.

However having said that, it is time that today we recognise the various loopholes that exist in the Panchayati Raj Act and take immediate steps to have these loopholes addressed. Naturally if you evolve a federation of Women Panchayats which I hope will spread throughout the length and breadth of the country, this federation will be a platform to advocate, lobby and bring about changes for grass root empowerment.

A dedicated band or federation of working Panchayati women who are newly entering local political structures to ensure that they have the necessary training and resources to fully participate in local affairs. It is hoped that this federation would be prepared to work in partnership with India's women leaders as they create their vision and plans for a new future for their communities and for their country.

By ensuring the inclusion of women in local government, the 73rd and 74th Amendments are bringing Indian politics a step closer to a full reflection of the needs and wants of all of Indian's people, both women and men. The amendments represent an opportunity to focus on the priorities of development that women state as essential to themselves, their families and their communities. Furthermore, this represents the possibility of rethinking leadership itself, so that it embodies the qualities of women in power, who value honesty, openness, patience, collective support, and accountability to the people they represent.

In order to participate in the Panchayati Raj Institutions, and in society at large, the Indian woman must first stepforth from the enshrouding conditions that characterize her life. Her successful participation in the panchyats is unquestionably linked to a process by which Indian society begins to breakdown the walls of tradition and custom that limit women's mobility and restrain their actions as key players in society.

Various societal supports, when created, can make room for women to act powerfully within society and thereby within its local political structure. To my mind district level federation would help the women in following areas:

Support within the Family

- Her husband and family encourage her participation in the Panchayats.
- Her husband and family assist her in household chores and family responsibilities, so that she has more time to engage in critical tasks as a Panchayat representative.
- Her husband and family accept the fact that she will be interacting with other men, and help her to overcome her shyness and reservation about doing so.
- Her husband and family understand the importance of her mobility, and allow her to determine her own movement outside of the home.

Support with the Community

- Local training programmes and workshops are created to empower women. They treat gender issues and build their confidence, as well as analyze the particulars of Panchayat operation.
- Local training programmes and workshops are developed to enlighten men, by building their cooperative skills and to treat of gender issues.
- Day care programmes are made available so that children can be cared for while the woman is at work.
- Women's organizations are created and strengthened so that women can exchange information and discuss ways to address their common problems.
- Women who have already served a term as panchayat leaders act as her mentors.

Support by Society at Large

- Government, NGOs and Civil Society institutions support her work by setting out funds for the Panchayats and making them easily accessible to women members.
- Government, NGOs and Civil Society institutions establish training brochures, satellite programmes, trips to seat of government and other special programmes to facilitate her work.
- Political parties make the participation of women in Panchayati Raj an important plank in their platform, and support Panchayats in their interface with government.
- Media creates a supportive environment for women members by letting society know about their accomplishments, and by influencing public opinion in support of women's reservation and rights.

Political empowerment and consequent decision-making roles for women ensures harmony in society and paves the way for undisturbed economic and social progress, and more vitally the woman is able to view herself not just as a wife or a mother but as a vital factor in solving social issues. Her self-esteem is much higher—a crucial factor in the development of equality. I want to recount a story of a woman elected to the Panchayat. She was asked to mediate a dispute between a Brahmin and different caste and she herself belonged to Brahmin community. She mediated the dispute successfully but when she came home her father-in-law was furious that she had given the judgement in favour of the other caste. That rural woman's answer lit a great hope in me. She said, "When I am in my official elected role I am not your daughter-in-law—so do not interfere in my work outside the home. When I am at home, then I am your daughter-in-law." In the event of existence of such a federation women will remain confident and can interact with each other.

Recently we heard of a small Gram Panchayat in Okha, Gujarat launching its own website. Such a federation would facilitate this kind of an achievement once again.

There is no doubt that women have traversed a long way in an uphill journey towards progress. However, they still have miles to go to achieve complete gender equality with social justice. Mere laws cannot ensure social transformation.

In the last five decades since India attained its independence, there has been a marked improvement in the quality of lives of many Indian woman. There is a new awareness of woman as a vibrant entity, who can no longer be ignored or marginalised. What is most significant is that the Indian Women's movement has made the political leadership aware that there is a desperate need for reform. This consciousness marks the beginning of a change. A spark has been ignited by Rajiv Gandhi and during the coming decades, it will become a cleaning fire.

Thus, today it is of great importance which could not only realise Mahatma's dreams but enable women from all corners to interact with each other on a common platform. Let me tell you that Gandhiji also said that it would not be easy and I quote: "Self-government depends entirely upon our own internal strength, upon our ability to fight against the heaviest odds. Indeed, self-government which does not require that continuous striving to attain it and sustain it is not worth the name".

12

Giving Power to Women

Crimes against women have increased in leaps and bounds. Patriarchy still of persists and deprives women of participation in many of activities. Many religious orders still do not have an entry to women. Traditions and superstitions are followed all over the country, which hampers the progress and growth of women. A widow is still a non-entity, marginalized by customs, practices and laws. Out of the 48 per cent of women's population (only 48 because of female foeticide, infanticide and preference of male child) only 1 per cent enjoy the fruits of freedom. Where is equality, where is freedom and where is the women's voice?

One of the affirmative actions that we envisaged at the Beijing Platform for Action, was political reservation of seats in the Parliament for women. The campaign for women's reservation in the Lok Sabha and the Legislative Assemblies had been going on for the past 9 years. This initiative is without question to establish political equality, which is guaranteed in our Constitution. The campaign that has been carried on by the National Commission for Women and other women's organizations has created sustained public interest and asserted the rights of women. The campaign signifies the social and political space created by women's movement and the National Commission for Women in India for building up an effective initiative for the rights of women. We have been striving hard to pave way for the networking and alliance with different groups of women activists all over the country trying to evolve the identity of women as one political constituency in India.

Today the government is debating and planning to change the previous women's representation bill to another bill. The very fact that we are envisaging a change strongly indicates the patriarchal way systematically depriving women of their rights.

What were the Highlights of the Previous Bill?

There should not be less than 1/3 seats reserved for women in Lok Sabha and Legislative Assemblies. The reservations are for an indefinite period. The reserved constituencies are to be determined through a draw of lots because for SC and ST's constituencies are reserved on the basis of the proportion of the population. Constituencies with a high SC/ST population are supposed to be delimited after some years. Since the population of women is unevenly spread throughout the country, this formula cannot be applied to them. The draw of lots systems means that every time a new set of constituencies will be declared as reserved for women. There is also a provision for parallel reservations for SCs and STs, which is to say women belonging to SCs and STs will be getting one third of seats reserved for people of that category, that is quota within a quota. The bill leaves out of its purview reservations in the Rajya Sabha and Legislative Council.

The new bill is now changing the whole perspective from the last bill that was introduced. Women throughout the country feel that to achieve our targets we will have to wait for a long time, as delimitation of a country as large as ours is not an easy task. Majority of the women feel that we need an immediate affirmative action and we need to honour the political commitments made by the UPA Government.

How is the new Bill going to affect women? The 73rd and 74th Amendments enabled over one million women to participate in the election process of local bodies and today we are proud of our panchayats, of the responsibility of governance that they had taken over. The government has to take the process forward and now in making a new Bill we have to have a constitutional Amendment Bill, then a discussion will have to take place whether to provide double-membership of 1/3 seats to the Lok Sabha and Legislative Assemblies will take place simultaneously or in a phased manner. Discussion will also have to take place as to the basis on which a part constituency would be made Double-Membership. Then again the question will come up of some of the constituencies have to be reserved for SC/ST. We are not sure whether once a constituency is declared double-member if it would permanently retain its unique status or would be on a rotational basis.

Several women's organizations had met recently and were unanimous on the following points: It was decided that the matter should be settled within a time frame. 180 seats increase is all right but how will this increase be done. Should there be a proportional addition from each state?

Population should not be the basis of this increase. Should there be double membership for one-third seats in the Lok Sabha and State Assemblies?

The government's move to bring in changes in the women's reservation bill; to increase the number of seats from 543 to 725 in the Lok Sabha is a commendable one. However, after having gone through the grit and grind of preparing the original bill and discussing the original bill, we fail to understand why the political parties are against it. The new proposal would need to start from scratch and this exercise would easily take more than four to five years. Once again women are being made pawns in the game of one upmanship where nobody is serious about giving power to women.

13

The Role of Women in the New Millennium

"If an ancestral treasure lying buried in a corner of the house unknown to the members of the family were suddenly discovered, what a celebration it would occasion. Similarly women's marvelous power is lying dormant. If the women of Asia wake up they will dazzle the world".

Mahatma Gandhi

The year 2000 has started with the hope that during this decade Indian women would attain further empowerment in continuation of the process initiated a few years ago at the grassroot level by adequate representation in the apex legislatures.

The last decade has seen some revolutionary changes in the way we think, work, do business and educate ourselves. For one, there is an unmistakable trend towards globalization with its opportunities and challenges also.

Second, technologies are changing at a breakneck pace and training in skills is often falling short of the speed of this change. Not just changes, technologies are often converging and merging into single units with multiple purpose.

Third, the right attitude for every job and a professional approach in every aspect you plan and execute are the other things, which are of great significance today. In an age of intense competition, globalization and growing consumer awareness, it is more than ever before, necessary for women to keep pace with the growing changes. So you cannot avoid going global, being techno-savvy and practicing high standards of managerial professionalism and precision in your work.

What is really empowerment? Empowerment to my mind is the process by which the disempowered, or powerless, people can change their circumstances and begin to have control over their lives. More important empowerment means the way we think of ourselves—to see ourselves not as victims of circumstances but as architects of our destinies. Why should women always look upon themselves as victims? They are the architects of their own destinies. They are the real Heroines. Empowerment results in a change in the balance of power, in the living conditions, and in the relationships. Perhaps the most important effect of empowerment is that the person says. Now I have no fear.

Empowerment is both individual and collective. Women in the informal economy are socially and economically weak and vulnerable, and it is only by the process of coming together that they can get empowered. This is the process of organizing. Attapady is a tribal village of Kerala where high incidents of alcoholic and drug abuse was prevalent leaving the women destitute. Anything they earned was spent on drugs and alcohol. Thaikulam a women's organization decided that they had enough of this and took the matters in their own hands and decided that they would either council or beat up the men who drink, so far they were the victims of violence, now they wanted the same violence targeted against man. The strength of their togetherness worked magic and the entire village swung into action against the men by beating them up and soon the total village was without liquor and there are no incidents of alcoholical beating there.

In the last two decades women's status in the society has undergone a tremendous change. The last decade has unleashed the strength and spirit of the Indian women and now they are able to control and manage their lives to a large extent and take independent decisions covering all aspects of their lives.

Although women constitute almost one-half of the population of the world, their social, economic and political status is lower than that of men in most countries including India. This being largely due to gender disparities and patriarchal mindset of the people. Women have been oppressed and marginalized for long and new initiatives by the UN and other women's movements have led to gender sensitisation through awareness programmes, policy formulation, enforcement of laws affecting lives of women for change and empowerment.

The changing social and political situation of our country offers us many serious challenges and opportunities. The most crucial among them are the challenges of poverty, exploitation and oppression experienced by the majority of Indian women. Guild of Service has been working for long in this area through vocational education and placement of young women, offering safe housing for working women, Rural Development Project, where girls and women are being helped to become self-reliant through non-formal education, awareness programmes on health and hygiene, promoting gender equality and equity upholding thereby women's rights to ensure a place of dignity and worth.

The changing times in today's world have encouraged many women to seek their own identity, the value and worth of their lives, through the contributions they make to the family and society at large. Increased awareness about rights has motivated the submissive and sacrificing woman to become conscious of herself as a person with her own identity and personality. She now wants to be regarded as an individual with feelings, aspirations, desires, in fact as a "human" person.

I would like to deal with today's socio-economic and political challenges faced by women which are bringing in changes in a dramatic manner today.

Legislation. As far as legislation is concerned today Indian women are marching towards liberty and equality. The National Commission for Women has, in the last few years, introduced several new bills in the Parliament from time to time towards eradication of many social evils. Some of the significant enactments are:

1. The Hindu Widow Remarriage Act of 1856

In the traditions at Hindu society there was a ban on widow remarriage. Ban on widow remarriage was one of the most important evils from which women in the traditional Hindu society suffered a lot. This Act allowed widows to remarry and Section 5 of this Act ensured that she would enjoy all the rights which a married woman did.

2. The Child Marriage Restraint Act of 1929

The practice of child marriage was another social evil from which woman in traditional Hindu society suffered a lot. Age at marriage for girls was 9 or 10 and after passing this Act the minimum marriageable age of women was fixed at 15 years. Later it was increased to 18 years.

3. The Hindu Womens Right to Property Act of 1937

In traditional society women had no property rights. In the eyes of law she was a minor or ward. This Act recognized a widow of a deceased person as his surviving personality with the same right as his in the joint property. Thus through this Act women in Hindu society received the property right to a limited extent.

4. The Hindu Marriage Act of 1955

This Act has recognized the equal rights of man and woman in the matters of marriage and divorce. Under the provision of this Act either the man or woman can present a petition in a court of law for divorce, the wife has got an equal right to divorce her husband.

5. The Hindu Succession Act of 1956

This Act recognized an equal right for women in the matter of inheritance of property. She can inherit the property of her father along with her brothers.

She can also sell or mortgage the inherited property or use it for herself. For the first time absolute ownership was conferred on a woman by this Act.

6. The Suppression of Immoral Traffic in Women and Girls Act of 1956-57

This Act aims to deal with the problem of prostitution and to promote the welfare of fallen women. Main objectives of this Act are to reduce the scope of prostitution and to reform prostitution under this Act. Every state is expected to set up protective homes and to appoint women police and women social workers. In protective homes these fallen women will be given training in tailoring, toy and basket making and other crafts so that they may earn for their maintenance in a proper way.

7. The Dowry Prohibition Act of 1961

The main objective of this Act is to abolish giving and taking dowry at the time of marriage. The term dowry refers to a valuable property or thing, which is determined by the parties to a marriage. The practice of dowry had produced a great deal of hardship. Dowry has become a social evil. Even though this Act prohibits dowry system, dowry cases have not been reduced. Still this Act makes some effort to bring in social change.

Above-mentioned are the important legislations, which brought upward trend in the status of women in India. Today the status women are enjoying is because of legislations. She is protected in every way of life. Thanks to legislations, women in India are gaining better status, recognition and respect.

I cannot escape talking about domestic violence against women, which has become rampant in India. Spouse abuse has become a cancer in our society and a recent bill that is going to be introduced in the Parliament on domestic violence against women is indeed very timely to safeguard women's interests.

Economic Empowerment

Economically women have also improved their status in the last few years.

June 2002 — The past decade has seen a powerful movement toward economic, social and environmental integration. It must be remembered that women's economic empowerment increases conversely with the perpetuation of patriarchal practice i.e. the more patriarchal a society the less option a woman has to be economically empowered. Kerala which has a long history of gender sensitivity shows that 78 per cent of the women work in non-agricultural services and their contribution is accounted for. On the other hand Bihar and Uttar Pradesh. show women in primary sector—agriculture based occupation indicating low state occupation and unaccounted for economic contribution. But while globalization has the potential to enhance lives, its promise has been unevenly realized. Broad divides persist between rich and poor; between information "haves" and information "have-nots"; between educated and uneducated people. Major gaps continue between the economic opportunities and status afforded to women and those offered to men in training, credit, employment opportunities, workplace roles and wages. Women's economic integration is a powerful impetus for economic, social and environmental progress. Improving women's economic status saves lives by promoting health, encouraging economic progress, and enhancing the social status of women.

Developments

- A series of human rights treaties and international conferences has provided the legal and international basis for ending gender discrimination and promoting equal rights for women. These include the International Women's Bill of Rights, formally titled the Convention on the Elimination of All Forms of Discrimination Against Women (CEDAW), adopted in 1979 and ratified by 168 countries.
- Women in the informal sector benefit from microcredit programmes, which provide seed loans for investing in an income-generating enterprise. Repaying these loans at a record rate, women are demonstrating that investment in women's economic power enhances their standing, their families' health and the prosperity of their communities.
- Studies show that increased earning power for women has a much more positive impact on family welfare than do increases for men.
- Women's wages can increase with little loss to male wages. As more people join the workforce, the economy grows, so that men's wages need not decline in absolute terms.
- Women hold about 3 per cent of top executive jobs and one per cent of top labour union jobs worldwide.
- The Final Outcome Statement of the March 2002 UN International Conference on Financing for Development in Monterrey, Mexico, called for gender equality in all areas, saying it was central to good governance and urging the use of microcredit programmes, especially for women; and for "sustainable, gender-sensitive, people-centred development" worldwide.
- Women are heads of state in only eight countries and are less than 14 per cent of the world's lawmakers.
- Gender disparities in education are declining. Girls' school enrollment has risen to almost 80 per cent. But of the 300 million children without access to education, two-thirds are girls. Two-thirds of the world's 880 million illiterates are women.

Examples

- A study in India found that productivity in the female labor force would be about 20 per cent higher if women's health problems were addressed.
- In South India, women barely keep any of their personal income for their exclusive personal use, while men keep up to 25 per cent of theirs.

Despite all the official proclamations about empowerment and the numerous government schemes designed to improve women's economic conditions, their material status still shows much cause for concern.

In India, improvement in the conditions faced by women has been among the explicit goals of government policy, alongwith growth, reduction of poverty and inequality and improved human development indicators.

Nevertheless, some of the data on conditions of women indicate that things may not have got much better for the bulk of Indias women over the past decade.

This is reflected even in demographic indicators, which tend to sum up health and living conditions at the most basic level of survival.

It is "therefore" a matter of great concern that the latest National Sample Survey has revealed not only a decline in per capita food grain availability in the aggregate in the country, but also a decline in per capita calorie intake in 1999-2000 compared to 1993-94, since this is likely to be associated with a disproportionately negative effect on women and girl children.

It is well-known tiiat intra-household distribution of food tends to discriminate by gender, usually because of self-denial by women and girls.

In terms of literacy and education, India still contains the largest number of illiterate people in the world, and also the largest number of illiterate women.

The progress of improvement in literacy has been very slow, which also shows that literacy among females remains substantially below that for males, and that even at present, nearly half the female population of the country remains illiterate. Furthermore, female literacy rates are much lower (usually between 50 and 70 per cent) among Scheduled Tribes and Scheduled Castes, as well as among certain minority groups.

Most of the women employed in India are engaged in agriculture, whether as workers in household farms owned or tenanted by their families, or as wage workers.

Yet it is precisely livelihood in agriculture that has tended to become more volatile and insecure in recent years, and women cultivators have, therefore, also been negatively affected.

In a positive sense, public infrastructure investment can directly feed into the lives and working conditions of women. Providing safe drinking water supply and better sanitation not only directly improves the lives and health of women but also reduces their workload in terms of provisioning and ensuring such facilities.

Access to affordable cooking fuel reduces the need to travel long distances and spend hours collecting fuel-wood. Improved transport connecting villages with each other and with towns can also directly improve living conditions as well as reduce unpaid labour and time spent m transporting items for household purposes.

Political Empowerment

As far as political empowerment is concerned we have seen a sea change in the past few years. With the introduction of the Panchayati Raj I think the greatest change that has come about is the fact that socio-economic conditions in a village change due to women in the decision-making process. It is the women who are most effected when they have to walk six kilometers for a bucket of water. So as a Panchayat member she makes maximum effort to ensure easy access to safe potable water. Thus an infrastructura change is effected.

(a) In the light of social background factors in caste, age, education level and other factors–the interventions by the various N.G.Os. brought all these women representatives under one umbrella. Caste and class barriers narrowed down. Purdah system, and shyness among village women have started disappearing. They have acquired courage to express their views both in formal and informal gatherings.

(b) The women started showing keen interest to learn more about Panchayat administration and community development.

(c) These changes amongst the women brought respectability for them in the community.

(d) With the help of the field staff they started taking initiatives to solve problems in the community.

(e) The women acquired the confidence to share their experiences and also learn from their peers.

(f) The women were encouraged to meet higher authorities of the government and represent their problems before them.

(g) There is a wind of change in the Panchayats as these women are acting as "agents of change".

The women's movement has been advocating 33 per cent reservation in the highest legislative bodies. A space is to be created for the women's voice to be heard. Most infrastructural inefficiencies and inequalities effect women most - lack of health care an insecure law and order situation - riots which leave women as the worst victims. So is it not essential that those who are at the receiving end should have a voice in the decision-making process of the country? What democracy can we advocate when 50 per cent of our population's voice is not heard in the Parliament?

For women to take their just place in society, we have to ensure

- legitimate political participation
- their voices are present in the decision-making process
- property laws are reviewed to do away with anomalies in the law, discrepancies between statutory law and customary law
- equal access to resources
- access to educational opportunities
- gender sensitivity at all levels of society

Is all this possible? Despite my gray hair, my dreams are young and I dream of a future for my 50 crore sisters in which they will hold their head high because they are women, not despite it. Will I see it in my lifetime? Perhaps not. Perhaps not even in the lifetime of many of you. But then I'm reminded of a story. An 83 old grandfather was planting elms and populars, trees which would take 8-10 years to mature. His grandson asked, "Grandfather why do you plant trees which you may never live to enjoy yourself. "The grandfather answered Son, did you plant all the trees that you see and enjoy around you" So let us plant many trees. The rest will follow.

14

Millennium Development Goals

The last decade of the last millennium was unique because it brought about a strong sense of global solidarity and the realization that half the world is hungry. If half the world is illiterate, if half the world has no health benefit, no good quality education, then a secure and just world is impossible.

It is time now to come together to the principle of share, care and look after the nations which are deprived. It is an investment in human relations that the rich nations will be making. However, this pledge by the world leaders to lift hundreds of millions of people out of extreme poverty can be achieved only if the developing countries and poor countries have a policy for reforms and policy for upgrading their conditions. South Asia and India has a large concentration of hungry people. It is not as if India does not have sufficient food grains but a great obstacle is our public distribution system.

Food security is basic to the right to live. A small increase in subsidy can provide the country and universal food distribution system at cheap prices which will serve the basic needs of the people.

We, as civil society, took the initiative to see when the new government was installed that a few obstacles that are in the way of the progress of our nations were included in the Common Minimum Programme. We had asked a commitment of the following:

1. A firm commitment to the passage and implementation of the Women's Reservation Bill.
2. Commitment to the passage of Protection against Domestic Violence Bill with the amendments suggested by the women's organizations and implementation of the various

recommendations of the Law Commission to reform laws concerning women.

3. Universalisation of PDS, Joint Pattas for women in land distributed and special work schemes for poor women in rural and urban areas.
4. Implemention of the non-coercive non-targeted national population policy as opposed to the coercive anti-woman policies in place in many states and strict implementation of the laws against sex selection and sex determination techniques and tests.
5. Commitment against the practice of dowry.
6. End to indiscriminate licensing for liquor vends as a revenue source and a comprehensive liquor policy taking into account the concerns of women.

If the adove commitments are implemented, we are confident that we will achieve many of the goals of the development programme. It will also ensure that Mahatma Gandhi's vision of wipping every tear comes true.

The civil society in India has been playing a unique role in addressing peace issues with our neighbouring countries. Needless to say that none of the millennium goals can be achieved if we do not have peace. Our strategies for overcoming obstacles to peace were dialogue. Our slogan was *"Goli Nahi Boli"*.

I am happy that the civil society has played, and is playing, a major role in people to people contact. We took several delegations to Pakistan.Bangladesh, Nepal etc. and the warmth and love that it has spread will go a long way in achieving the millennium development goals. Peace really is not absence of war. It means that when peace prevails there will be more development in the country. Water, electricity, food will be available and also when there is goodwill generated, trade and commerce will flourish.

The civil society in the recent past has been very active in the issue of gender equality and empowerment of women. Strategies that we have followed are economic empowerment, where Self help Groups have come up and created the economic boon to my daughters and sisters who are now financing their husband's small enterprises hand in hand with an economic support. Indian women are realizing the needs for education and more girls are going to schools but this is not enough. We need to create a gender-just society. After having lived under patriarchal subjugation for so many years, there is a need to sensitize the judiciary, the police, the bureaucracy and the society. Only when such sensitization programmes reach the grassroot then can we expect violence against women to stop and the society together in partnership with women and men will achieve the millennium goals. Civil society has been taking training programmes for the elected Panchayat members and thereby helping to overcome the many difficulties faced by the rural community.

While I talk about empowering women, I must not forget to mention that half the population is deprived at the policy-making level in the Parliament. We, members of the civil society have been fighting for affirmative action in the Parliament. The same patriarchy, which is an obstacle to our progress, is depriving that affirmative action in the Parliament by not giving us our due—to be in the Parliament. It will be impossible to achieve the millennium development goals if women are left behind in the highest policy making body.

What makes a nation strong? Not the weapon it has, not the wealth it has, not the thousands of years of cultural heritage it has, not the big population. Health to my mind is the greatest wealth that the nation can have. I strongly feel that even the Olympics that we have not won is due to reasons of health. Does the little child have nutrition, balanced diet and vaccinations in time? I am afraid the civil society in India has been totally negligent of these and child mortality still remains a dilemma.

Many members of the civil society are working towards barefoot doctors and nurses aid programmes but this component needs to be taken on a war footing. The human development report says that the poorest nations have more than one billion people living in extreme malnourished conditions.

How are we going to overcome this big obstacle? When I go around the village HIV Aids is like a Demon devouring the Nations. When I went around many brothels in India, my survey showed that 80 per cent of men who visited the brothels were college students.

Since then I have been advocating awareness programmes for Aids to colleges and to men everywhere. Civil society needs to address this issue urgently as this is spreading like wild fire and needs urgent attention. Of course all of you will laugh if I say abstinence is a strategy. It is not impossible and it could be tried!

I am particularly worried with the status of my sisters in prostitution and girls who are trafficked. Trafficking is really a billion dollars industry and is a major obstacle towards empowerment and controlling Aids and promotion of gender equality.

In India civil society has shown a great concern for environment and I am not going into the details you all about the Chipko Movement where women ensured that environmental resources are not lost. No nation can live without water yet half the population is still living without access to safe drinking water.

Over the last 6-9 months some of us — women's organisations—have been listening deeply to women's unheard voices in different slums, in different cities, and in different rural areas, about their terrible experiences of 'water and sanitation'. I must admit that listening to these voices has shaken my soul, and has made me question concepts and concerns of development that need to be addressed.

Decade after decade, governments (and international agencies) have promoted initiatives that are—known to have failed again and again. The poor women are not seen as agents of changes but as passive recipients of favours to be bestowed by people in power.

After listening to these many voices, I have now come to realize why international projects and our own projects have largely failed so far – they have not listened to the 'voices of women' and how to deal with their problems. We need more realistic policy and action framework.

The civil society has been trying strategies of water, harvesting etc. However, this is going to be one of the major obstacles and we will have to address water and sanitation urgently.

Apart from all that there are a few very serious obstacles to achieving millennium goals. The rampant corruption that society is steeped in from top to bottom is a destabilizing factor. We have to at once address this issue and find ways and means to stop this rot.

Another very serious obstacle is judiciary and law enforcement agencies, which are not able to deliver. The third very major obstacle to our progress is unemployment of the thousands of youth who are passing through the colleges.

15

The Death Penalty: An Affront to Humanity

On I5th August 1997 India was celebrating the 50th year of its independence, was sitting in the National Commission for Women's office planning the programmes for 15 August. Suddenly, I received a frantic phone call from the relatives of Ram Shree who was imprisoned Mathura Jail and was to be hanged the next day on the I5th August. My colleague Padma Seth and myself sat through the whole night sending telegraphic messages and phone calls to the Allahabad High Court asking for review of the case. We also sent Swaraj Lata Goel at once to Mathura to meet the Jailor and see that the sentence was not carried out. We also sent urgent communication to the President of India for pardon. Our efforts bore fruit and Ram Shree's case was successfully represented by Ms. Indira Jaisingh and her death sentence was stayed and later commuted to life imprisonment.

At that time Ram Shree had a two year old baby who was being breast fed. We as women were horrified to even think of what would happen to that baby. Of course at that time, being in the Women's Commission I strongly condemned death penalty to women. As I felt that we have no right to destroy a woman, a life giver and a creator. As we had no right to take the life of any human being.

Today I find it very difficult to advocate death penalty even if it is a rapist. There are many crimes, which are gruesome but if we start imposing capital punishment there will be no end to it. Indian State has the authority to make and amend laws keeping pace with changing social conditions.

Several countries in the world have either abolished or are in the process of abolition of capital punishment.

Our country today is debating whether death penalty should be given to the rapist. The government of the day has spoken about it in the Parliament and certain women's groups have welcomed this. The judiciary has been awarding death penalty from time to time. India is a party to the International Covenant on Civil and Political Rights (ICCPR) that required a progression towards abolition of death penalty. Needless to say that the death penalty violates human rights and is a cruel punishment.

Nearly 120 countries have signed the statute creating the International Criminal Court which has rejected the death penalty as a punishment for genocide, crimes against humanity and war crimes.

An Unjust Justice

It is often said that capital punishment is given to those without capital. The death penalty is always an unjust method justice. It is applied unfairly death row cells are filled with people from impoverished and ethnic minority backgrounds, those least able to defend themselves in court. Millionaires are rarely found among them. The death penalty is applied arbitrarily, depending on such random factor as the competence of lawyers, the strength of evidence, the tampering of proof the capacity of witnesses to sustain cross examination, the integrity of the witness, plea bargaining or pardons granted. Whether someone lives or dies can be a lottery. And the death penalty always carries the risk of ending the lives of people innocent of any crime, either because it is used as a political tool to silence government opponents for good or because of inevitable miscarriages of justice.

Prisoners facing death sentences are often represented by inexperienced lawyers or by lawyers appointed for political reasons by the state, or even by no lawyer at all. Defendants may not understand the charges or evidence against them, particularly if the proceedings are in a language they do not know. Sometimes they are denied the right to appeal to a court of higher jurisdiction or to petition for clemency. Some prisoners are tried before special courts lacking elementary safeguards. As a result, many prisoners are condemned to death after unfair trials, some of which are a travesty of justice.

In the above context the denial of an automatic right of appeal to the Supreme Court in a case of confirmation of death sentence by the High Court requires to be examined.

We need to review the right of the High Court to reject death sentence appeals. To prevent tiie miscarriage of justice the death sentence awardee should have an automatic right to appeal to the highest court in the land

There is no automatic right of appeal to the Supreme Court where death sentences awarded by a trial court get confirmed by the High Court. It is only where there is a reversal of acquittal by the trial court and awarding of life sentence or death sentence or a sentence of ten years or more by the High Court that the Cr.P.C. and the Constitution provide for an automatic right of appeal. While it has been a general practice that the Supreme Court will not summarily reject a special leave petition where it involves a death sentence, a recent instance makes real such a possibility. In that event there would not be really a right of appeal on the question of sentence, which, gets confirmed for the first time in the High Court. This may be inconsistent with the ICCPR treaty requirement to which India is a signatory.

Uncertainty of the Mercy Jurisdiction

The power of the executive to grant clemency is vested in both the President and the Governor under our Constitution.

In Maru Ram v. Union of India, a Constitution bench of the court held that the power under Article 12 is to be exercised on the advice of the central government and not by the President on his own, and the that the advice of the government binds the head of the state. The government's advice however, altruistic it may be, may still be governed by political ideologies. Ideologies can not be allowed to govern death. This was reiterated in *Kehar Singh* v. *Union of India* in which the challenge was to the order of the President declining clemency to owe of the accused in the Indira Gandhi assassination case on the ground that he could not go into the merits of the case finally decided by die highest court of the land. The court here explained that the question as to the area of the President's power under Article 72 falls squarely within the judicial domain and can be examined by the court the way of judicial review. The court clarified that the order of the President cannot be subjected to judicial review on its merits except with the strict limitation defined in *Maru Ram.*

Such cases highlight an essential fault of the death penalty—that it is irrevocable. Mistakes cannot be rectified, death cannot be reversed. Yet mistakes are inevitable in all systems of justice, however scrupulous the process and however honest to the participants.

A further problem is that around the world it is not just that inadvertent mistakes are made or feat a few corrupt police officers pervert the course of justice. Often, international standards to ensure fair trial are routinely flouted in capital cases.

Narrowing the Scope of the Death Penalty

Fortunately, the world is increasingly rejecting the legitimacy of the death penalty. One indication is the growing consensus that the death penalty should not apply to certain types of people such as juvenile offenders, the elderly and the mentally ill. There is support for these exemptions even in countries where the public and state officials favour the use of the death penalty.

The exclusion of juvenile offenders those under 18 years old at that time of the offence is now so widely accepted in law and practice that it is approaching the status of a norm of customary international law. The International Covenant on Civil and Political Rights (ICCPR –Article 6(5) and other major human rights instruments prohibit sentencing juvenile offenders to death, which has been ratified by almost all UN member states. The very few states that do put to death juvenile offenders provoke widespread condemnation.

International standards also hold that the mentally ill should be excluded from the death penalty. UN safeguards approved in 1984 by the Economic and Social Council (ECOSOC) guaranteeing protection of the rights of those facing the death penalty ECOSOC safeguards state that executions shall not be carried out on "persons who have become insane." In 1989 ECOSOC recommended that UN member states should eliminate the death penalty "for persons suffering from mental retardation or extremely limited mental competence, whether at the state of sentence or execution". Sadly, these exclusions have been ignored in some countries, including the USA.

International standards have established that in countries which have yet to abolish it, the death penalty should be used only for the most serious crimes. The ECOSOC safeguards state that the scope of these crimes "should not go beyond intentional crimes with lethal or other extremely brave consequences. In a few countries, however, people face execution for a wide range of offences, which pose no threat to life, including crimes against property and peaceful political activities. In China, for example, the death penalty continues to be applied for a variety of violent and non-violent crimes, including that of fraud, counterfeiting, embezzlement and corruption. In June 1998 Luo Feng, a manager in the Beijing Xiwang Computer Company, was sentenced to death for embezzlement, accepting bribes and using company funds to "play the stock market", despite an apparent lack of coherent evidence.

In the United Kingdom injustice was meted out and young, homeless poor people who would face the gallows within a week's trial. However, as society developed, especially in the post-war period such miscarriages of justice were unacceptable in the modern society. As a result of a pressure in 1965 a the law was passed and capital punishment was abolished in case of murder.

Ironically it was retained for treason and sedition and it was only in 1999 that the law changed in England and now there is no capital punishment. The pressure at that time was brought about by International conventions specially the European Convention of Human Rights in 1950 to which England was a signatory and later the Human Rights Act of 1988. European convention deals with capital punishment in two ways.

It deals with right to Hie and provides that every one's rights shall be protected by law. No one shall be deprived of this right internationally, save the execution of a sentence of the court which was provided by law.

The capital punishment was on the statute book of many signatory countries and a protocol was provided by the convention protocol No. 6 and it was signed by 38 countries. The protocol said that death penalty shall be abolished and no one shall be condemned or executed by such penalty.

Campaigning Against the Death Penalty

Among those campaigning against the death penalty are some of the very people that capital punishment is supposed to help - victims of crime and their relatives. In the face of increasing evidence that capital punishment does not act as a deterrent against crime more effectively than other forms of punishment. Proponents of the death penalty have increasingly claimed that it is needed to help the process of recovery of murder victims' families. It is true that some relatives of murder victims do find consolation in such retribution. But many others do not. Some relatives have reported that the execution of the murderer makes it more difficult to come to terms with their loss.

Countless other human rights defenders and other activists also campaign against the death penalty, by promoting the arrjuments against the punishment and by appealing on behalf of people under sentence of death or in imminent danger of execution, catting for clemency, pardon, commutation or retrial. Each year such appeals result in the threat of execution being lifted.

The March Towards Worldwide Abolition

Every year more countries abolish the death penalty, the pace of abolition has been especially remarkable.

In 1889 on the eve of the 20th century, only three states had permanently abolished tbe death penalty for art crimes Costa Rica. San Marino and Venezuela. When the Universal Declaration of Human Rights was adopted in 1948, the number stood at eight. By the end of 1978 it had risen to 19. During the past 20 years the number has almost tripled. In 1998 the trend continued, with Azerbaijan, Bulgaria, The Russian Minister of Justice stated that the Russian Federation would abolish the death penalty by April 1999.

By the end of 1998, 67 countries had abolished the death penalty for all offences and 14 for all but exceptional offences, such as war time crimes. At least 24 countries which retained the death penalty in law were considered abolitionist in practice, in that, they had not executed anyone for at least 10 years or had made an international commitment not to earn, out executions. Some countries reduced the scope of the death penalty. For example in Tajikistan the number of crimes carrying a possible death sentence was reduced in 1998 & from 44 to 15.

International treaties to abolish the death penalty altogether continue to attract new states. During 1998, Belgium, Costa Rica, Liechtenstein and Nepal became parties to the Second Optional Protocol to the ICCPR, aiming at the abolition of the death penalty, bringing the number of state parliers to 35. Belgium, Estonia and Greece ratified Protocol No. 6 to the European Convention for Protection of Human Rights and Fundamental Freedoms (European

Convention on Human Rights) concerning the abolition of the death penalty, bringing the number of states parties to 30. Costa Rica and Ecuador ratified the Protocol to the American Convention on Human Rights to Abolish the Deatn penalty, bringing the number of states parties to six. A number of other countries had signed one or another of the protocols, indicating their intention to become parties at a later date.

In April the UN Commission on Human Rights adopted resolution 1998/8 calling on all states that maintain the punishment" to establish a moratorium on executions, with a view to completely abolishing the death penalty". The resolution was co-sponsored by 66 states, a marked increase over the 47 States which co-sponsored a similar resolution at the Commission on Human Rights in 1997, response, 51 others states circulated a statement at the UN Economic and Social Council dissociating themselves from the resolution.

While over 90 countries can still be said to retain and use the death penalty, the number of countries which actuary execute prisoners in any one year is much smaller. During 1988 at least 1,625 prisoners were executed in 37 countries and 3, 899 people were sentenced to death in 78 countries. These figures include only cases known to Amnesty International; the true figures are certainly higher. As in previous years, a small number of countries accounted for the great majority of executions.

A few countiies have taken steps to expand the scope-of death penalty or to speed up executions. Jamaica. Trinidad Tobago, Guyana, Yemen etc., have withdrawn from optional protocol to the ICCPR.

Despite such developments, growing international opposition to the death penalty was symbolized in 199 per cent with the adoption in July of the Statute of the International Criminal Court. After much debate, it was decided to exclude the death penalty as punishment for what are arguably the most heinous crimes of all genocide, other crimes against humanity and war crimes. The clear implication is that, if the death penalty should not be used for the worst possible crimes, then it should not be used for lesser crimes. In other words, it should never be used.

The Home Minister mentioned in the Parliament the possibility to award death sentence to the rapist perhaps a few of the women

NGO's might think it an appropriate thing to do. Though I know many of the NGO's on a National seminar discussion held at New Delhi on "The Law, The State and Capital Punishment" had voiced their concern about extension of the death penalty to rape cases I had pointed out at that point of time that one of the reasons that they did not approve of extension of the death sentences to the new offences, is because we must try to curtail it as far as possible. The other reason particularly in the rape case, which I thought was a relevant matter, was that it enhances the risk factor as far as the victim of the offence, is concerned.

Rigorous imprisonment can be awarded to the rapist. Even that is not being awarded and conviction rate under the tape law is as low as 1%. Punishment may be made stringent. But implementation of law has to be speedy and efficient.

I had a case where a tribal woman had killed two of her infants. There was convincing evidence that she had done it. On that even the defence was not able to contend otherwise. The circumstance in which she did it was very important she killed both the children because they were crying for milk since morning. Her husband was a drunkard he used to take away all the money she earned and then he was the one who would be shouting at her that she keep the children quiet. And the only way she could keep them quiet was to throttle them. She killed both of them. Justice Ahmad who was the judge says."I remember I was in a very very awkward dilemma. I couldn't say that there was no crime I could not have any way to say, I could not have way to get out of the situation, I might have written a judgement, which was not very accurate, but there was very strong convincing evidence. So I was in the horns of the dilemma. This is where the problem arises with mandatory punishment and minimum punishment. I had no option but to convict her and sentence her to life. I had only one option and I wrote a strong piece saying this is one of the fittest cases where the Governor should exercise his power and commute the entire sentence and only when that happens would I be able to overcome the trauma of sentencing this woman. This is how mandatory sentences sometimes operate and I think this was a very important question.

Even when the death sentence is given there should be a chance for the criminal to speak up for himself on his sentences so that matters, which have not come out properly during hearing will all come out. In one case the judge said that the criminal was asked but he didn't have anything to say.

As societies develop we move away from barbaric practices so that criminals are punished, but more important they are corrected. When the courts award death sentence, then human right is violated –the right to life that is to be enjoyed by all human beings. Can justice be carried out by violating human justice? Corrective efforts are vital to change mindsets, of course punitive justice is vital in a social milieu. But we have to draw the line before violating irrevocably human rights.

Many of the inputs to this article have come from the Syposium organised by the Guild of Service on "The Law, The Slate and Capital Punishment" on 26 Februar 2000 at New Delhi.

16

Elderly and Policy-Making

Way back in 1971 after the Bangladesh war I was told by several hundreds of Jawans dying in the various hospitals "do not worry about me but take care of the one's I leave behind". I had to organize on a war footing the War Widows Association and I felt very inadequate both in experience and exposure to organize a big activity for the war widows throughout the length and breadth of the country. It was at that time that I was approached by several retired government servants, judges, lawyers and industrialists that they could help me in this venture. But for the intervention of the elderly at that time the success that War Widows Association achieved in delivering many services to the widows would not have been possible. I still remember Mr. Soni who had retired from the Audits and Accounts, 65 year old coming daily to the two rooms make shift office in the President Bodyguard and help with the total accounting of the organization. He taught us the system of filing, the system of keeping things in order and above all office management.

It is obvious there is an urgent need to tap the potentials of the elderly towards national development. Here I would like to mention my recent experience with the widows of Vrindavan. There was a time when mothers of Vrindavan with tonsured hair, emaciated look, were begging on the streets. On the 13th of May when the whole country was observing solidarity with the sisters of Gujarat, they were not to be left behind. Today their empowerment has reached such a pinnacle that not only are they self-supporting, economically empowered with a strong sense of self-esteem as symbolized by their coloured sarees, but they are also taking active participation in nation building. Today their concern is no longer the next meal as before but it extends to empathy for those in distress.

Needless to say we often think that the only role a woman can play is her reproductive role - bearing, rearing and caring for children. If given an opportunity, they could be the most sought after important women. Given the opportunity to play a role commensurate with their background and life experience, older women can be utilized as excellent resource persons in the community and in the national development process. Unfortunately, these opportunities have not been given in the past, nor envisaged in the National Policy for Older Persons possibly due to the mindset that elderly women are a force. Older women are broadly in two categories—the rich literate elites needing no support and the vast majority of middle class and the poverty stricken for whom old age homes and old age pensions are the only answers.

It is often forgotten that a country like India where motherhood has always been respected and revered is slowly becoming unwanted, uncared for. Although India in 1999 adopted a policy for the aged, in a vast country like ours I fail to see how we could operationalise any of those policies. The constraints are of course economic, of how and from where to get financial support for millions of eiderly population in India. Today our elderly population has doubled and tripled. Those between the ages of 60-75 can be utilized in several fields of activity. I would like to give an example of one such activity that has been successful.

Old widows in Mathura and Vrindavan are left to the mercy of the public to eke out some sort of existence. The only way to get them out of this state is to empower them with some self sustaining skills. Guild of Service has now been working with these widows for the past ten years and is familiar with their problems. During a free cataract eye camp held in March/April 2000 at Mathura, for widows, by the Guild of Service a group of widows were recruited to help in nursing of patients. Their performance was quite satisfactory and indicated that if trained, these women could become nursing assistants. Four batches of these women were trained. Inspite of handicaps like lack of formal education and age these women have proved that these criteria are irrelevant when a person is determined to acquire skills. Confidence in their gait is clearly visible.

Today, we have more elderly women than men inspite of low nutrition given to them. Inspite of load of morbidity accumulated during their reproductive age, inspite of menopausal and post-menopausal traumas, inspite of all these they outlive the males as has been seen by the large number of widows.

How many a times I have seen women becoming healthy and shedding ali their depressions, when proper action is taken to keep them occupied, it is amazing to see the poor, illiterate widows of Vrindavan who have lived in extreme cases of neglect, yet are taking responsibilities in a home on various issues.

We can utilize the services of elderly women as a grandmother in supervising and assisting activities of children in homes like the SOS and other establishments where day care centre are needed or where the lady is working outside the home. There are two categories of elderly women. One, those who are educated, have financial resources, yet are lonesome because their children are not with them and the other kind are those who are illiterate, economically deprived and need care and protection.

Today the Government. of India runs several ICDS programmes, Anganwadi programmes, Primary Health Centres, Adult Literacy programme, Panchayati Raj, Poverty alleviation programmes, slum development programme, services of the elderly should be encouraged and utilized in these programmes. There is an added advantage in utilizing these women as they are content with the specific job given and not always hankering for the attractions of the urban city and also not tempted to look around for other jobs with higher emoluments.

At Vrindavan when we talk to the elderly widows, they are keen to look after the dairy industry where each widow would be given charge to take care of a cow and a cooperative dairy would give them a source of livelihood and at the same time, their time will be spent in caring for the cow. The amount of milk thus collected could be utilized in producing good quality butter, butter milk and also give care to the cattle and occupation to the aged women who want to stay at home and work.

The Panchayati Raj has great potential as older women are found to be experienced, conscientious and free to take care of community development work of the Panchayat.

Running an NGO for Women since the past four decades I have found the usefulness of eldaly is tremendous in running various welfare activities. We were fortunate of elderly in having the services of Mr. Puri who is 80 years of age. He has been with our NGO since the past 20 years and yet he is diligent, honest, sincere, and punctual. Services of such older people would make them feel wanted. At the National Commission for Women I had the privilege to have the services of at least a dozen consultants in the age group of 65 to 75. The librarian Mr. Sahni was 78 years old and it was only his commitment that saw *a* good research library at NCW. Mr. Ravindran was 72 and headed the complaint cell at NCW, where I would get 200 complaints a day from across the country and he not only replied to each but brought them to my notice and for redressal. Dr. Menon was 65 years old and he would see to the target section of women in agriculture and with his vast knowledge had brought hope to thousands of tribals and agricultural women by policy changes. The list is endless but I would like to share the experiences with you. It would not be out of place to mention that 60% of our parliamentarians are in the (60-80) age range. Of course the ethos of national development is not a high priority in the Parliament, otherwise their potential could have been far better utilized.

In India the old have always been considered as repositories of wisdom gained through experience. They have graduated from the school of life. A predominantly consumerist culture changes all that. Aggression, success, fast track are the key words in a world where human value is measured in terms of the contribution to the GDP of the country. Is human value to be measured in cold human figures? It is time we found answers to these questions on our terms based on our cultural ethos, not on the borrowed parameters of alien concepts.

17

Second Widowhood

Thirty-two years ago, the newspaper had headlines screaming 'Plane Missing'. A young girl named Shammi, beautiful and intelligent holding two small children came to me to the War Widows Association. An IAF Plane carrying 98 defence personnel from Chandigarh to Leh disappeared into thin air. She was desperate.

Tracing back, on February 7, 1968 Indian Air Force plane AN-12-BL-534 was flying from Chandigarh to Leh. It was a routine flight and the passengers inside - a mixed crew of 92 Army and six Air Force personnel were getting ready to disembark as the aircraft approached its destination. Everything proceeded according to schedule, when ground control radioed the pilot to turn back. Weather conditions were simply too bad and landing the plane at Leh would be too hazardous under the circumstances.

AN-12-BL-534 made a U-turn and was returning to Chandigarh when flying over Rohtang Pass—only a few seconds from the Pakistan Border—it suddenly lost contact with ground control. Weather conditions not with standing, it was expected that the missing blip would return in a jiffy. It did not....

Shammi was only 19 when she was married. Five and a half years later her husband, Squadron leader Malhotra, co-piloted a sortie on a regular trip to Leh, he never returned.

Shammi visited me day after day refusing to be called a widow, kept a vigil and waited sure that one day her husband Squadron Leader, Prem Nath Malhotra would come back.

My son was studying at that time in Mayo College and my heart went out to 7 year old Sajid, Shammi Malhotra's little child. After a great deal of persuasion, Sajid was admitted in Mayo College.

There was no trace of the plane since then the family had faced the worst. However frequent stories about the presence of Indian prisoners of war held in Pakistani jails appeared in the newspaper.

By now, little Sajid had grown up after passing out from Mayo college did his masters from America and now works at an internationally reputed firm in Dayton, Ohio. As time would have it, he went on to become an American citizen. Suddenly he received information that his father could be in one of the Pakistan jails, he wrote the following letter to General Pervez Musharraf in 2002. Following are the extracts:

"What advice do you give a son? I do not want to give up and believe, with this appeal that I have the best opportunity to get an honest answer as to whether my father might be alive. As you may imagine, I am willing to do anything to reach a resolution.

Needless to say, I am forever indebted to you for taking the time to read this and assist in any possible way. Please advise."

Sajid also wrote a letter to the President of America. Following are the extracts:

"Now, there are frequent stories about the presence of Indian POWs being held in Pakistan.

If true, then after more than thirty years, these prisoners are no longer an information source. They are also not there because of any action the current government took. Therefore, the acknowledgement of their existence, should not be a source of embarrassment for the present Pakistan government. Arguably, it could help diffuse the tension and show goodwill on the part of the present regime, in Pakistan.

In the meantime, I wrote to Asma Jehangir and Mr. George Fernandes regarding the release of Indian POWs. I am mentioning all this to highlight the trauma and suffering that the widow undergoes in the uncertain knowledge of whereabouts of near and dear ones.

After 35 years, Shammi Malhotra w/o Squadron Leader. Prem Nath Malhotra is reliving the tragedy. She is shattered and inconsolable. The remains of flight AN-12-BL-534 have been traced, the mutilated body of Sepoy Beli Ram who died in the air crash 16,000 feet was found on the south Dakka Grlacier in Lahaul-Spiti.

The tragedy has struck the families of the 98 Defence Personnel once again. Shammi is a widow all over again.

The Air Force says that it will retrieve the wreckage of the plane. The families want to see signs of near and dear ones.

On the 6th of August 2003, I received an email from Sajid and I quote, "This is most likely the end of the road for our family. Can you please help us to get in touch with the right individuals so that the families can pay their last homage these soldiers deserve?

I am at a loss for words in reaching out ...."

In the present softening climate both governments must put needless acrimony and suspicion behind and take an upfront stance.

If prisoners exist, then maybe the best step forward in this road to peace is to exchange the prisoners. Both Indians and Pakistanis will be convinced on the workable nature of the road map to peace. Can expect this humanitarian gesture as transcending all petty consideration from our politicians?

(Mrs. Mohini Giri, is the founder trustee of Women's Initiative for Peace in South Asia)

18

Widows: Lifetime Prisoners of War

For 15 year old Ranjita, widowhood became a harsh reality even before she had seen the dreams of a bride. Married on 1st July 1998 to Gunner Jyoti Kumar, she was with him for exactly 24 hours, before he left for Ladakh. He came home in December 1998 for a 15 days leave. Ranjita knew wifehood for 11 days—11 days to get to know her husband, 11 days shared by innumerable relations. Because in the dusty village far away from the highway of Meerut, privacy is an unknown commodity. 22nd May 1999 Jyoti Kumar died at Kargil leaving behind a 15 year old widow to whom he never even wrote a letter.

Social conventions demand that Ranjita cries for a man she hardly knew. She cries, ... but more for her fate in being trapped in hostile surroundings. Tradition demands that Ranjita spends a life time of suppressing herself, adhering to a strict moral code of taboos. What a heavy price to pay for 11 days of marital life!

The support system of the Armed Forces, the regimental help, the payment of gratuity and pension all ensure that Ranjita is comfortably well off. Both her parents and in-laws are engaged in a tug of war, for the privilege of taking care of Ranjita. Privilege, because who ever takes care of uneducated Ranjita will gain access to the money that she gets as a war widow. At 15 years Ranjita has realised that as a golden goose, she has no parents or in-laws. All are out-laws—out to deprive her of a life of dignity, all in the hypocritical garb of sympathy.

As soon as a woman becomes a widow it is not only the loss of the beloved one which troubles her, but multi-dimensional issues economic, social, physical torment her. Financial security does not automatically lead to her empowerment and although finances are a major constraint, that is not the only consideration. Economic assistance does not necessarily improve her status. Major factors that inhibit place her in a disadvantaged position are ignorance, powerlessness and vulnerability. It is a sad indeed that border skirmishes or war only effect the people who are left behind especially women.

Financial aid to enable the war widow to be economically self-supporting is absolutely vital. But this aid unaccompanied by socio-legal changes ensures that she is a prisoner of her circumstances. The money given by the government ranging from Rs.3 lacs to 10 lakh to enable her to live a life of dignity makes her a puppet in the hands of greedy relations. Lathika a war widow of 1971 aggression was horrified to know that her in-laws planned to marry her off to her student brother-in-law. Obviously this crude method was to get control of her money. Of course taking care of Lathika's future was just incidental to their plans. Fortunately for Lathika good sense prevailed before she was sacrificed to the dangerous intentions of well meaning relations. The officer's widow is in a better position since her education may protect from being duped. But the Jawan's widow is absolutely a prisoner of her money and conditions. Very often she has little access to the finances. More often than not, she is dependent on the mercy of her in-laws, brothers or father for the financial dignity that is rightfully hers.

Most social organisation and NGOs feel that the war widow is dependent on her relations for shelter. Herein lies the root of exploitation. Being dependent on someone else for a roof over her head, she has to trade off her financial independence. Of course housing allotments are made by the Government and Armed Forces. But the benefit reaches the very few. As a principle if a small apartment be allotted to each war widow by the government in tandem with the state government, then she is in a better position to safe guard her financial position.

The attitude of the government at the Centre and State and to an extent the social organisations has been woefully myopic. Aid is made available to the war widow. That's it! Everyone feels very sanctimonious. The problem doesn't stop there. In fact it just begins. The social organisations and NGOs with the help of Zilla Sainik Board have to keep a constant vigil to ensure that the hapless widow is not being taken advantage of—for at least such time that she is capable of handling her life herself. She must have the confidence that there are non-interested parties to whom she can go for aid, advice and guidance.

The trauma of being a war widow goes much beyond financial insecurity. Today in India there are approximately 33 million widows that is 9 per cent of the total women's population. Of this approximately 20 thousand are war widows of 1962, 1965 and 1971 aggressions. To this is added the compounding all of these difficulties–the monumental task of being a single parent. Many of the war widows do work to supplement their incomes. This syndrome often fuels a guilt complex in the mother, in not being able to give enough of her self to her children - that too, children who have lost their fathers. In trying to assuage the guilt, she bends backwards to adjust and accommodate, resulting in having maladjusted children. Society would of course insist that these children suffer from the lack of a father figure. They probably suffer from having too much of a guilt stricken mother figure.

A definite social change alone can alleviate the trauma of a war widow. Media must stop projecting the traditional image of the white clad Indian widow, hapless, helpless and an easy prey. Media may be reflecting society, but it is high time to stop distorting reflections. In a patriarchal society like ours, change has to emanate from the man. Very often women are helpless witnesses to the atrocities committed in the name of preservation of morals. A war widow has to be treated normally - neither with kid gloves or with a whip hand. She is a victim of an unfortunate circumstance who needs economic, social and legal help. She is neither a candidate for sainthood nor a temptress. She needs social encouragement to get over her trauma and pick up the threads of her life again in terms of remarriage or taking up a career.

Social organisations need to work over time to bring this enlightenment, particularly in rural India where often being a widow is equated with punishment for a sin. There can be absolutely no religious stigma attached to an unfortunate circumstance. After all a widower is considered to be more sinned against than sinning. Specific social reforms and collective actions need to be set in motion immediately keeping the crisis in view.

1. Women need an identity as autonomous individuals and as citizens of the country.
2. Women require a time and space at the grassroots level to meet, organize, and unleash their own power for change.

3. Non-governmental organisations should be sensitized to examine the actions they are taking to support widows, their own role in perpetuating patriarchy.
4. Existing schemes need to be redesigned to include mechanisms whereby women have better control over resources.

Social security must be made available to every war widow regardless of her education or economic strata.

1. .'Anti-poverty measures', under which widows should be given preferential treatment: land redistribution; allotment of house sites and houses; health schemes; public distribution; employment guarantee and self-employment programmes; credit schemes.
2. 'Pro-women measures', which would benefit widows as well as other women, e.g. female education, enforcement of laws relating to minimum age at marriage, and protection of women's property rights.
3. 'Rehabilitation measures', targeted specifically at widows, such as vocational training, adult education, awareness camps, legal counselling, provisions of assets for self-employment, residential housing for elderly widows.
4. 'Social security measures', which are designed for and/or targeted at widows, including: survivor benefits (in the form of social assistance provided by the government, or subsidized life insurance extended to rural areas); calamity insurance (e.g., insurance of housing, land, animals, tools, trees and other productive assets); unemployment insurance (e.g., unemployment compensation for working widows); pensions (monthly allowances for all widows, or for widows without adult sons); short stay homes for widows.

A multi-dimensional approach has to be encouraged by the government in tandem with state governments NGOs and social organizations.This alone can correct any imbalances that arrest the war widow's attempt to lead a normal life.

It's highly cronic that socially politically and lagally sati is banned in India. But a throughly outdalted social attitude a male in clined system of rights and a rather myopic approach to the problem makes the was widow's life a burning hall. It'a time that in the new millennium, we change them for all times.

(*Names have been chaged to protect the identities of the people*)

19

The Unsung Brave

Kargil has been cleared—so the press tells us. It is been a great victory for India—so the government tells us. But in war there are no winners. There are only losers—loss of property, resources and precious human lives. The soldiers have made their ultimate sacrifice leaving behind bereaved families. The war has just begun for them—war against deprivation, poverty and loneliness. They are the unsung brave. It goes to the credit of the government that once the first shell shock had worn off, they quickly got their act together for aid and succour to the bereaved families. The Hon'ble Defence Minister convened a committee to put forth certain recommendations which the government accepted. The broad gist of the rehabilitation measures are:

- Fast Track procedure for speedy payment of ex-gratia compensation. Controller General of Defence Accounts to settle all cases within 48 hours from date of receipt of claims.
- Ex-gratia lumpsum compensation payable increased from Rs. 2 lakh to Rs.7.5 lakh along with family pension equal to last monthly salary drawn by the deceased soldier.
- In addition to ex-gratia payment of Rs.7.5 lakh in case of death and Rs. 6 lakh in case of injury Rs. 5 lakh would be given to families to acquire – dwelling with an out of turn basis by housing projects or state housing boards.
- Rs. 2 lakh additionally would be deposited in long-term fixed deposits – the interest would go towards education of children.
- 500 petrol pumps and LPG dealership have been reserved for the bereaved families.

It is certainly a laudable effort on the part of the government to incorporate the families into the mainstream of life. But the problem has so many ramifications and there are so many slips and red tapes between the policy and the execution, that the families are never able to fully reap the benefits of the government's rehabilitation measures. Pushpa Rawat widow of Kripal Singh Rawat (4055826) of 18 Garhwal Rifles, mother of 5, lives in a rented house in Karbala, New Delhi. The landlord threatens to evict her from her house. When will the Rs. 5 lakh set aside for her dwelling reach her? For pregnant Mukesh widow of L/NK Satbir Singh (2886165) of 2nd Rashtriya Rifles, a separate dwelling unit away from her in-laws is a must since her life is threatened by them. At the moment she has got a reprieve on life because the sonograph showed that she was carrying a son. The wheels of the government may move too late for Mukesh. The government needs to fix a time limit for disbursal of the money for a dwelling unit.

Available Options

On a personal interaction with the bereaved families it was clear that only 2 options existed with the widows:

- To continue staying with in-laws or parents.
- To stay in an independent unit.

The advantages of the first option are the continued relationship with the husband's family and a possibility of the children getting a share in the property. Of course in-laws and parents could provide the emotional support if – only if they are not blinded by greed for the compensation. On the other hand in the first option the widow trades away her financial independence for the shelter provided. She is also likely to be swindled of her money – as is the case with Vimlesh widow of L/NK Ravi Karan. Mother of 2 children, she is caught between the devil and the deep sea. Vimlesh on the one hand faces the jealousy of her in-laws since the total compensation is in her name. On the other hand she faces the greedy pressure from her parents, 2 unemployed brothers, and an unmarried sister. Most of these widows particularly in the states of Rajasthan, Haryana, Punjab and parts of Uttar Pradesh are pressurized to marry their brothers-in-law. Manoj Devi widow of Sepoy Naresh Muskoh (3179697) of 17 Jat will almost certainly be married off to her brother-in-law. After all her other-in-law a 16 year old widow of 1971 aggression was married off to her brother-in-law!

Many of the widows prefer the second option of staying in 2 room tenements provided by the government in Regimental centres or cantonments nearest to their villages. Even though she would be away from relatives, she would not be beholden to anyone for her shelter. The financial independence is secure. Vocational training, educational opportunities, employment facilities are facilitated by this arrangement. The support system provided by other sisters in her plight would lessen the emotional trauma.

Role of Big Brother

What has clearly emerged from a detailed study of the bereaved family is that the armed forces would have to take an even more pro-active role in the case of the families. If in individual regimental centres or cantonments, 2 room tenements can be provided, the forces would have at one place the families needing their care. One of the major obstacles in the disbursal of aid, and the followup on rehabilitation measures is the sheer distances. A congregated community would make investment guidance, educational opportunities, vocational training, employment facilities, counselling etc. practical and viable. The forces could make use of the services of retired officers, JCO's and the welfare centres to facilitate this role of a guardian. Reema Begum widow of L/NK Hussain (2690297), with only a coolie father-in-law for support can turn to the armed forces alone for support, guidance and care.

Financial fall outs: The compensation given is certainly generous and the government is making every attempt to ensure that she is not swindled of her right, by depositing the cheque in the name of the widow. But the money itself divides her away from her-in-laws. For those who adopt the options of staying with the in-laws, some part of the compensation must be made available to them. The compensation attracts the greed of relatives and an illiterate widow is very easy to dupe. Illiterate Malhori Devi widow of L/NK Kharak Singh (3180920) does not even know/how many zeroes are there in Rs.7.5 lakh. The welfare institutions of the armed forces, NGOs, Bank and financial institutions must ensure that proper and viable investment guidance is made available to them.

The complete expense incurred by injured soldiers in any private institution is borne by the government. Often children of deceased soldiers require specialized treatment which sometimes the army hospitals may not be able to provide. Kamlesh widow of Naik Soran Singh of Rajputana Rifles has a 6 year old son with a hole in the heart. He needs specialized treatment. Possibly the government/armed forces could provide special medical cards to the bereaved families which could obtain treatment for them in any private hospital or institution.

The armed forces must with all firmness work out a system by which marriages are registered in their own records, and this should be accepted by the civil authorities too. Ideally still, dual registration both with the armed forces and civil authorities must be compulsory and immediate nominations too should be made simultaneously. Many widows share the plight of 18 year old Sunita, widow of Sepoy Gajpal Singh (3189532) of 17 Jat who has still to get her compensation as her name had not been nominated in the official papers. The Government while granting compensation must make the tax status clear. This alone can prevent petty officials from making a profit from ignorance. Finanally all ex-gratia payments must be uniform for all state. The soldiers were Indians fighting for India. Why should there be a distinction between a soldier from UP and one from Rajasthan?

Zilla Sainik Boards

These boards certainly need to be rejuvenated to take a more pro-active role. The very composition needs to change. These male dominated Zilla Sainik boards, with a strong gender bias can hardly be a focus of emotional counselling for the widows. How would these gunghat clad women ever confide in them? More often then not, these boards want to settle matters quickly by joining hands with the family in pressurizing the widows to marry her brother-in-law. As Geeta widow of L/NK Rishi Pal is being pressurized in village Sonali Khend, Panipat. There must be a woman member in the Zilla Sainik Board—ideally an educated war widow from that region and an NGO representative. The Boards have to take on the role of counsellors. Kalpana widow of L/NK Naresh (3185589) of 4 Jat received the mutilated, tortured body of her husband. Yogendra Singh's (2893507) parents too received the mutilated body of their son. Their agony is difficult to fathom. Tremendous and consistent emotional counselling is needed to exorcise their grief and rage.

New Paradigms

The governmental perspective of the rehabilitation measures must undergo a qualitative change – to make the package more viable, more in keeping with the demands of the new millennium. The attitude earlier was to see the widows as beneficiaries. They must be seen as primary authors and actors of their own development. The strategy should not be to just provide services, but to empower and mobilize self reliant action by providing an enabling environment. The rehabilitation package must seek with the help of NGOs and Armed Forces to make the war widow a self supporting entitity. Aid should not be seen as a one time availability. Care of the bereaved families is a continuous process as the Armed Forces itself has realized. Most of the widows are between the ages of 18-25. Any programme created for them has to be long-sighted keeping future options in view. This alone is the dignity that we can accord to the unsung brave.

20

Wish We Could Stretch Out and Touch Your Hand

We were standing at the Wagah border on August 14, 2002 at 5 p.m. People were thronging on both sides, perhaps 2000 on our side and 5000 on theirs. Pakistan and India celebrate their independence days on August 14 and 15 respectively. Music filled the air. Indian side played the same patriotic songs over and over: *"Mera rang de basanti chola" and "Ye desh hai veer jawano ka".* Music could be heard from the other side as well. The path we were directed to skirted around the visitors galleries and ran alongside the Pakistan side. An identical 'Pakistan path' runs parallel to the Indian path for about 30 yards where both peoples virtually 'walk together'. We could see women and men from the other side looking at us with great curiosity. We must have appeared equally curious to them. Suddenly we stopped in our tracks. Wonderstrack. The three slight figures on the other side who were smiling and waving at us were–Asma, Salima and Shahtaf.

These are dear friends and fellow travellers with whom we have spent many days in many parts of the world - including India and Pakistan. Could they stretch out their fingers and touch us? We were reminded of Michelangelo's painting on the Sistin Chapel - God and Adam reaching out to one another across the heavens. In the painting they are stretching to touch the tips of their fingers. But we Pakistanis and Indians cannot bridge the inches; we are forced apart by the might of the two states. Here 'across the border', we were blowing kisses at each other. Some eyes became moist. Kuldip Nayar said *"Tum ro rahi ho".*

A small bunch of us with Kuldip, our *"Marg Darshak"* had gone to Amritsar to light candles at the Wagah border. This was our 7th year. We had heard people snigger and sneer at us. "A bunch of peaceniks who light candles for peace, so futile and infructuous". Said a former foreign Secretary at a meeting this summer at India International Centre. "Don't you have anything worthwhile to do than light candles at borders and invoke peace?" Friends, well-wishers, opinion-makers have asked over the years. Then the usual jibe: "A bunch of fools go all the way—but no one ever appears on the other side. Where are your friends, peaceniks of Pakistan?" The first time we had gone, there were Nikhil Chakravarty, Vinod Mehta, Justice Sachar, Rajiv Sethi all walking to the edge of India, lighting candles within two metres of the gate with the sign "Welcome to the Islamic Republic of Pakistan".

That year Kuldip had patiently answered the volley of media questions *"Kahan hain apke dost?" Wahan se koi aaya?* "When we told them that they had been, physically stopped 4 kms before they could reach their own side, they looked at us with scorn and disbelief. Last ear again, as we leant later, they were stopped again, only this time there were rough and ugly scenes with the Pakistan Rangers. But this time they were there and we watched them with eyes brimming with tears. Niti, a student who was part of out team heard people say, *"Wahan inke rishtedaar honge!"* Faiz Sahib expressed it the best when he wrote:

Ek ek kar ke huey jatey hain tarey ranshan

Meri manzil ki teraf terey qadam atey hain

One by one light up the far off stars

Your steps to me are moving from afar

Suddenly the music stopped on both sides. It was time for both flags to be lowered and the gates opened on both sides. It remained so for about 10 minutes. On both sides the men who were to 'Beat the Retreat' had been hand picked. Tall, stern, stiff and fierce, dressed in the best regalia of BSF and Pakistan Rangers, they rushed from either side stamping the earth with their massive boots as if they would break open her bosom. They were grown men who had been told to spew venom and hatred with every gesture of their hand, every stamp of their foot and every expression on their face. A few days ago Dr. Kamla Chowdhary had visited this drill and witnessed this display of intense loathing. "I wish they would stop this abomination and embrace one another", she had said. To us it seemed as if they would devour each other.

"I have never seen anything more absurd in my life" said Shreva a Class 11 student, one of our party. The Sardars, one of our hosts, were waving at the Pakistanis. "See that one in green shirt. He is my friend. Often comes to Amritsar." The "green shirt" and his friends were waving madly. We were searching in the crowd for our friends. "Please send Asma" we implored a photographer on the other side. "Please... please". He looked at us and shook his head. Later we were told by our BSF that Asma and others were "taken away" by the Rangers. We managed to inch our way back to the path.

None of our friends were there. Those who were sitting around deliberately looked away, as if they did not want to meet our eye. "We have a message from the crowd," our hosts said. "They are saying *"Kuldip Sahib se kahiye hamko hath hilaen*" Kuldip raised his hands. Hundreds of hands went up on the other side.

Suddenly we felt a sense of cohesion among us. Ten of us who had come from Delhi, some of us had met for the first time, and 14 of our hosts- the best and the warmest Amritsaris. We looked at each other and said "We wish these gates would open and people could flow back and forth. The Jiyalas of Lahore and Gabru Jawans of Amritsar; the girls from Mall Road and Hall Road arm in arm at Hall Bazaar and Bano Bazaar".

The night was sheer magic. Over ten thousand people from all over Punjab met under the umbrella of Hind Pak *Dosti Manch.* From 7 pm onwards the music started at one end, while *langar* arranged by committed people and generous donors started from the other. Singer after singer came on stage and celebrated the vibrancy and vigour of Punjab. This time we noticed that the stage had been built closer to no man's land'. We could almost 'see' the Lahoris sitting on the other side in pitch dark, swaying to the music.

At last came the moment every one was waiting for—Hans Raj Hans.

Hans Raj Hans has become a cult figure, his music is heard across the country from Kanniya Kumari to Kashmir. He started with a poem of Shiv Kumar Batalvi. "People ask me why do I come to the Sarhad? say I come here because here comes a man who lights a candle 1of hope. This is my khidmat, my contribution to his cause. I only have one humble request from both sides. Can you pass a law, which makes it incumbent for every Minister, every

President, every Prime Minister, and all the *'mahaan hastis'* to send one son in the military... to be killed in war. Let this happen. Then they will understand what mothers, sisters, wives and daughters on both sides of the border feel when the dead bodies are brought home.

The audience laughed, wept, danced with Hans. He sang his famous "*Voh jo silli silli aundi hai hawa*" "That damp breeze that comes across—someone must be crying on the other side". He had spoken for all of us 10,000 on this side and many on the other who were listening with bated breath.

At the stroke of midnight the candles were lit. Media surrounded us with questions. Do you feel you have brought about a change? What about cross-border terrorism? Do you blame Pakistan? Do you think one day we will say with one voice, Hindustan-Pakistan Zindabad?

Kuldip's vision this year had transcended India and Pakistan. He spoke of a South Asian identity. Bangladesh, Sri Lanka, Nepal. Pakistan, India. The people of Punjab understood what Kuldip was saying. Hans Raj's music was reverberating the same sentiment. But the leaders of both sides are still unable to understand the power of a regional identity. It does not suit them to let the people come together. It raises too many inconvenient questions. It draws attention to their colossal failures. They cannot risk it. So they stop the bus, the train, the plane, clamp the gates in the face of thousands who would rather see them open. One small 'tilli' holds the massive gates shut against human traffic while the birds, the clouds, the breezes go merrily back and forth. The small tilli is probably symbolic of the very fragile endeavours of the two governments to hold the friends back from the borders. But for how long? To what avail?

Last night the scene at Wagah confirmed our belief that leaders on both sides can delay peace; they can no longer stop it. This overwhelming mass of humanity, when it is clamouring for peace, for exchanges, for sharing... how long can they plug their ears against their demands? Wagah is not the achievement of a handful of people from Delhi. It is the victory of people of India and Pakistan that they their voices have disturbed the complacency residing in the corridors of power. We felt that there were definitely some solid achievements. There was personal warmth and bond between people and the very fact that it has sustained for over a period shows that the peoples movement is gaining strength. It was heartening to note that the movement was not confined to the Wagah border but had spread to the Husainwala Border and as far away as USA where Indian and Pakistanis were also lighting the candles.

Our belief in collective voices had strengthened and we were happy that there was equal reciprocity of both sides.

Can we hope that the sterile boardrooms of foreign offices will be left far behind to rummage through their musty files and impotent agreements. It won't be long before the people of both countries, the bearers of candles and torches, together, usher a new dawn.

The Hind Pak Dosti—Folklore Research Academy - International Cultural Society Punjabi Forum Janwadi Lekhak Sangh Amritsar and with the cooperation of all the people of India and the people of different region resolved on that night:

(a) To appeal to both the Governments to solve the Kashmir problem peacefully and that Pakistan Government puts an end to terrorism.

(b) To appeal to both the Governments to have a treaty not to use nuclear weapons.

(c) Both the Government should start train, air and land services so that common man can come and go.

(d) Both the Governments to lessen the tension at the borders and to withdraw the forces from the borders.

(e) The demand for the exchange of artists, writers, intellectuals. They should be given visas liberally.

Today there will be two rows of candles on both sides of India. Pakistan borders. We have to choose between the electrified fence and candles. This is what people would choose. But sometime there will be a single row of candles some day... sometime...

21
Crossing Divides

Today when the very fabric of world peace is torn by communal strife, fundamentalism and terrorism, we were overjoyed *to* receive an invitation from the ASR, Pakistan for the two-day peace conference on June 29-30 to be held at Lahore. The response to the invitation among the Indian civil society was tremendous. The need of the hour of course was for some sane Indians and sane Pakistanis to join hands for peace at this crucial hour.

The invitation letter from sisters in Pakistan said "We are sure that you will all agree that we cannot work for a better and just society, in our country and in the region unless we are able to work towards peace. By this we do not mean just the absence of war but a society in which there is equity at every level; that is provincial, linguistic, religious, sectarian, racial and gender. This would mean that we work towards eliminating hegemony of any particular class, province, religion or sex and that we work towards a democratic just, tolerant and demilitarized society. We are convinced of the fact that all these are equally important for ail of us in the region particularly South Asia and Afghanistan, in which millions of people suffer because of conflicts within our countries and between our countries. In these conflicts women invariably pay a greater price; during the conflict as victims of war and as refugees with no right of citizenship; and their voices and their needs are not reflected in either conflict resolutions or in reconstructing the society post conflicts".

Naturally this gave the Women's initiative for Peace in South Asia a golden opportunity to raise our voices together at a larger forum in a stronger voice so that our voices are heard in togetherness and has an impact on micro and macro politics, in Women's Initiative for Peace in South Asia we strongly believe that:

- People to people contact is the surest way to build a pressure of public opinion for peace which no government can afford to ignore.
- Women though not part of the decision process when it comes to war or foreign relations are an integral part of the decision for peace. In fact for the first time women initiated a peace process which is now snow balling at such a swift pace.
- Historical, cultural and social commonalities ensure that a direct link of understanding can be built.
- Kashmir is an issue that troubles the peace process. But the optimism is high that a pragmatic process of compromises can solve the problem.
- The pragmatic view that half a century old distrust must be put behind.
- The approach that India as a vibrant democracy with an industrial, educational and commercial infrastructure has much to offer other South Asian countries.
- The vital need to build a cohesive South Asian identity that will ensure a greater negotiating muscle on the global stage.
- Above all the realization that despite what successive governments in Pakistan have reiterated India has no hegemonistic design on Pakistan.
- The vital realization that peace in South Asia is no longer a choice but the only reality left for survival.

However to our great disappointment our hopes were not realized as we could not get permission from the Home Ministry to cross the Wagah border just yet to attend the peace conference on 28th and 29th of June. We had hoped that the people's voices would perhaps open up a viable media for opportunities and create an environment for peace. But we have to strive harder to cross the borders of suspicion, distrust, short sighted approach to progress and above all the cacophony of war rhetoric.

History tells us that those who instigate war will eat their own evil foods. The 21st century is a home for 6.3 billion people and we should see that this figure is not affected by wars like the last century where humankind experienced two world wars, more than 30 regional wars, above 150 internal wars, border disputes and skirmishes, death due to fundamentalism and now we face the greatest threat to humanity by the fear of the nuclear explosion and imminent war. Absence of peace can only bring death and destruction.

A time has now come when both women and men have to step together in pursuing an agenda of peace along with the women's movement in both India and Pakistan. Needless to say that the strength of the women's movement is often countered by hostility from divisive forces such as religious fundamentalism and patriarchy. Today it is most important that we from the women's movement link women's issue to human rights issues and come up on a common platform in the women's struggle for survival.

It has been the endeavour of Women's Initiative for Peace in South Asia to bring about various voices in the country through common mobilization like the Manila Millennium Mobilisation where peace chains were formed throughout the nation on the 19th of December 1999 just before the turn of the century. Women throughout the length and breadth of Asia came up with the slogan of "empowerment for peace and peace for empowerment". We had also endeavoured to bring women's voices together by including various groups in the people to people contact delegations that were taken to Pakistan and in return Pakistani sisters reciprocated their gesture in the same way to initiate a habit of dialogue arid discussion in the region, talking to each other on issues of mutual concern, facilitating movement between two countries in South Asia.

Our endeavour has also been to offer and advocate the conceptual gap between our countries by emphasizing the role of writers, creative thinkers, musicians in developing a shared ideology. Experiences of women in political, economic and cultural spheres in both the countries seem to be transcending the forces of militarism, patriarchy, religious fundamentalism and in one voice women speak up on this issue of violence faced by women. Some of the resolutions at the Conference of Asian Parliamentarians for Peace and Cooperation were:

1. Promote concerted regional efforts for prevention and resolution of conflicts in the Asian continent.
2. Support the United Nations in its central role in conflict prevention and resolution.
3. Recommend that the Association of Asian Parliaments for Peace may examine the establishment of a regional early warning

system for effective detection, prevention, resolution and transformation of violent conflicts.

4. Recommend a multidisciplinary approach for peace building, based on active participation of, and cooperation among, government, parliamentarians, NGO's, private sector, media, and others in civil society.
5. Recommend also the use of multi-track diplomacy for establishment of favourable conditions towards prevention and resolution of violent conflicts.
6. Urge countries to consider reducing their defence expenditures in order to commit greater resources towards the welfare of their peoples.
7. Promote the development of research for peace, conflict resolution and combating terrorism, including state terrorism.

Women's groups across the country and in the South Asia region need to start listening to the voices of women who have been directly and indirectly affected by armed conflict and lend a hand in helping them cope with adverse circumstances and help in formation of peace action committees where concerned women themselves express a need for peace.

Virtually every country in our region has been affected by armed conflict. In our own country, India, from Kashmir in the north to Andhra Pradesh in the South and in virtually ail the North Eastern states, barring Arunachal Pradesh and Mizoram, armed groups are engaged in fighting with the state, or with each other. Most of these armed conflicts are a result of people organizing around the issue of identity - in Kashmir, in Assam, in Nagaland, Manipur, Tripura and Meghalaya. In Andhra Pradesh and parts of central India, the extreme left or Naxalite Movements are fighting a class struggle, with the state apparatus.

But, in this process, hundreds of innocent people, and people who do not necessarily subscribe to the armed resolution of conflict, are caught in the crossfire between these opposing groups. In India wherever there is prolonged armed conflict, a dangerous trend is the shrinking of democratic spaces. People who raise their voices against violence and injustice are immediately considered threats and attempts are made to silence them, by both the state and the armed opposition groups, if one is critical of the governments actions then one is termed "anti-national", and if one dares to question the terror tactics of extremist groups then one will be dubbed "an agent of the state".

Women have been affected in different ways by this low intensity warfare that is taking place. In some cases they are direct victims of rape, torture, and death. In the majority of cases they are the ones who are *forced* to take a hold over themselves during and after the fighting to pick up pieces and rebuild their lives and those of their families and communities. Sn many cases they have been forced to flee their homes and live as refugees in another place.

As I have earlier mentioned networking among all the women's groups is of paramount importance *today* because very often women and men who may want to initiate effort for peace alone by themselves are singled out and harassed. It is vital today that we link up to national, regional and international networks who can act as a visible support group and be effective in prevention of Human Rights violations. Today women need to go beyond picking up pieces and patching up lives to determining what kind of society and what kind of life do they want. To do this we need to broaden our horizons. The time has now come for new thinking in South Asia. For too long we have been linked with a fear of possible impending conflict. This kind of a feeling has resulted in the region lagging behind the world. In meeting the legitimate aspirations of its people a new approach and a new mindset is necessary for us to go ahead and make a new beginning. We have to play a larger role in political, social and economic life of the country and naturally the key to all this is that we do advocate the passing of many of the pending bills whether it be for 33% reservation or domestic violence bill or the property rights of women in the Parliament, the crux is empowerment of women on a large scale.

It is only when we are empowered we will be able to put an end to the culture of violence that threatens to engulf humankind and work towards a no war, *goli nahi boli* situation for a peaceful world. If only we had strong linkages, one powerful empowered voice, it is not just a Wagah border that we could cross but beyond the seven seas.

22

War at What Cost

Headlines everyday make us shiver to think of what will happen to those thousands of wives whose future depends on what our political pandits decide about waging war.

I still remember visiting Chirawa on July 19th, 1999 after Kargil operations along with Aruna Dalmia and Tripat Kaur, widow of 1965 operations to visit families of those killed during operations. Our journey took us across 400 kms. to various small hamlets of Jhunjhunu, Chirawa, Churum and Sikar. We traversed through dusty, bumpy fields for days together sometimes by foot and sometimes in a jeep covered in dust and grime to reach those tiny hamlets from which our brave jawans came. We would visit at least six families a day and each visit left us stunned by the magnitude of the grief, helplessness and the waste of life.

For Brijesh Devi of Dhambada Rajasthan the tragedy of her husband's death hit her only when his mutilated body came back home and during cremation a bullet was discovered among his ashes. When we met Brijesh Devi she was clutching the bullet in her hands and placing it at the place of worship. The bullet she says will be a constant reminder of the futility of war. There are of course several thousand widows in a similar situation.

I often wonder can we draw a line between national security and social security. Although women suiter the most they are considered outside the realm of politics and matters of national security. Needless to say no national security can be built without social security as the two are interdependent. If a society suffers and does not feel secure then what is the use of building up national security? Today it is nearly 37 years since the 1971 war destroyed several thousands of families and shattered the lives of hundreds of women. Since then they have till today never felt secure. Roopa was only 26 when her husband was declared missing. She had two small sons. For several years she refused to accept the fact that she was a widow. After great deal of persuasion we made her accept the pensions etc. that were given to the war widows in 1971. One day in 1972 she suddenly came and told me that she was going to China to hunt for her missing husband. I had tears in my eyes. I knew that her search was futile. "However" she did go to China. She came back and told me that she went to every nook and corner, looked at every beggar to see if she could find her husband anywhere there. Such is the insecurity and trauma that a woman faces.

Time and again we have discussed the importance of dialogue and specially so after the Indian and Pakistani nuclear tests in May 1998 steadily deteriorated the relations between the two countries. Each time civil society and peace loving people bring forth the importance of confidence building measures, war history is created on a war footing. Knowing how important it is to safeguard the interests of women we had launched the Lahore Bus Yatra. We were trying to create a counter peace hysteria. We found that the traditional approaches to building confidence were not people oriented. We wanted to avoid military means of achieving transparency and bring forth a psychological milieu in which the two nations conduct their relations. Therefore we presumed that if South Asia is to benefit from prevailing emphasis on confidence and trust building measures an alternative approach favouring a psychological solution and people to people contact needs to be employed.

While we traversed through the desert land of Rajasthan and met Dhanpati, Kushalo Dev, Dhanni, Gyan, Malhori Devi each one's family in their own simple language told us that the Indo-Pakistani hostility is the creation and the perpetuation of so many myths surrounding each country which were determining factors for the hostility. Each simple villager acknowledged mat this hostility was a creation of the media, the governmental authority in both countries and several folk myths, I learnt from several war widows that building confidence therefore would require not a Simla Agreement or not the Agra Summit but on altering the commonly held myths about the other through facilitating people to people contacts, interaction with media, interaction of school children with each other and most important these contacts should not be restricted to the elite alone but it must broaden its scope to include a large number of ordinary citizens specially women and children.

After several visits we came to the conclusion that in order to help widows and the future generation. It is important that conflict resolution and initiatives for peace have the intellectual and moral solidarity of human kind. Human solidarity can only be expressed with the full participation of women and taking into account women's particular experiences and needs. The creation of a culture of peace must be addressed with priority at all levels of society. In today's increasingly globalised economy and networked world, it has to be led first and foremost at the international level where actions are a major determinant of regional and national environment.

Alter working with the cause of war widows, child widows, religious wodows, political widows, widows of natural calamities for so long I realized that war is really necessary to make us pine for peace! Why is that so? Peace without question is a crucial factor for human development. Arms can only be bought at the cost of bread in people's stomach, at the cost of development and the cost of human lives. Even when we mourn the loss of precious lives and limbs in hostilities our hearts go to those thousands of families who are uprooted, destroyed and traumatized.

One of the major problems in South Asia is the pathetic position of those women who are widowed and who constitute in India alone 33 million women, 9% of the women population. They are victims of social, cultural, religious and political discrimination. Even though the constitution of every country guarantees equality to men and women, the discrimination against widows, even now in the 21st century makes one feel that they belong to no human category. Her human dignity is trampled upon and the human right of freedom of expression is snatched away. Her physical security is at stake and she is tortured both physically and mentally. This state of affairs is present in almost all South Asian countries. The main focus of deprivation is:

- Social Discrimination—this discrimination is given the approval of traditions and religious sanctions.
- Economic Deprivation—the traditional breadwinner is no longer alive and she herself is not equipped to earn.

- Legally marginalized—Unaware of her rights and incapable of asserting herself, she has no judicial recourse.
- Lack of support—very few governments and NGOs view widows as a special category with individual problems and a specialized status.

In order to bring about a vital gender bonding in the South Asian region and to empower the single woman. It is inportant that South Asian Women Summit meet to talk. We hope many of the problems faced would be addressed by social activists, religious leaders, media representatives, members of the concerned governments, institutions as well as widows who have experienced social economic marginalisation.

23

Religion is it Operate from Politics

As a little child I often heard my mother recite a "mantra" which said "even as waters from the clouds, meandering along different paths return to the same ocean, so does one's prayers to different forms of God ultimately reach the supreme being". That one mantra laid the foundation to a strong belief that all religions and scriptures did influence one's way of thinking, behaving and acting. Since the Vedic days to the present day thinkers, we find an unbroken continuous history of philosophy of the people of India. All hues of thought, be it idolatory, theism, monotheism to atheism all, find a place.

Vedas affirm that there is something sacred in all life and all nature, that divinity pervades the entire universe. According to any tradition or scripture that recognizes such a spiritual component to life and to the world, it is always profoundly respected. My guru-bhai Swami Chidanandji often said that "various religious systems that exist and prevail in this world today are ever so many ways of approaching the one supreme cosmic reality... Who is transcendental and cannot be encompassed within the confines of the limited experience of our finite sense, of our finite inner cognizing instrument of mind, intellect etc. That supreme is known as PARA, which in the Sanskrit language means that which transcends, that which goes beyond and that which is beyond.

Within the context of the Vedic religion the different paths of yoga one through feeling... one through reasoning... one through concentration one through active service... although apparently different are recognized as being of the one Supreme non-dual cosmic reality.

All religions therefore exist and prevail in order to raise the human spirit toward its essential divine status. Godly status so that man's nature becomes filled with the God like qualities of love, compassion, kindness, purity and with everything that is sublime, beautiful, holy and sanctifying.

The very fact that we all debating to understand if religions have influenced our political, social and cultural directions is proof enough that even when we see spiritualism corroding we are striving to reach out and hold on to those spiritual values. Today man has reached the moon, but global wars are still continuing with all this venom and destruction... robots are moving in as humanism is moving out. We are paying the price for advancement and civilization by moving in the direction of conflict and strife. We keep inflicting wounds aided by more weaponry and atomic finesse. We must stop here right now and contemplate for there is something fundamentally wrong in man's thinking as we have failed to learn lessons from the two world wars. A peculiar trait of religion is that it has often been a source of division, conflict, bloodshed and war. Examples of these can be found in the Crusades, the wars of religion in Europe, "Ethnic Cleansing" in the former Yugoslavia, and in India we have the Kashmir problem fueled from across the border.

The Women's initiative for peace in South Asia, went through the heartaches and silent cries of millions of sisters of South Asia who were the victims of enmity between two neighbouring countries. This women's group was influenced by the higher values of spiritualism. Our motto was "GOLI NAHIN BOLI" "no bullets but dialogue". Thus in the summer of 1999 WIPSA was launched with a conviction that women would be able to bring peace in the Indian subcontinent. We resolved to look within our souls and behold we found bliss, pulsating there; we knew a spiritual era was on the threshold of humanity once again. The task set to our generation was to reconcile the varying ideals of the converging religious patterns... weave them together to sustain and support, rather than combat and kill one another. We realized that we are living in a world of free interaction and we have no business to trample on the toes of our neighbours. We wanted to work toward building up a cohesive entity in South Asia. We know that people to people contact would bring that understanding and love between countries 41 of us decided to take the bus journey from New Delhi, India to Lahore Pakistan.

Later, this journey came to be known as the Lahore peace yatra. A whole new world of opportunity, advocacy and good will opened up. Our sisters in Pakistan welcomed us with open arms, warmth, love and of course songs, these were the moments of joy, for the first time sisters from two countries converged in harmony and goodwill. We also understood that we women who suffered the consequences of war the most are never invited to the negotiating tables. I am today very proud to be a part of history.

The step is in keeping with the aspirations of the people of both countries, particularly the women who suffer the most in conditions of conflict and who have the highest stakes in peace. WIPSA's endeavors to keep this continued contact on a sustained basis has in some measure corrected perspectives about each other on both sides of the border. So today peace initiatives do begin in an environment relatively free of preconceived notions and misrepresentations. WIPSA is hopeful that the visit of the General will open a new chapter bearing the simplest and most profound title, PEACE, in the book of Pakistan-India relations and that this chapter will then underpin the hopes of future generations of South Asians.

Spirituality teaches patience and patience is what the people of Pakistan and India have exhibited in the 53 years of hostility. In the hope that the next year, or the next month will bring the nightmare to an end. But the nuclearisation of both countries, each claming to have outdone the other, had brought that proverbial patience to an end. It dawned on us women that in this game of one upmanship between both the governments, the people have been forgotten. Inexorable facts such as ... it is the people who make countries, people who chalk destinies and it is the people who install governments have become embedded in the popular imagination. Religion teaches us that centrality of people can never be overlooked or undermined, it is people who are at the heart of decisions. Consequently, the argument that political decisions should be detached from public sentiment is flawed logic that needs to be expunged totally. It is for this reason today that civil society in general and women in particular are demanding a space for intervention in the process of normalization of the relationship. A clear direction comes from ancient scriptures that there should be peace and no bloodshed and a commitment by the governments that the nuclear button not be pressed now or ever. No longer are people willing to be mute witness to their being written and rewritten and destroyed by governments. We are no longer hesitant to stand up and be counted; we women today are determined to make the world a safe place for our children. The spontaneity with which people of both Pakistan and India responded to "the people to people contact" charted the course for an action oriented strategy. Needless to say this called for channelising political sensitivity in both countries.

We who pride ourselves in being a secular modern society have sometimes to pause and think whether social integration and a just society can exist without "spiritual capital" derived from religious precepts. If we discard the spiritual sources as old and outdated, where do we find the source of growth, brotherhood or social justice?

While our scriptures are of the point of view of "sarvadharma sambhavana" that is treating all religions equally it is however felt that this is not secularism. The state should distance itself from religion but it cannot totally separate. Sometimes to reform the state or political system we need the moralities or idealistic appeal of religion. And when religion degenerates the state is under obligation to intervene. Of course, one must expect politicians to appeal to religious identities and hatred to get votes. A direct ban on such activities is at best futile and at worst encourages authoritarianism. This does not mean that those who uphold the ideals of secularism and those of democracy based on mass suffrage should give up hope. One should abstain from vain preaching. Freedom of dissent and freedom of expression is another principle, which must be unconditionally applied to promoting secular ethos.

Religion and Culture

As far back as the 5th century BC, Budhism had a sweeping effect not only on the cultural and social day to day life of that civilization, but the rulers of that time adapted the principals of Buddhism in their administrative setup. So much so that Ashoka the Great influenced by the teaching of Buddha, gave up the path of violence and adapted ahimsa or non-violence as the main motto of his administration.

Waves of rejection of dogmas and decay of religion and ethics at various stages of development gave rise to a new thinking and many religions like Jainism, Buddhism and Sikhism emerged. All these were bora of the Indian thought and culture that could amalgamate the different styles of thought. Even religions that came from outside the country like Islam and Christianity found an honoured place in India.

During the period 1192 to 1596 Sufis gained particular support through poetry and in the media of local languages. The most favoured and popular Chiti order of Sufism professed the Sufi teaching theory of unity of being, oneness of existence, Yogic definition of Unity of Being was similar to thoughts from Persian poetry.

15th and 16th century poetry developed through poets like Kabir, Nanak and Surdas.

In Sikhism, Nanak incorporated good points of Hinduism and Islam.

Not so far back in the 16th century Akbar the great, the Mogul ruler of India was influenced by the dictates of all the religions and declared his state religion to be "Deen-E-Ilahi" which was really the essence of all the religions based on peace, good will and non-violence.

In modern times Mahatma Gandhi was a symbol of integration, brotherhood and non-violence. The Mahatma was greatly influenced by the Bhagvad Gita and various other scriptures. He adapted the percepts of truth, courage and non-violence in his daily practical life. It was because of his non-violent satyagrah that India won its freedom from the mighty British Empire. However, we have come a long way to the 21st century, to the days of gross materialism. There is a general feeling that religion does not play much of a role in our lives today. More often these religious ceremonies are looked at as rituals. Take for instance, visits to churches, temples and mosques... What really happens? Some who visit these are firm believers and fully conscious of what is happening, while some have scant knowledge and awareness of what is happening. And yet there are those with no knowledge and also perhaps fundamentalist. When we talk about religion we should also bear in mind the tremendous role-played by faith. In my country they say that faith can move mountains, suggesting the great expectations which faith can generate. I would like to illustrate something that happened in India not so long ago when our national media came out with stories about a miracle surrounding milk drinking idols of Lord Ganesh. These stories even received international attention. May be some of you would remember that a number of believers rushed to those temples and those who went there went because of their belief and faith. Although, many of us tried to find a rational explanation for this phenomena... Pious believers remained unconvinced that what happened was not a miracle. Although religion and festivals linked with religion do play important roles in our lives the materialism we have seen in the last few years of the 20th century seems to have overtaken religion as a binding force within the family.

From the present perspective and contemporary study, it seems that our attitude, our way of life, our cultures and our civilizations of the past are so different from today's way of life, that they are creating divisions rather than unity. Many of these ways of life have been too narrow, too restricting and too inhibiting. It is noticed that these may lead to a stunting of personal growth and social development. Recently in India it was the spirituality of the common adivasi people, which led to their coming together in protest against building big dams, which would not only submerge their land but also destroy their culture, their way of living and indeed their indigenous medicine. Hence we see that the rapidity of technological change has given rise to a number of social and psychological problems, which make the modern world for all its technological marvels, an uncomfortable and unfulfilling place to live. There is a growing feeling that the modern acquisitive society often prevents human beings from cultivating the warm affiliative side of human nature.

The question, should religion be separated from politics, culture and social development is a very important one. Today, the future of mankind depends on how we answer this question. The choice is to go ahead into the computer age or regress to medieval times or to combine both. Today we are just now at its fringe and it requires immediate attention. What is required urgently is the need to develop a morally informed consciousness, which lays emphasis on self control and asks basic ethical questions to guide human kind in socially constructive use of knowledge. And for the discovery of these moral values and ethical norms we must return to religion and spirituality. By religion I do not refer to any particular sect or creed but to the eternal and universal religion, which lays emphasis on the essential onenness and unity of all human kind. There are alternative spiritual paths available, paths supported by different philosophical systems to guide us in our quest for self-perfection and social good through the judicious mix of self-study, self-control of body and mind and righteous conduct. But basically they all explore the same fundamental truths although they use different idioms. Thus spirituality is a quest for inner and outer perfection to face the challenges of life and promote action and striving on law of dharma, to transform the world. It is a quest to evolve a design for living, informed and guided by the divinity within us, which is what gives our life a meaning and a sense of purpose.

Throughout history, religious thought has been a powerful factor in shaping the course of human evolution. I see it, as the key to make a powerful contribution to the evolution of a truly universal civilization of the future, based on both reason and spirituality. It should be the common endeavour of all of us who are engaged in the interfaith dialogue to evolve a truly universal value system for guiding human conduct in the increasingly interdependent world which we live. Religion, the spiritual source of our inner life, links us to each other, to our society, and because spiritual truths cannot be stopped by national boundaries, to the international community and social order. But the integrating force of religion is only one side of the picture. On the other side is a component of our culture, the daily routine of raising a family, selecting a way of life, and our interacting within and outside the community.

24
Communal Peace

"Sometimes I think I am the most unfortunate woman in the world. But next to me in the camp lives a woman who has lost her mind after her daughter was raped by fundamentalists, I go to her every day, and, upon seeing her anguish, I forget mine, which is insignificant compared to hers"—Wahida, aged 45, war widow fvam Afghanistan 1998

Marginalized and rendered as a footnote all through history, women's voices have been rarely heard in security concerns. But as events in the recent history of war have borne out, the need for women to move beyond the humanitarian front of the war story and claim a seat at the negotiating table has become imperative. Issues of genocide, and security for all affect them as well, and their presence is necessary for building a "just" and enduring peace, reconstruction and reconciliation.

I had always felt great pride when people exclaimed and said "you have the highest and most beautiful Himalayas in your country". With a sense of shame I realize that what does exist is the mountain of hate, mountain of animosity, mountain of discrimination.

Why does one human being be so cruel to another? I think it may be worthwhile to launch a study, which can help us to understand the roots of such cruelty.

It was 25th December 2000 Hijacking of the Indian Airlines plane to Kathmandu. It was the 11th September 2001 terrorist attack on World Trade Centre, it was the 13th December, 2001 terrorist attack on Indian Parliament House, it was the Gujarat Carnage etc. what is the cause for all this? In our country we are preoccupied with putting out "bush fires" and have little time to understand the causes leading to such fires at frequent intervals.

What is the reason for the gradual erosion of tolerance and rise of the love of diversity and pluralism in human societies, in terms of gender, religion, caste, class, colour and political belief?

While I was thinking of these issues Huma Ahmed Ghosh asked me suddenly what can women do to "prevent war" —why are women called upon to clean up after the mess. This question started a process of thinking. Today more than ever is the need for women in India and Pakistan to raise voices in unity and solidarity before we see body bags on both sides of the border.

The questions to, which we are seeking answers, are:

1. Why does a lack of awareness exist particularly in the developing world about understanding and resolving conflicts?
2. Why has the state been a source of conflict formation?
3. Why has the civil society failed to play an effective role in settling the conflicts?
4. What has been the response of media?
5. How does education at grassroot level create conditions tor managingand resolving conflicts?

While it was generally felt that women are never heard still the question kept coming back of what is really the women's role in preventing war. While we were debating on these issues to our great surprise we received an e-mail from Pakistan just then from a group of women who were also trying their best to answer the question of women's role in preventing war. The letter from this women's group read as follows:

"We are sure that you will all agree that we cannot work for a better and just society, in our country and in the region unless we are able to work towards peace. By this we do not mean just the absence of war but a society in which there is equity at every level; that is provincial, linguistic, religious, sectarian, racial and gender. This would mean that we work towards eliminating hegemony of any particular class, province, religion or sex and that we work towards a democratic just, tolerant and demilitarized society." They invited us to participate so that we could become instruments of conflict resolution.

While we of the women's movement have organized ourselves in peace movements why aren't we active before the out break of wars?

We are only asked to clean up what is left after the war. Women are recognized as nurses, social workers, caretakers and compassionate people and are asked, in the "service of the nation" to once again perform their domestic duties!

While working with several thousands of war widows I have realized that they could be key players in the process of reconstruction, reconciliation and democracy building and must be treated as equal participants in decision-making at all levels of society. Since in many countries a high percentage of adult women are war widows, their voices must be heard.

Peace definitely needs an integrated approach to incorporate the traumatized people in the mainstream of nation building. The futility of all the efforts made by women was loudly proclaimed the other day in the newspaper (Prime Minister refuses to meet women's group). How strange that people in power in our country do not want to engage with the impact of war on women. Women's misery and suffering during war are seen as peripheral to war even though they are the largest victims. Rape, homelessness. widowhood and poverty are direct outcomes of war. It is not just about women but also children who are brought into a world similar to their mothers.

Women, who are directly victimized by the conflicts, have always been used as the vote banks and rally muscles. Their difficulties and problems have always been overlooked. A broader vision is required to uplift the status of this *marginalized group and bring them to the development mainstream* where human rights, gender equity, nationalism and human values are respected and a sustainable peace has been established with the presence of this half sky.

We should really look around and see that widows, particularly those of armed conflict and war are living symbols of what absence of peace can reduce human life to. The strength of their anguish, the value of their experiences and their ferv-ent wish that there has to be a let up in suffering must be channelised. No other women should suffer due to governments taking nations mindlessly to war, or state's incapability to maintain law and order and provide the civic necessities of life in the 21st century.

This is the hour for all women's groups to come together and protest the government agenda. When we see what wars do to women, we cannot continue in terms of religion, caste and other political hierarchies.

Women as a constituency have to be much more savvy in how they vote. War as a political agenda has to be shunned by all women. Women's strength to effect change has been proven in anti-dowry and anti-alcohol movements and chipko movement.

Women's groups in India and Pakistan (rest of South Asia) have to reach out to international women' organizations concerned with war and peace issues worldwide. The power of cross-border and international network is essential to give voice to the atrocities perpetrated against women during wars.

Centuries of war has wreaked havoc for all. Not one instance of war has brought about resolve. Human suffering has only increased and perpetuated further violence.

For women worldwide the horrors of war have been abysmal. Never has their situation been given attention. Today, when two nuclear equipped nations are threatening war, it is the urgent responsibility of women of India to unite and prevent further suffering and destruction.

One solution is dialogue but how can we make this dialogue meaningful and an instrument of reconciliation? The general public is asking questions of the Government, about it, passive response to the recent terrorist attack on the Parliament and in Jammu. The solution is not in violent retaliation or war but in creating a more effective format for dialogue. Public consensus has to be created with constant bombardment of distractive images of war. Information about the abuses of war, its lack of resolution has to be imparted to the younger generation. Neighbourhood and community meetings have to be organized. Women's NGOs have to prepare for such education.

Politicians have to be lobbied and make publicly accountable for their decisions. Relentless persistence by women's groups is the only solution not by a selective group of women's groups but by all.

The concept Common Security emphasizes that security could not be unilateral and lays down six principles, which are to form the basis of common security.

- All nations have a legitimate right of security.

- Military force is not a legitimate instrument for resolving disputes between nations.
- Restraint is necessary in expression of national policy.
- Security cannot be attained through military superiority.
- Reduction and qualitative limitations of armaments are necessary for common security.
- Linkages between arms negotiations and political events should be avoided.

Only that tree that bends a little can face the storm. Is it too much to ask the politicians in both countries to bend a little, and face the storm to save lives and countries?

25

Creating a Culture of Healing

We are all gathered here today from different experiences, different back grounds, different languages but we have one things in common .... it is our belief in the imperative of peace and out commitment towards a violence free society. We have all witnessed the results of war and conflicts, communal riots and terrorism that has had a brutal effect on the lives of survivals and women and children. The heavy toll that women and children pay leaves the society crippled and the society pays for its mistakes.

We are all also gathered here in making the world a more secure place.

According to statistics obtained from he World Bank, about 113 million total, numbers of women are missing as a result of female infanticide

In the year 2000, an estimate of seven lakhs to two million women and children throughout the world were subjected to trafficking across international borders annually.

According to the 1998 Unites Nations Study on the Status of Women, one women is raped every 26 seconds.

Today poverty, homelessness, exposure to sexual violence and abuse from male relatives, the inevitable issue of HIV and AIDS further stigmatizing them - harmful traditional of women and victims, whose situation often worsens in the aftermath.

The majority of conflicts are taking place in traditional patriarchal societies where, even in peacetime, the status of widows is low. Oppressive traditional practices, ineligibility to inheritance, denial of ownership of land reduces them to paupers. However, in the post-conflict environment, these injustices are vastly exacerbated. It is desperately important that widows' legal rights are prioritized in new constitutions and laws.

The global village has become a virtual reality. It excites us to think of global citizenship. Global ethics, global civic society are words peppering most seminar presentations. The excitement becomes somber when we think of global war and globalizations of violence. There is undoubtedly global hurt. There is across the world deep pockets of hurt, wide areas of inequalities and innumerable conflicts being sustained by feudalistic, patriarchal structures. Within India, there are caste conflicts, land conflicts, communal conflicts, religious clashes, conflicts arising out of unequal and inequitable accessibility to material and intellectual resources, armed conflicts being sustained in more than nine states. The list is frighteningly endless. We do know that the world is at war at many levels and dimensions. But we also accept that a world with war is a world without peace. And that is the surest way to break the global village into pieces.

"While entire communities suffer the consequences of armed conflict and terrorism, women and girls are particularly affected because of their status in society as well as their sex". (Platform for Action of the Fourth United Nations World Conference on Women).

Conflict is a gendered activity: women and men have different access to resources, power and decision-making before, during and after conflicts.

The experience of women and men in situations of tensions, war, and post-conflicts reconstructions is significantly different. Approximately 80% of today's civilian casualties are women and 80% of all refugees and internally displaced people worldwide are women and children.

Women are thus caught in a vicious paradox: while, on the one hand, they are the main civilian victims of conflicts, they are, on the other hand, often powerless to prevent them, excluded from the negotiating tables when it comes to their resolutions and marginalised in the post-conflict reconstruction and reconciliation's efforts. The general exclusion of women from decision-making positions prior to, during and following violent conflict, reinforces their victimization. Some generalisations can the victimization:

- A vast majority of women affected by conflict are widows as a direct or indirect consequence of the violence.
    * Most of them are displaced from their place of residence and livelihood.

* Perforce they are left with very little or no means of income generation.
* Accessibly to resources is minimal.

  Despite this they have to take care of their children.
* Ill equiped as they are, they have to head households.
* They are further handicapped by the trauma of conflict and its fallout-rape, brutal violence, genocide, ethnic cleansing, forced pregnancy etc.

Very often their victimization is reinforced by the social ostracism.

We researched three sets of problems including emotional stress, sexual harassment and social undesirability. The second set of problems, are related to mismanagement of home affairs, losing control over children and inferiority complex while the third set of problems are associated with loneliness, physical insecurity, over-burden of work and compulsion for remarriage.

Hence in the post conflict scenario there are large numbers of women who are triply traumatized -as widows as the poor and needy.

Women are more than just victims, they are fighters. Widows are survivors. Mothers are peace builders

Women represent an untapped resource in peace building. Stereotype images of women as passive victims overshadow their agency and contributions to peace building and underplay their complex experience of conflict situations. It also robs them of legitimate avenues to progress. Since women often play an "informal" role their immense contributions are neither recongnized nor tapped. It is stripped of its political meaning and rendered, like much of women's work, invisible. Women remain marginalized, their problems ignored, their experiences unanalyzed, and their skills under-utilized.

A majority of women affected by conflict are widows. To the process of peace building they bring sensitivity tempered by their personal loss, a sense of immediacy since their families' futures are at stake and surviving skills against all odds. These qualities once tapped while accelerating the ownership of the process of reconstruction will help them individually to overcome their personal traumas.

To heal, reconciliation is the process through which a society moves from a divided past to a shared future.

The peace-building process comprises several stages including conflict prevention, conflict resolution and post-conflict peace-building and reconstruction. Sustainable peace requires the full participation of women at each of the stages of the peace process.

Conflict prevention comprises measures taken and efforts made to prevent the breakdown of peaceful conditions. It aims to prevent existing tensions escalating into violence and to contain the spread of conflict when it occurs. This may include measures to prevent the collapse of the social fabric and resulting fragmentation of the society. Preventive action is an area where women, in countries or regions with strong civil societies, could make a mark by expressing their views on conflict through their direct participation in the negotiations between the parties to the conflict.

Women are often the first who detect the signs of potential conflict, but because they have no direct access to the decision-making positions, they have few opportunities to inform on the necessity of preventive actions.

Gender-sensitive indicators should be regarded as an important part of early warning system analyses. Recent research has shown that the status of women in a country is associated with the country's level of stability. Those countries, where the percentage women are very high, are considered as countries at risk of conflict. Such violations of women's rights as rape, trafficking, domestic violence and military-related prostitutions could also be regarded as indicators in these early warning systems.

Women play a particular role in the prevention of conflict, as they are the main bearers of tradition and carry a special responsibly as educators of the young generation. As educators, women should be aware of the positive and negative influence they may have on their children's behaviour towards "the other" in the transmission of values and attitudes.

Traditional 'feminine' values of tolerance, listening and openness to dialogue and survival skills will have to become accepted as values of society. Such a paradigm shift alone will pave the way for reconciliation and greater democratic spaces

Friends, we are here today to find solutions to heal a hurting world. The priority is of course peace. It is my great pleasure and privilege to address you to this conference, which is born out of out commitment to intensify peace efforts by enhancing and ensuring recognition of the crucial role that women can play in healing a hurting world.

We are gathered here with sisters who will be revealing our experience and tireless drive for peace. Creating solidarity and networking for making voices of women heard in the many initiatives of civil society.

I share with you all our commitment for promoting peace and removing obstacles in violence against women. I am eager to learn more about your ideas and how we can collectively move ahead. Today is the time that with the opportunities that we have we must transform and build new and equal societies where women and men can join and enjoy equal rights.

Women make up half of the world populations. They should be able to exercise a corresponding share of political influence to create a more peaceful world. This conference is an important opportunity to make both women and men more aware of the decisive role that women have to play in securing a peaceful world.

Friends, let us be bold and decisive - dialogue for peace to heal the wounds of war.

26

Courage, Peace and Diplomacy

Four months ago I was suddenly informed by K.T. Chen, Director General, Taipei Economic Centre that huge shipments of ambulances, medicines, food etc. were flown from Taiwan for the earthquake affected brothers and sisters in Gujarat. I was told that I should be present at Hyatt Regency in a ceremony to receive these articles. Of course I knew that India and Taiwan do not have any diplomatic relations. However not to have good neighbourly relations was unimaginable. It was with a great sense of shame that I witnessed the generosity and charity being accepted with bad grace by a country whose motto has always been large heartedness and gratitude. 24 ambulances were presented by President Annete Lu of Taiwan and million dollars worth of foodgrains, medicines, bandages which still lie on the docks of Bombay port. I believe that the people of Taiwan went into action to collect help for India within 24 hours of the earthquake. Doctors were kept ready at the airport to be sent to Gujarat only to be told that they will not get visas. I was surprised to know how arrogant and how weak we are as a nation. Rice grains so kindly sent by Taiwan could have been used to feed the thousands of homeless people of Gujarat. However even to accept a gift we need grace.

Then I was suddenly invited to Taiwan to attend the Global Peace Assembly and I was surprised to see how Taiwan has emerged as a nation of genuine democracy with an acceptable record on human rights. This I found was mainly due to its courage coupled with low key diplomacy. Taiwan's courage is revealed in its ability to adapt itself to a system of genuine democracy where I found that it was people who were viewed as the highest authority in the land. The top officials of the government including the nations Vice-President who had invited us are elected by the people and they will serve in office until the people decide otherwise found Taiwan's secret of democratic process lies in its ability to recognise higher laws like the divine positive law, the natural law and to respect them and to protect them by all means.

A lush green country with broad roads and avenues with flyovers and disciplined traffic was a dream to be achieved by India found that civic-law in Taiwan had only one major objective to protect its people. The government officials of this fascinating nation many of whom I met had all recognised that human beings are composed of body and spirit and with proper care people would lead a happy and satisfied life. I found that economic progress of a nation was not enough unless it was accompanied by spiritual growth which enables people to develop a strong character and pleasant personality. At the Kinmen islands, in the night bazaars, in the cultural programmme we found the qualities of love, charity, humility and patience among the people.

It was indeed a very sad reflection that a country where such genuine democracy was practiced, where human rights were well protected has not been allowed to become a member of United Nations. It is indeed ironic that there are many countries who use tyranny as a method of government and do not protect human rights and yet they are members of the United Nations. This often makes me wonder as to what may be coming to this world body.

World war II ended on the 15th of August 6 decades ago! Did it really end Since then we have been battling to see how to rid the world of arms, weapons, and nuclear power. Peace conferences, peace forums, peace assemblies, are actively wanting to find solutions but with mighty forces of violence spread all over the globe, peace seems to be a far cry. The rapid development of modern technology has given mankind material comfort; however it has also led to the destruction of the environment, moral deterioration, disease, disaster and war, a nightmare which mankind has not been able to leave behind.

Imagine the unfriendly attitude of India where a genuine democracy exists and yet we ignore them. It was with this background and with a positive mind I attended the 2001 Global Peace Assembly at Taiwan on the 15th of August. The gathering had local and foreign peace activists from across the world. Among them were congressmen and the five Nobel peace laureates-former South African President F.W. de Klerk, U.K. anti-nuclear advocate Joseph Rotblat, U.S. anti-landmine activist Jody Williams, former president of Costa Rica Oscar Arias Sanchez, and former president of Poland Lech Walesa. It was a once in a lifetime occasion for me to meet so many Noble Laureates at the same time.

The Global Peace Meet started with the ceremony of ringing the bell of peace. The ceremony of ringing the Bell of Peace is a cultural heritage passed down from ancient times, preserving the good part of traditional culture. The greatness in human beings is that they comprehend the importance in respecting Heaven (tian, sky) and earth, cherishing all creatures, and admiring the law of nature. The significance of the ceremony of ringing the Bell of Peace is in respecting heaven and earth. Only with heartfelt sincerity can people appeal to the protection and safety of all creatures. The cultural function of the ceremony is as important as the concept of Tian-tan (Sky altar), which served as a sacred place for ancient emperors to show respect to Heaven and to pray for peoples, fortune and happiness. The resounding of the Bell of Peace is to remind people to follow the laws of nature. May it inspire mankind to have a heart of kindness and may it unite all peoples together to help and have great influence on the others in order to make the most of fraternity and sublime love. May the sound of the Bell spread the message of peace throughout the world, and reveal our sincere appeals for a world in which there is no suffering, no fear, no war and no pain. There was indeed such a similarity in the ringing of our temple bells where we invoke the god to spread the message of goodwill, and understanding throughout the world.

The Vice President of Taiwan Annette Lu emphasised and reemphasised that peace was no longer a slogan but an issue related to common interests of all people around the globe and across the Taiwan Strait. She symbolised Taiwan as the soft gentle cartoon character "Ketty" while China was a strong and aggressive lion. Peace was a matter of life and death. She said that Taiwan is not a trouble maker but a peace-maker. She said that peace is not a dream and it will become a matter of fact as long as we have wisdom, action and determination. She said that children should be formally taught that there are many non-violent ways to reach an accord and to avoid savage confrontation. Love not hate, cooperation not war are tenets by which we live together and support each other.

The Peace conference, which was, attended by so many heavy weight political figures, peace advocates was all in search of a creative resolution. It would not be out of place here to point out that the cross strait relations by nature are relations between military invasions and counter invasion measures adopted by each side. Accordingly China seems to be playing the role of an aggressor with her 300 missiles, aimed at Taiwan with her constant and open threats. The question is will China use her military forces to attack Taiwan. If the situation is so created and Taiwan will have to act as a nation which has to resist the aggression and preach the doctrine of non-violence.

Another interesting question that arose was if the concept of non violence is possible to practice between two countries. Unfortunately Taiwan and China are not sitting at the same table to carry out a dialogue and solve the problem. We found that this was an unequal relation and difficult for Taiwan to negotiate. For me as a delegate from India it was interesting to grasp a situation of two unequal partners one for non violence and one for aggression and realise how difficult it must have been for Mahatma Gandhi to have practiced the concept of non-violence many years ago at a time when peace forums and peace assemblies were not as active as they are today. It also made me think as to what made the concept of non-violence viable? It was tremendous patience that Mahatma Gandhi showed and the various strategies of Satyagraha that made the mighty British Empire give up their hold on India.

At Taiwan I spoke about this non violence that would eventually lead both sides China and Taiwan to set up a much needed confidence building mechanism. I also felt the need for a structured mechanism for peace to be introduced and implemented. Women's Initiatives for Peace in South Asia has been acting as a pressure group and the role of civil society becomes important as a pressure group to protect the dignity in life of the common people. At the Global Peace Assembly held at Taiwan there were about 100 foreign and local peace activists to exchange opinions on stability in the Asia Pacific region throughout the world.

President Chen Shui-bian of Taiwan hoped that goodwill towards China will be responded to by China also and said that learning from history we should realise that war brings nothing but casualties and harms our loved ones.

The 1997 Nobel laureate Jody Williams, a long time anti-landmine activist was there and told us that she had received threats on phone call and e-mail from someone from China who did not want to put the strength of her voice in the call for peace. Amidst great applause the landmine activist said that she was not afraid of anonymous threats and the more she was threatened more she made up her mind to attend the conference. She shared her experiences in promoting the movement to ban landmines as well as her role as the coordinator of the International Campaign to Ban Landmines. She felt that there were very few countries that have the resources to clear mines and campaign on banning landmines needs to be strengthened. Jodie Williams also urged and said that no one should underestimate his or her strength. She said "it is great to feel compassion for others but compassion without action is irrelevant".

Apart from the Nobel laureates Ms. Eliane Valdov, President of International Institute for a Culture of Peace and Non-Violence for children of the World said that it is possible to change things and that we need 10 per cent of the military budget of every single country to help children. Valdov who has dedicated herself to nonviolence and children's rights campaigns pointed out that there were approximately 30 million refugees or one among 30 people in the world are refugees. About 90% of the population in major refugee camps were women and children. She told the audience that every moment she claps, a child dies of inadequate food and health in the world and in every minute that she snaps her finger, the world community has spent over US one million dollars on the military.

Another panelist Nicholas Lardy, Senior Fellow of the Brookings Institution predicted that China which is currently the world's seventh largest global trading country will overtake France, Canada and United Kingdom to become the fourth largest trading country in the next few years. He said that China is likely to surpass both Japan and Germany by the end of the decade and become the world's largest trading nation. He pointed out that the main risk in this forecast is the possibility that advanced industrial countries will not maintain relatively open markets.

Mr. Antoniol Beatonto President of World Institute of Development and Peace said that this forum could reach every man and woman to shoulder the responsibility of peace. Former President of Costa Rica, Oscar Arias Sanchez said that in a civilised and rational world no conflict should be solved with military force. He felt dialogue reduces barriers and that you need to look into the faces and eyes of other parties and for that you naturally have to sit at a table. To my Indian context it seemed relevant when he said if you do not succeed the first time try again and again. He said you need to be patient and humble to understand that the essence of dialogue is compromise. He proposed a closer look at the dangers to world peace—poverty, illiteracy, environmental degradation instead of starting a new arms race. He questioned how can we live in peace if half the worlds population lives in poverty and without potable water.

Dr. John Montgomery, a professor from Harvard University said that China is a regional superpower. He said peace is something you have to achieve and it is done by building forces to support peaceful initiatives and restraining military confrontations.

Dr. Klaus Rupprecht, Director General from German Institute cited the example of unification of East and West Germany saying that the unification was achieved because both governments opened up to each other. He said that Germans could not imagine that they could unite with each other some day. Yet they did.

Another Nobel laureate of 1984, former President of Poland Lech Walesa hoped that this Conference, the Global Peace Assembly would achieve its aim of creating world peace.

One would wonder if there was any positive outcome by attending any of these conferences. On August 15-16 2001, international figures—including prominent Nobel Peace laureates, parliamentarians, NGO representatives, and scholars - gathered together in a spirit of "peace and love" offering their insights, experiences, and inspirations to not only preserve peace and security across the Taiwan Straits, but also around the world. Conflict and violence are not inevitable, for there is a peaceful solution to even the most complex problems and disputes. Even though over three hundred missiles are aimed at Taiwan by the PRC, Taiwan is searching for a peaceful resolution.

The positive fallout of the conference was that peace is an issue that we all should be concerned about. It needs to be a global effort. We call upon each individual to take responsibility for peace making. Let us work together to set up institutions for peace by first creating a culture of peace within our respective countries. The dawning of the 21st century is challenging the people of Taiwan and their friends around the world to find peaceful solutions to the ever-expanding threat of war and ultimate destruction.

During the Assembly, the people of Taiwan gathered together with thse prominent global leaders and activists to hear about resolving conflicts in India, Isreal, South Africa, Central America, Korea and Germany. Taiwan is committed to achieving peace with the PRC by sharing Taiwan's experience in developing the principle of "soft power" which includes democracy, human rights, high-technology, peace and love.

The distinguished participants highlighted six principles of peace-making that can be applied to resolving the conflict anywhere. These six principles and their direct recommendations are as follows:

1. Acknowledge that problem can only be solved through negotiation: Taiwan should renounce the use of force, the PRC should also renounce the use of force and threats of war, and both sides should be prepared to compromise;
2. Build trust and confidence: both sides should encourage further exchanges within civil society and uphold principles of parity and mutual respect in the negotiation process;
3. Create win-win outcomes, both sides should abandon one-sided solutions that disregard the current reality;
4. Establish concrete mechanisms early in the peace process to avoid deadlocks in negotiation: both sides should find ways to keep moving forward in cooperation to maintain dialogue;
5. Practice patience and never give up trying: both sides shall accept that obstacles will arise and be creative in finding new approaches;
6. Establish mechanisms for conducting the peace process: both sides shall invite Nobel Peace Prize Laureates to suggest possible methods to resume constructive dialogue and ultimately to achieve a lasting and permanent peace.

All these dialogues are also applicable to our talks with Pakistan. I firmly believe that we can create a new culture of peace, a renaissance of the knowledge age in the 21st century. This culture can be accomplished by unifying the cultures of east, west, north, south synergistically combining cultures of spirituality with those of the most advanced science and technology. This to my mind will bring everlasting peace and we could realise a border less, harmonious global village.

Throughout the conference it was felt that men should transcend the ways of animals, which usually settles disputes by force if they think they will win and take flight if they lose. The only way that mankind or Homo sapiens would rightfully claim superiority is to settle disputes through dialogue, negotiation and cooperation.

27

Women and Torture

When a woman is assaulted she may not stop to think in terms of himsa or ahimsa? Her primary duty is self-protection. She is at liberty to employ every method or means that come to her mind in order to defend her honour. God has given her nails and teeth. She must use them with all her strength and, if need be, die in the effort

Gandhiji, Harijan, 1 March 1942

The problem of crime against women is not new. Women in Indian society have been victims of humiliation, torture and exploitation for as long as we have had written records of social organization and family life.

No serious attempt was made to explain why the Government, public and the scientific communities alike ignored for so long the varied evidence that women were being greatly exploited in our society. The attitude of indifference and negligence can be attributed to three factors: a lack of awareness of the seriousness of the problem, the general acceptance of man's superiority over woman because of which violence acts against women were not viewed as violent or deviant, and the denial of violence by women themselves due to their religious values and social attitudes. Laws and attitudes have been dictated by men, so it suited them to perpetuate the image of the superior being.

South Asia is known all through the world as the continent of 'missing women'. We must be honest and recognise the harsh reality that no other continent denies its female population life chances from birth to death, in the manner that we do, in South Asia. The fact that many of us come from environments where we have been loved and supported to realise our full potential, must not prevent us from recognising the evil of gender based discrimination in our societies.

Lawyers and judges have to function and fulfil their responsibilities in the context of this social reality. I would like to give a cameo picture of domestic felicity. The air smelt of honey dew, the expanse of green tea gardens made one feel in total harmony with the creator... the entire scenic beauty was so picturesque that it felt unreal. The little cottages tilted on the slopes of the holiday resort were a reminder of tranquility, peace and harmony.

Shattering this silence suddenly came the repeated sounds of a whistle... unmistakably the sound of a pressure cooker — of course it could not come from the far away kitchen of the holiday resort, hence I followed the trail of the whistling to cottage number two and to my utter disbelief I heard "Move your lazy lump, useless woman. Does it take you a lifetime to make sambhar..." I heard the sounds of physical violence. To my utter amazement I realized the wife was there on a holiday— to cook. Wasn't this really harassment and domestic violence against women?

After 50 years of independence women of India do not enjoy a life free of torture. The foundation for this can be traced in our pious institution of family itself. Specific gender-based oppression has its roots in a patriarchal social order which constitutes the mainstream model of family life in India. It is, therefore, not surprising that much of the violence women suffer is executed within the family. Although the excessive forms of this violence now frequently come to light, other silent forms reflected in high incidence of neurosis, depression and other psychosomatic disorders are yet to be given wider recognition. Thus violence continues to be seen and interpreted through crime figures which do not necessarily cover the entire gamut of stresses experienced in interpersonal relationships within the family. Even on the basis of crime statistics, it can be shown that violence within the family, the primary unit responsible for maintaining the social order, has increased. So much so, that a law has to be enacted to curb domestic violence.

In the process of socialisation, violence is a means by which discipline is enforced and values instilled. In addition to this, self-effecting subservient attitudes are enforced through strictly prescribed norms and moral prescripts of 'good' behaviour. For the Hindus, it is best summed up within the parameters of Manu's Code which continues to form the basis for laws governing Hindu women. Ironically the upper-caste norms are being emulated by others. These notions of subservience and seclusion prepare the ground for acceptance of subordination, within the family and outside. Thus, non-acceptance of these norms by a daughter-in-law would itself be seen as an act of 'defiance' by a society which has for decades now put up with bride-burning on account of a daughter-in-law bringing insufficient dowry. Wife-beating and abuse are imbibed by young males as inherited forms of consciousness/behaviour, alongwith other notions of macho image. Internalisation of such forms of consciousness are a major factor for a large mass of women still accepting these without any complaints and for crimes executed within the family still largely unreported.

Women's life experiences across the world and statistics and writing on women are testimony to the fact that violence against women is the gravest and most pervasive form of violation of human rights. This fact has been reiterated at several forums over the years, but its enormity and severe implications have begun to be recognized only in the last decade. To quote the Beijing Platform for Action, "VAW violates and impairs or nullifies the enjoyment by women of their human rights and fundamental freedoms". It is a blot on our collective conscience.

Torture of women is observable in the following forms.

Wife battering

It is ironical that in a country where womanhood has been put on a pedestal for worship, incidence of wife battering, molestation of women in various forms like rape, eve-teasing, abduction and bride burning among others keep on increasing year to year. Women find no security in the home, where they are ill-treated by husbands and in-laws, they have no security in streets and workplaces where they are vulnerable and fall prey to police, anti-socials, moneylenders, men colleagues and bosses and are subjected to innumerable indignities perhaps in higher frequency than in most civilized societies. Today the general perception among the people is that the crime against women has increased to such a great extent that women are not able to move freely and participate in the community. Women are rarely treated as personalities in their own right - either as dream goddess or as sex symbol. So the reaction is in proportion either veneration to illogical extents or the attitude towards a toy - play, destroy or throw away.

Discrimination leads to common occurrence of wife-beating as a means of enforcing subordination. Although, often the act of violence is committed after a drunken bout, it would be wrong to see alcoholism as the underlying factor rather than as an additional factor. Transgression of prescribed norms of female behaviour, or accusation along these lines is often an excuse to spark off violence. With the increasing pressure on the family due to economic change, the woman's attempt to change the family budget is also a cause of tension, as reflected in the anti-arrack agitation in Andhra Pradesh.

Rajulu complained that her husband would come home drunk every night, take away her jewellery and also force her to sell illegal liquor. So much so that many times she was a victim of police aggression also. These women are in dire need of an entire range of crises intervention for her immediate protection like shelter, medical aid, treatment, counselling and lawyers. Many of the children from violent homes end up believing that:

- It is the accepted norm for husbands to hit wives.
- Violence is a way to win arguments.
- Big people have power they often misuse.
- Men are bullies who push women and children around.
- Women are victims and can't take care of themselves or their children.

Cases of domestic violence are usually, but not exclusively, associated with liquor consumption by the husband. Liquor, foreign and indigenous is freely available in most Indian states. Men drink with callousness and gay abandon. The hard earned money of both the husband and wife is devoured by alcohol. Consequently, the wives resort to taking up extra jobs and hiding their income. Deaths due to the consumption of alcohol are increasing but there is no statistical data available. It is estimated that the number of deaths due to spurious liquor exceeds the deaths due to communal riots. Many cases, however, are not reported .The death of the husband due to liquor consumption places a heavy burden on the wife. She has to assume the entire responsibility of supporting her family if she has no grownup children. At times, men have been blinded as a result of spurious liquor. This too equally cripples the family. (Extract from the book Women Against Violence, ed. by Shri Kudchedkar Sabiha Al-Issa, 1998)

Dowry

The march of history towards the development in the field of Science and Technology has changed the life styles of the people and the man's lust for unattainable comforts at the cost of women's life has made things worse. Adding fuel to the fire is the fact that in many of the incidents of dowry harassments while some women are being killed, few others commit suicide and many more prefer to leave the matrimonial house and become destitutes or liabilities on the parents. If at all in rarest of the rare circumstances a woman prefers to take recourse to police and judiciary the system is so cumbersome that she has to move from pillar to post and will get justice only after years. The most discouraging provision which make women to suffer rather than taking resource to the judiciary is the awarding of a meagre amount of Rs. 500/- as maintenance under the Code of Criminal Procedure after divorce. What a dismal picture; What then is the scenario? Will the Indian women have to suffer and die in the name of dowry even after 50 years of Independence? The answer is a clear no.

Taking into account the enormity of the situation I decided that there has to be quick coordinated action to save the woman from further trauma and harassment. We developed a very innovative method of speedy justice to women in a coordinated fashion. Idea of Parivarik Mahila Lok Adalat is the result of all the anguish that I suffered because women in large numbers were left deserted and destitute. Many women could not bear the heavy cost of litigation with its accompanying cumbersome procedures which left women in a trauma—how to seek justice. Women would not be isolated from their families and therefore I looked around for a mechanism that could resolve family disputes and domestic violence.

Dowry deaths and other forms of harassment, torture on account of dowry, remain a major factor contributing to violence against women. As has been established by numerous studies, as well as the experience of legal-aid cells run by women's organisations and the Crimes Against Women Cell run by the police in Delhi as also elsewhere, the incidence of this crime has continued to rise, despite consistent campaign against it.

Some Pertinent Facts Regarding Dowry

Although giving and taking dowry is prohibited by the 1951 Dowry Act, a single day does not pass without newspaper headlines

Population and Health Policies

The violence being inflicted on women through hazardous contraceptives and a coercive "population control policy" is a matter of great concern. Long-acting contraceptives, including injectibles which promote infertility are being thrust on women without any thought being given to the effect of these on women's health. Further, at the level of governmental policy, as well as 'aid' coming from the first world, the views that this 'surplus' population is the reason for India's poverty and the 'population explosion' will spell disaster are widely subscribed to. Both are wreaking havoc in women's lives and are being resisted by the women's movement. The fact remains that women are hardly in a position to assert or exercise any kind of 'choice' in these matters; that 'informed consent' is missing altogether and today the government is encouraging disenfranchisement on grounds of a third child.

Repe

Rape and rape-related murders are on the rise. Marital rape has never been defined in India, rape was one of the first issues on which women expressed and articulated organised resistance to gender specific violence. It became clear at a very early stage that in societies such as ours, where human life and dignity were generally at a discount, the security of women counted for very little. The concentration of 'power' in the hands of a few made women particularly vulnerable to sexual attacks.

Rape by the husband is not as yet a cognisable offence in India. Women are conditioned to play a submissive role especially in the matter of sexual relations. Most husbands feel a sense of exclusive possession with regard to their wives. Hence in sexual relations, the wife 's consent is rarely taken. Cases have been reported of deviant sexual behaviour of the husband, for example beating the wife prior to the sexual intercourse, burning her with cigarette butts or thrusting hard objects in her vagina. Refusal to give into the insatiable sexual desire of the husband is interpreted as the result of her extramarital relations. She is therefore 'doubly punished.

There was a case of murder of a young housewife in Delhi some years ago. She had been married for two months. Her husband was impotent but this was not disclosed to her prior to her marriage. In his efforts to cure his impotency, the husband forced her to have sexual relations with his friends in his presence. Gradually her brother in law and father-in-law to began to rape her. On one occasion when she strongly resisted her father-in-law's advances, he strangled her and then threw her out of their sixteenth floor apartment. This case would have been registered as suicide because the in-laws made a statement to the police that the woman was mentally deranged. However, the timely intervention of a casual spectator, who happened to be a nurse, changed the entire complexion of their case. Cases of cruelty by the husband and her relatives have increased from 11603 in 1989 to 15949 in 1991 (Social Welfare, Vol. XXXIX, 12, Feb. No. 11 Mar. 1993). Rape as a 'tool of war' is a familiar behaviour of the 20th century. It is the psyche of superiority that the victorious army exhibits. What a warped sense of superiority?

Sexual Harassment

Despite the fact that the vast mass of women in India are involved in contributing to the economy in various ways and are engaged in paid work for a living, recognition of sexual harassment of women at the workplace has come in only recently. The Supreme Court judgement relating to sexual harassment has been a landmark aimed to curb this reprehensible behaviour. Today as the economic crisis deepens, more women are being driven to the job market. These women are concentrated in the unorganised sector and employed as casual labour by contractors. They look for work at low-paid, low skill levels since they have been denied any formal training for a vocation. Many proponents of the new economic policy argue that it would open up new possiblities of work for women. But even new jobs are in the most low-paid and insecure sector of the economy. Amidst ever-increasing unemployment the need to cling on to even the ill-paid jobs is great.

Prostitution

Another crime against women which often involves violence is prostitution. Some parents sell their daughters into prositution due to poverty Child prostitution is on the increase, more so as options for economic survival shrink further. Although some discussion with regard to 'choice' is being raised, the reality of a poverty-ridden, third World society such as ours and the absence of any kind of social security makes a mockery of these notions, particularly in view of the large number of minor girls forced into prostitution. The cultural image of the 'virtuous' Indian woman frustrates efforts at 'rehabilitiation' of even the children of prostitutes, leave alone the prostitutes themselves.

Child Marriages

Child marriage was banned as long ago as 1929. Nevertheless, the practice continues in many parts of India, and is today caught up in the web of identity politics, with some claiming the right as a 'tradition'. The incidence of crime is high particularly in the State of Rajasthan, where on the occasion of 'Akha Teei' child marriages continue to be performed on a widescale, and State level ministers have been known to defend the crime.

Religious Fundamentalism

In the wake of the rising tide of religious fundamentalism, there has been a hardening of attitudes with regard to assertion of freedom by women. This has led to a conservative backlash which draws on religion to justify itself and to justify the cobweb ridden notion of male superiority.

Sati

The rising tide of fundamentalism has gripped the majority community in a big way. This was witnessed, as early as 1987 when an incident of *Sati*— widow murder in a remote village of Rajasthan was sought to be defended and glorified as a customary rite. Not surprisingly, the State colluded with the fundamentalists, to allow the whipping up of passions and a section of the media used this as an occasion to attack women activists.

Communal Violence

Violence experience by entire families during communal riots is not an entirely new phenomenon, but it is to be noted that in the course of riots unleashed after the demolition of the Babri Masjid in Ayodhya, women of the minority community were the focus of sexual attacks. Both the police and para-military forces, themselves influenced by communal as well as patriarchal ideologies (e.g. the PAC in U.P.), made no intervention on behalf of women in the course of these riots.

Caste Violence

Women from disadvantaged social groups—lower castes, dalits, tribals and the landless—have been vulnerable to sexual exploitation over a long–period in Indian history. In recent years sexual violence has been resorted to more openly as an instrument of subjugation. There is an increase in the incidents of stripping and parading of women from lower castes, a blatant display of caste-based prejudice and violence.

Witchcraft

Labelling women as witches and subjecting them to every possible torture on that ground is not uncommon in many rural pockets.

Procreation

Women unable to bear children are also not allowed to lead life in dignity irrespective of the fact the reason for sterility lies with the husband.

Widows

This is probably the most marginalized section of society 9 per cent of the women's population are widows who lead a life of sexual exploitation and social ostracism. The piteous case of the widows of Vrindavan is well-known. It is horrifying to note that this happens in a society that treats its cows better!

Conclusion

No women's movement contrary to the popular misconception seeks to create an Amazonian society. There is no question of woman being superior or man or vice versa. The need is to create the environment of equality of mutual respect. This in itself, I am convinced will bring down the crime rate by more than 60 per cent, since most crimes are gender based. Surely we owe to human civilization that we go into the 21st century with our women not as down trodden victimized masses, but as dignified partners in progress.

28

Shortlived Joy

Little Arti was dragged into a small congested room. Her toys were the screeching sounds of the looms, the coloured thread scattered all over. She fiddled with looms in between. Whenever she wailed her mother Shanno Devi would pick her up, stick her to her breast till the child closed her eyes. What was the joy of living? What was childhood? The life started and ended in poverty and deprivation.

Children are the future of this country and what are we giving to the country in terms of human resource? The well-being of the children is indicative of the well-being of the society. In almost all countries, children, as a demographic category, constitute a vulnerable group physically, economically, educationally, and socially. Their vulnerability is caused due to their dependency for their own well-being on the elders, families in short, and on the society at large. They have been identified as the 'at risk' groups in terms of the growing infant mortality rate, school dropouts and the rate of child labour.

The birth of the child which duplicates the evolution of the species is ordinarily a joyous and festive occasion. But regretfully the joy is shortlived. Right from the moment the child comes out of the protective warmth of the mother's womb, it is subjected to the gruelling stress and strain of the world outside. Even before it saw the light of the world, the foetus is subjected to the most heinous test of amniocentesis, and after it saw the light it is not spared the trauma of discrimination.

The discrimination grows with the growth of the child. It is manifested in day-to-day life style, minimum needs, food, dress, and human interaction. It is forgotten that to be able to grow into an active, skilled and confident woman a girl child should be nurtured in an environment of dignity and opportunity. Regretfully for the average girl child in India, the privations of poverty are significantly compounded by the value systems, norms and social mores which define and not infrequently disparage the role of women.

Every year about 12 million girls are born in India. Three million or 25 per cent do not survive to see their fifteenth birthday. A third of these deaths takes place in the first year of life.

Around 105 males are born for every 100 female births. The sex ratio (female per 1000 males) for children upto the age of six is 945 a figure which keeps declining as girls advance in years. Several acts of omission and commission account for lower survival rates of females and the most prominent amongst them are genocide which includes female infanticide and more recently female foeticide. Both represent the sinister face of cultural negation of women.

Girls as compared to boys are at a greater risk of dying during infancy in the states of Bihar, Gujarat, Haryana, Himachal Pradesh, J&K, Karnataka, Madhya Pradesh, Punjab, Rajasthan, Tamil Nadu and Uttar Pradesh.

Region, religion, caste and poverty exercise an ominous spell over mortality rates. The lower the status of women, the lower the expectation of life at birth. A girl born in Uttar Pradesh can expect to live for 54 years, 20 years less than her peer in Kerala whose life expectancy is 74 years.

Studies also indicate that in situations where higher percentage of girls than boys are ill, lower percentage of girls receive medical treatment in the group under 15 years of age. In fact, better and more timely medical care for boys is an important factor explaining high survival among males compared with females.

Access of the girl child into the world of basic knowledge and information is an important component of social development with several beneficial results such as lower fertility rates, lower infant and child mortality rates, lower population growth rate, higher age at marriage, higher life expectancy and higher rate of participation. These benefits notwithstanding, there is a gap between the participation rates of boys and girls in elementary education. Gender disparity in participation rates and specially in rural areas reflect the discriminatory social attitude with respect to the girl child.

Reasons for girls non-enrolment in formal school systems are varied: lack of equal access to educational opportunity, early assumption of domestic responsibility, conservative cultural values and fears for security, early marriage, demand for dowry, unwillingness of parents to send daughters to co-educational schools where there are no female teachers, belief of parents that education is of little value to a girl, perceptions that curriculum of education institutions do not enhance the productive capability of girl children and adolescent girls.

With the advent of puberty a young girl is seen to be more vulnerable, numerous restrictions are imposed on her as far as her movements and behaviours are concerned. The trauma reaches its climax when the female child is given away in marriage at a time when she needs to play, run, sing, dance and also read and write, parents throw them by the wayside like throwing dolls. Marriage is reduced to a mockery. It spells the end of education, premature assumption of domestic (including child care) responsibilities and severely restricted physical mobility. The girl child is deprived of an outlet for little relaxation, zest and joy. The petals of childhood wither away before blossoming into the maturity of youth and womanhood.

Child Labour: International and National Scenario

In November 1989, a historic convention on the rights of the child came before the 44th session of the U.N. General Assembly. The convention recognised the special vulnerability of children and addressed their civil, political, economic, social, and cultural rights as constituents of interdependent provisions. It also professed that although a child may be adequately nourished (survival right), its right to develop fully are not adequately protected, unless the child is educated (a cultural right), shielded from such things as arbitrary detention (a civil right) and from exploitation at work which is a socioeconomic right.

In the wake of the convention, a Declaration and Plan of Action for "Survival, Protection and Development of Children in 1990" was unanimously adopted by 150 nations including India on 30th September 1990. It was also resolved to provide children with better future and special protection to working children and abolish illegal child labour.

The girl child population today demands an immediate and serious attention. The volume of child labour throughout the world is huge enough to generate manifold problems though they are not manifest in their fullest magnitude. This is mainly because the inhuman conditions of child labour have been overlooked by the adult society which frames and implements policies which are unconcerned with the problems of children.

The International Labour Organisation points out that a decade after the International Year of the Child (1979), the abuse of child labour has gradually been reduced in formal sector but has pushed children into the precarious conditions in agriculture, urban, informal and domestic work. Among these three, the most vulnerable and exploited is the domestic work.

A massive national and regional media campaign has been launched to sensitise the society against child labour. Several TV programmes and films on child labour have been produced. Funds have been allocated to districts identified as child labour endemic to conduct surveys to identify child labour and also to take up awareness generation programmes to sensitise employers, parents and working children on the issue. Funds have been provided to set up projects in 76 districts to rehabilitate 150,000 children withdrawn from work through special schools.

The total withdrawal of children from work and ensuring their rehabilitation is a major challenge facing India. The country has the largest child labour population in the world. The 1981 census put it at 13.65 million while the 43rd round of the National Sample Survey conducted in 1987-88 estimated it to be 17 million, showing an increase.

However, child labour is not peculiar to India alone—it is a global phenomenon. According to an estimate of International Labour Organisation (1975) there were 52 million working children in the world. Asian countries accounted for 73 per cent of the child labour population. Although India has the largest child labor population in the world in terms of absolute number, the proportion of working children to the total labour force is lower in India than many other developing countries. Child labour constitutes 5.2 per cent of the total labour force in India.

Another aspect of child labour is that it is much more of a rural phenomenon than urban. Approximately 90 per cent of the working children are in the rural areas and employed in agriculture and allied activities. Cultivation, agricultural labour, livestock, forestry and fisheries account for 84.9 per cent of child labor. In the urban areas, manufacturing, servicing and repairs account for 8.64 per cent of child labour. Of this only 0.8 per cent of child labor work in factories.

India has enacted a comprehensive national child labour policy in 1987.We are happy to know that child labour is an issue placed on the national agenda. We in India have always followed a protective policy in the matter of tackling the problem of child labour. A national concern is of course reflected in the following.

Article 23

Prohibition of Traffic in Human Beings and Forced Labour.

(1) Traffic in human beings and *begar* and other similar forms of forced labour are prohibited and any contravention of this provision will be an offence punishable in accordance with law.

Article 24

Prohibition of Employment of Children in Factories, etc.

No child below the age of fourteen years shall be employed to work in any factory or mine or engaged in any other hazardous employment.

Article 39(e) and (f)

Certain Principles of Policy to be Followed by State. The state shall, in particular direct its policy securing

(e) that the health and strength of workers, men and women, and the tender age of children are not abused and that citizens are not forced by economic necessity to enter avocations unsuited to their age or strength.

(f) that children are given opportunities and facilities to develop in a healthy manner and in conditions of freedom and dignity and that childhood and youth are protected against exploitation and against moral and material abandonment.

Article 45

Provision for Free and Compulsory Education for Children

The state shall endeavour to provide, within a period of ten years from the commencement of this Constitution, for free and compulsory education for all children until they complete the age of fourteen years.

Article 51(c)

Promotion of International Peace and Security.

The state shall endeavour to -

(c) foster respect for international law and treaty obligations in the dealings of organised people with one another.

However legislative policies will not be able to prevent child labour in the country. The act of course bans employment of children under fourteen. Also it

- lays down a procedure to make additions to the schedule of banned occupations or processes;
- regulates the working conditions of children in occupations where they are not prohibited from working;
- lays down penalties for employment of children in violation of the provisions of this act, and other acts which forbid the employment of children;
- brings out uniformity in the definition of "child" in related laws.

But will all these legislations really make a difference in the country? Laws are either not known or not implemented. Child labour is a problem basically economic in nature hence legislation alone is not likely to remove it. Poverty, illiteracy, the existence of large families leading to land holdings reduced to uneconomic sizes, landlessness, lack of skills to earn a livelihood are some of the reasons for children being sent out to work. To contain and reduce the problem, more avenues for adult employment in rural areas need to be created. While India is committed to complete eradication of child labour, our immediate efforts are focussed on ensuring prevention of child employment in hazardous occupations.

The status of the girl child in India is deplorable, with general lack of access to opportunities, and little choice or control over her own life. From the prenatal stage to adulthood the girl child is subjected to a series of traditional social malpractices which germinate, breed and reinforce discrimination, which in turn perpetuates her low status in society.

The Family and the Girl Child

Role of the family in determining the status of the girl child within and outside the family is very significant. Preference for a male child, arising from social and cultural biases and sanctions, cuts across caste, class, and state lines. After birth celebrations, discriminatory food and nutritional practices, low investment in health and education are some of the parameters which reflect the real status of the girl child in the country. Restrictions on the girl child's mobility as she grows up which have an adverse effect on her personality development is an important area of concern.

The position becomes worse when both the husband and wife in the scenario of rural poverty and unemployment have often a subconscious and intense desore for male offsprings who are expected to bring more income through employment. This leads to second marriage, large families (procreation often continues unchecked till advent of a male offspring in the family) and strained marital relationship.

In case a young girl is widowed, it becomes almost impossible for her to remarry. A girl widow also is castigated as an inauspicious object and is deprived of the right to participate in festive occasions. Early marriage enlarges a girl's fertility span; malnourishment combined with early pregnancy makes her a physical wreck. The situation gets further compounded when underweight babies with reduced chances of survival are delivered. The resultant high infant mortality rate provides the impulse for further pregnancies which result in even further biological depletion.

Girl children are thus helplessly vulnerable to the wanton cruelty of a society which is altogether callous and insensitive to their needs.

References

1. Varma A.P., Rehman M.M.; Chauhan P.S. (1996) Women Labour in India Noida: V. V.Giri National Labour Institute.
2. Kudchedkar S;.Sabiha A. (1998) Violence Against Women - Women Against Violence -Delhi: Pencraft International.
3. A Report on the Consultations held in Madras and Jaipur (1993-94) Status of the Girl Child in India: National Foundation for India.
4. A status report on Indian initiatives towards the elimination of child labour (1996) Noida: V. V. Giri National Labour Institute.

5. Dr. Regina B; Dr. Gokilavani S. Bonded Girl-Children as Domestic Labourers –Centre for Women's Studies, Alagappa University, Karaikudi.

6. Country Report - India (Feb. 1997) - Convention on the Rights of the Child - Deptt. of Women and Child Development, Ministry of Human Resource Development, Govt. of India.

29

Reassertion of Woman's Place in Society

Sharada from the prestigious South Delhi University Campus came to me and said that she was doing her Ph.D. under the guidance of a renowned professor. Each time she would try to get his help at the University Campus he would call her home and make advances. She tried very hard to tell him that she would rather work at the campus premises but to no avail. Ultimately one day he tried to molest her and she has to complain to the National Commission for Women. The National Commission for Women at once took up the matter but could not proceed very much in the matter due to lack of evidence. Thousands of such cases are reported every day but due to lack of evidence and threat to the security of the girl, do not see the light of the day.

The saga of the Indian woman is riddled with cruel inhuman, pathetic attacks on her physical, emotional, social, political and even spiritual growth. The struggle continues from womb to grave without respite.

Sexual harassment is a humiliating and degrading experience which undermines the confidence and dignity of those affected by it. It can interfere with an individual's ability to work and can lead to serious health problems. Sexual harassment can also contaminate the whole working environment and affect the morale of entire workforce.

Millions of working women, in the fields, the forests, the factories, the offices, the schools and the colleges are under constant threat of being deprived of their honour, dignity, safety and security. Appropriate counselling when needed by the harassed women provides remedial routes. If one is ignorant about legal remedies, one cannot go to the court to seek redressal of grievances and justice.

Traditionally, Indian women's occupational profile has been associated with the family and the attitude of particular communities towards working women. After attaining independence, definite and positive changes have been occurring because of what may be termed as 'modernisation'. This has occurred, particularly because there have been tremendous opportunities for women; there has been substantial rise in educational levels and to some extent attitudinal changes at family and community levels. The working woman in the real sense, is not an addition to the Indian scene. In the real economic sense, women of lower strata have always been in the category of working women. Others work at home and it's related fields but these were not recognised. It will be agreed that the level of economic equality and independence are the true indicators to determine the status of women. Employment of women, therefore, is a necessary corollary to achieve gender equity, gender equality and gender justice. No doubt, there are many occupational hazards in case of working women, the prominent among them being 'harassment' because of personal greed, lust, indecent and inhuman behaviour on the part of male colleagues, superiors and others. In the context of recently introduced economic reforms and structural adjustment programmes, there has been a demand from women's movement in the country that in addition to providing safety nets and reducing hardships caused by the new economic policy, it would be essential to explore approaches, in which women are at the centre of the policy changes. It cannot be doubted that research studies and documentation on various facets of employment of women and the nature, extent and consequences of their exploitation and harassment in different settings are not quite adequate. In this connection, I would like to emphasise that the knowledge of concrete local experiences lend credence in formulating specific gender related policy formulations whether it be poverty, employment or harassment. In one recent publication migration the gender–specific causes and consequences of seasonal labour, graphic details of exploitation and harassment are given. A reading of the book arouses at once a feeling of dissatisfaction with the systems. Then there are the woes of the contract women labourers. Their condition in work sites is deplorable and their exploitation knows no bounds. I feel that there is a need to enquire and study in depth the rural scene in all its manifestation where women toil for their livelihood amidst harassment and exploitation.

Some important positive developments which have recently taken place in the context of working women. Firstly, the Supreme Court judgement upholding the Constitutional validity of Andhra Pradesh Government orders on reservation of quota for women in public services in the context of the Constitutional provision under Article 15(3).

Secondly, the judgement of the Supreme Court in Ms. Radha Bai V. Union Territory of Pondicherry and others, which is about harassment of working woman. The judgement delivered by Hon. Justice K.S. Paripoornan indicting the Union Territory Administration observed, I quote, "It cannot be gainsaid that the modesty of a woman is very precious to her from all points of view and when attempts were made to molest her and also thwart the genuine attempts made by her to set right the undesirable happenings in the shelter home for women, any person placed in the position of appellant will certainly feel annoyed and ashamed. There is every reason for the appellant to feel greatly humiliated. There is bound to be moral indignation or resentment". We are all happy that at last justice was done to her, though belated, after all the good prevailed over the evil.

Thirdly, the directions of the Supreme Court to the Government of India to formulate guidelines to check sexual harassment at the workplace on a public interest litigation filed by a non-governmental organisation called "VISHAKHA" against the state of Rajasthan.

Fourthly, the concern and sensitiveness displayed by women parliamentarians in the matter. A Bill was moved by Ms. Kamla Sinha in the Parliament in May 1994 to provide for the prevention of sexual harassment of women employees at their workplaces. In the statement of objects and reasons, it was explained by Ms. Sinha that in almost every field of economic activity women form a large part of the work force. The number of working women is increasing everyday. At the workplace women are compelled to work in the most disadvantageous service conditions. They are harassed sexually at the workplace by their male colleagues, bosses, employers and others. Cases of sexual harassment of women at the workplaces occur but more often these are not reported for threats and discriminatory treatment. Though this offence like physical assault and molestation has been made punishable under the Indian Penal Code, yet working women feel insecure since all aspects of sexual harassment are not covered by that Code. Accordingly, an urgent need is felt to deal with the situation more stringently. The Bill therefore takes care of the offences related to sexual harassment of women at the workplace.

One incident in Jaipur—I rushed to the scene of sexual harassment. The girl Radha used to get phone calls during her work. Ultimately one day she was waylaid by a Maruti car which was driven by four young men and taken to the University campus of Jaipur. She was repeatedly gang raped by seven students in an unoccupied hostel room. A large crowd of students outside the University Hostel room witnessed the process of gang rape. After our intervention and investigations, for the first time not only did the University give compensation to the girl but also formulated a code of conduct. Now many other Universities of India have also formulated such a code which is helpful in solving problem.

It is hoped that these various Bills which are pending in the Parliament would soon be introduced and a step towards empowerment could be realized.

30
Securing a Future

Strenuous efforts have been made in the last fifty years to ameliorate the economic and social conditions of the backward sections of the Indian society. They continue to suffer from gross economic deprivations and social humiliations. They form a major chunk of the population and causes of their backwardness have been varied. The major segments identified among the backwards have been the Scheduled Castes and the Scheduled Tribes. Of late another segment has been identified as the "Other Backward Classes" or the "OBC". Cutting across all the class and caste distinctions, women as a group, form a major chunk that suffered economic and social deprivation in a male dominated society. The reasons for their backwardness have been varied, mostly historical. One major single cause of their social and economic backwardness has been identified as lack of education. From the educational angle women as a group suffered the most since female education did not get the desired attention on account of various social factors even among the otherwise socially and economically advanced societies. Over the last half a century concerted efforts have been made with varied success to remove the backwardness of the identified segments like the Scheduled Castes and Tribes and other castes. Since education was considered as the one most important single cause for the backwardness of most of the backward groups, greater stress has rightfully been laid on providing education. It has been the feeling that education could erase the stigma of backwardness, since once a person is educated he/she begins to move in a higher circle with some ease.

Women on the basis of their educational, social and economic backwardness could be classified into several groups, based on caste, creed, religion, region etc. However cutting through all these divisions and distinctions there is a group of women who have been historically oppressed, economically exploited, socially stigmatised, culturally deprived, and socially ostracised, sexually drained off, legally bereft of civic rights, and pushed to the margin to get in the stink and stench of the society which gives them nothing but takes away all they have. They are the prostitutes or in modern parlance the sex workers who are said to be practicing the oldest profession in the world. They are the victims of the lust of man who uses them and then throws them to languish in the dustbin of the back and bylanes of his cities. These unfortunate women are socially the most neglected lot who have been cheated of their homes, their security, their relations, their youth, their chastity, and left at the mercy of the most cruel pimps, touts and brothel keepers who use them as money making machines and discards them when they are no longer fit to earn for them.

(a) There is no authentic census of the children of the prostitutes or of the prostitutes themselves, which could quantify the problem. But according to one estimate 883 prostitutes give birth to 1056 socially handicapped children. It would be fair to presume that every prostitute bears at least a child or two in her working life. According to a very rough estimate there are 17,00,000 prostitutes whose children comprise 45 lakhs. Almost fifty to sixty thousand women enter this profession every year. This in itself is a staggering picture.

(b) According to a survey of commercial sex workers in Andhra Pradesh conducted for the National Commission for Women in 1997 it was found that 77 per cent of the prostitutes in Andhra Pradesh were themselves illiterate and 70.5 per cent of them had children. Majority of them, 58.23 per cent, reported that their children lived with them at their place of work and only 15.88 per cent reported that their children were staying with their relatives.

(c) The main victims of the profession of prostitution are their children since they are born with the social stigma of being "illegitimate". They stay in isolation from the mainstream and are deprived of a normal life.

(d) They are born and brought up in the uncongenial environment of the brothels and suffer from health problems from their very childhood.

(e) The mere fact of their being born to a prostitute denies them equal opportunities of all kinds including educational.

(f) Due to the influences to which they are exposed at an early age they constitute a potential material to those interested in the propagation of flesh trade. They become both disadvantaged and vulnerable. The girls become victims of child prostitution at an early age in their life and boys take to pimping and other kinds of anti-social activities.

(g) The children who live with their mothers at their place of work, live in small rooms in overcrowded, ill-ventilated localities. Lack of time and poverty prevent the women from cooking fresh and nutritious food either for themselves or for their children. They maintain most irregular timings. They sleep during the day and work during the night. The time is not theirs, they live in fear of the police who they fear would not only take away their money but also their children. This life of fear and dread of law and society results in many psychological problems for the women and also their children.

(h) The children living with their mothers in the brothels come into contact and under the influence of the anti-social and undesirable elements very early in their lives. These elements too become the role models for the young minds. The anti-social elements, the machos not only exercise disproportionate influence on the prostitutes for their nuisance value but also manipulate their children to their advantage and use them as errand boys. They easily take to smoking too early in their lives, and get hooked to opium and drugs.

(i) They are the rich recruiting ground for drug peddlers. The girls among them are the easy victims for girl prostitution finally landing into a life of complete prostitution.

(j) These children are vulnerable to the ways of the trade right from their childhood and at every stage of growing up. They witness drunken brawls and their mothers' involvement in relationships with various men, which frequently entails rough scenes. They also see their mother being ill-treated by the brothel keepers, which at times reaches the heights of cruelty. It is commonplace for them to see their mothers haggle with clients and settle the rates. The curiosity of a growing male child about these issues make them learn many undesirable things too early in their lives prematurely and in a distorted perspective. This in turn creates a compelling urge to molest and eve tease and even indulge in sexual relationships rather too early in life.

(k) Besides their own handicaps and proneness to deviation, the children constitute the potential source of strength to those who are interested in the propagation of the trade. The female child is taken to prostitution or the allied profession of singing and dancing or is made to do so by familial forces of environmental compulsions. The male children receive training to play the necessary supportive role in trade management like pimping and procuring besides acquiring proficiency in other underworld activities.

During my visit to Ujjain I saw a group of young children–boys in the age group of eight to twelve –surround men and beg customers to take their mothers for Rs.10/- and another boy would say Rs.8/- and there was stiff competition among the boys to barter their mothers. In the process, they are unable to rise above their situation, and instead are nurtured to carry on anti-social activities, which is detrimental to the social balance.

Looked at in the above perspective, it would be observed that the children of the prostitutes suffer from innumerable disabilities imposed on them by reason of birth, environment, social stigma, denial of equal opportunities, lack of education of their mother, lack of security due to absence of fatherly affection, loose control of the mothers on the upbringing of their children due to the peculiarities and hazards of their trade and business, the attitude of the brothel keepers towards them etc. The pace at which urbanisation is taking place is too fast. Urban centres with their ever growing floating population give rise to prostitution and the concomitant problem of their children. Therefore the need for their proper upbringing and education becomes obvious if these children are not to be lost to society and swell the ranks of the anti-socials, criminals, and delinquent children roaming the streets of the metropolitan cities and major semi-metros.

In the normal household the children grow up, through parental love and care and are unconsciously prepared to go to school. They have no difficulty in doing so as soon as they have attained the school going age. According to the financial status and standing of the family, the children find entry in appropriate schools. This certainly is not the case with the children of sex workers who grow up neglected from the day of their birth and just grow up with time without any particular care or consideration that they have to go to a school at some stage. Hence it is necessary that the children of the sex-workers be provided with the facilities from the age of infancy, that they, at the appropriate age, find themselves on the road to a school. Unless this was ensured, these, children staying in the unnatural climate of the brothels, would have no urge to go to school at all.

The question of education for these children has to be tackled in two stages. Stage one would be their upbringing from the age of one year or even earlier to the age of five when they are ready to enter a school. The first would appropriately be called the preparatory stage or State I. In State II they are ready to go to a school and get the education that would prepare them to stand up on their feet and give them the ability to fight social disabilities that are part of their unfortunate inheritance.

The State I is that of upbringing. Though upbringing and education go hand in hand and cannot be divorced from each other, in the case of these children upbringing assumes much greater importance. The children from the day of their birth suffer from a stigma and are unwanted by the people around even if the mother has a different perception. They do not have a family that would celebrate their birth or make merry. Therefore the problem of their upbringing is from the day they are born and the question of their education comes much later. Unless they are rescued from the morass immediately on birth the question of education may never arise. Hence the importance of their segregation from the environment in which they are born immediately on birth, and to bring them up in a manner that they are made ready to receive education at the appropriate time.

Given the special problems and disabilities that these children suffer from, are the mainstream day schools the answer to their needs? If they are, as some people may be led to believe, the problem is simple and easy. There are schools available in every nook and corner of every big and metropolitan city. The Supreme Court judgement of 1993 has removed any hurdle in their joining the mainstream schools. It is no longer necessary that the children of the prostitutes must have the names of their fathers for admission. But this enabling judgement has failed to solve the problem of the children of prostitutes.

The children can stay in the day schools only for a certain number of hours and not beyond. Such schools can take care of the children for four to five hours in the morning and forenoon only. This is also the time when there is very little activity in their place of residence. But the return of the children from school coincides with the timing when the business in the brothels, starts picking up and when the need to isolate them form that shady life is most acutely felt. Their mothers become unavailable to them to provide the necessary care. The pimps and the goons who provide the protection to the business become active and would like these children to run various errands or at least not be seen around and become a hindrance in the business. Their mothers who are under the discipline and control of these elements are helpless and unable to provide them the protection because the economic demands find an overriding priority over all other factors. They have neither any place for after-school studies, nor any place to play or playmates, nor any place to isolate themselves from the activities of their mothers or other goings on. That apart, these schools can only provide them education three R's only while they need total development of the body and mind, for emotional, intellectual and physical development.

Apart from other factors, the importance of education can hardly be discounted. It not only adapts an individual to the existing or emerging social situation, but it has also a creative role. It has the potential for liberating the child's mind from the shackles of the environmental and established culture. It is therefore inevitable that the dose of education is imparted from the very beginning before the children develop any cynicism to education and society and their mind has been won over to easy ways of life, which in the long term could cost them their future irretrievably.

The problem of this category of children has to be tackled at two levels. First the mothers must be made to realise the need for keeping the children away from the trade and environment and there by providing conditions for basic minimum healthy development and groom them so that they are equipped to lead a respectable life. Without generating the requisite motivation among the mothers little can be done for the children because the decision regarding their future lies with the parents, who in this case are none other than mothers, their one and only relation. But the mothers can only be motivated, once they are assured rather convinced that the alternative being offered is so attractive that they find it impossible to ignore. No force can be exerted on the mothers to surrender their children just because we feel that they are unable to provide them with the proper upbringing. The mother-child relationship has to be treated humanely and it would be tragic if in one's eagerness to solve the problem of the child, the mother is alienated creating an altogether new emotional problem for her.

The development of a child is a long-term problem and has no easy or short-term solution. The change of environment seems fundamental to the liberation of the children of the prostitutes. Environmental changes could come about either by placement of the children under institutional care, or adoption or placement in a family. The Juvenile Justice Act recognises that "much greater attention is required to be given to children who may be found in situations of social maladjustment, delinquency or neglect... There is also need for larger involvement of informal systems and communit-based welfare agencies in the care, protection, treatment, development and rehabilitation of such juveniles." The Act defines a "neglected juvenile" as a juvenile who lives in a brothel or with a prostitute who frequently goes to a place for the purpose of prostitution or is found to associate with any prostitute or any other person who leads an immoral, drunken or depraved life. Both the Act and need for social justice recognise the urgent necessity for the children to be provided the right type of environment for their healthy growth. The social activists abhor any use of force legal or otherwise to separate the child from the mother even if the welfare of the child is the ultimate goal. They feel that the prostitute mothers would find it impossible to face the Juvenile Welfare Boards and justify their ability to take care of their children in the circumstances they are placed. When children are forcibly taken away from their mothers by invoking the law, it leaves a trauma behind for the mother. Similarly when the children are separated under duress from their mothers they suffer the pangs of separation and yearn to be reunited and the new environment however pleasant, becomes oppressive and retards the healthy growth of the children and they suffer emotional instability just the reverse of what is intended.

From the above it follows that if a healthy and integrated growth of the children both physical, mental and emotional are to be ensured, it is necessary that they are taken out of the environment of the brothels which reek of human degradation and shame and placed in a healthier environment that could ensure their all round development. Since it is recognised that the most impressionable years of the children are between five to ten, it is essential that they do not grow in the shadow of their mother in the brothels. Besides the impressionable years there is the need for saving the children from malnutrition and disease in the earlier stages of their career.

It would be considered desirable that these children are removed from the unhealthy climate of the brothels as early as possible even from the age of one year and earlier if possible. This is the time when it is possible to separate the child from the mother and put him from breast feeding to bottle. These could not be just day care homes but total homes where they are able to get hygienic environment, nourishing and nutritious food, motherly affection right from the earliest stage to the time when they are ready to enter a school. It may be hard on the mothers to part with their children when they have hardly opened their eyes. But unless the children are removed from the brothels from the very beginning they cannot be ensured a healthy growth. The most difficult time during the day for the children is after sunset till they go to sleep whey they hanker after mother's affection and care the most and that is the time when their mothers have the busiest of time and could give the minimum of care. Hence the chances of the children getting neglected and traumatised early in life are the greatest thus impacting their psyche the hardest. This could adversely affect the mental and psychological growth of the children for the rest of their lives. Hence the need to completely segregate them.

Such Homes for the infant children could be on the pattern of the SOS Children Homes, with suitable modifications to meet the peculiar needs of this section of the children. In a normal SOS home the children once brought in, their parents or relations are not allowed to keep contacts with them. Other friends or well wishers are also barred from having contacts with the children. In fact till about the age of fourteen the children are not even told if they have any one of their blood relations living. The children live in exclusive homes with foster mothers who look after their total needs, and for all practical purposes act as their mothers and the children are expected to look up to their wardens as their own mothers and other inmates as their brothers and sisters. The children who are brought to SOS homes are destitute, impoverished, orphans, indigent and delinquent. The point to note is that they are needy and brought to the Homes and the Homes do not go out to seek them. The fact that their relations if any are not seeking them out makes it easy for the Homes to give them a new life and new relations particularly a new mother. The adaptation of the children to these homes becomes that much easier.

In the case of Home for the children of the sex workers it would be necessary to maintain a link between the mothers and the children so that the mothers are assured that their dear ones are not lost to them. Some link between the mother and the children even if it is tenuous is absolutely necessary. There is the mother who needs the child and is willing to undergo some sacrifice financial or otherwise for the child's sake. She feels herself responsible to the child for his upbringing and the child to that extent is not a destitute or orphan. Thus there would be a primary need to motivate the mothers to send their infant children to the Preparatory Homes by assuring them that their children would be taken care of during their infancy and well prepared for the school stage.

Once the infant children have attained the age of four or so they would be ready to go to the regular schools from their base in the Children's Home where they stay during their school stint which could last till they have attained the age of 16 or 17 years. They have not only to be completely cut off from the brothel atmosphere but also the company of the managers and other connected with the running of the brothels. That they need to be provided with the basic schooling to prepare them for the life is beyond any discussion. Only education can equip them to fact the world and gain the confidence to overcome the social stigma and economic backwardness. The social ostracism that falls to their lot by virtue of their being the children of the prostitutes cannot be eliminated and overcome without building them psychologically through an all round educational programme. Only after they had gone to school they would be enabled to over come their social stigma, emotional instability, educational backwardness, and be able to win freedom from want and disease and finally win for themselves an honourable place in society. Since the prostitutes are deprived of economic stability particularly in old age and they look to their children as their assets and insurance for old age, a chance of a stable and profitable career after the school stage would be a sufficient motivation for the mothers to send their children away from the unhealthy and humanly degrading environment of the brothels that offer hardly any scope or chance to their children of a decent life then or later. They would have to be assured a constant interaction with their children during their school period. Constant interaction between the mothers and their children would also give the latter the much-needed emotional stability. This would also ensure flow of funds from the mothers to the children for meeting the recurring cost of their living and education. The mothers howsoever, economically weak would gladly and happily volunteer to share the cost of upbringing of their children.

What type of schools do we need for these children to start their educational career? Should they be exclusive schools or the normal boarding schools, which are also attended by children from other strata of society? This question has been more or less finally settled by the Supreme Court in its judgement in the case of *Gaurav Jain V. The Union of India* in July 1997 when it directed that while these children "should be segregated from their mothers" they should "mingle with others and become a part of the society." The Court ordered that "Children of the prostitutes should, however, not be permitted to life in inferno and the undesirable surroundings of prostitute home". This was felt particularly so in the case of young girls whose body and mind are likely to be abused with growing age for being admitted into the profession of their mothers. The Court rejecting the idea of separate hostels for children of prostitutes, felt that "accommodation in hostels and other reformatory homes should be adequately available to help their segregation from their mothers living in prostitute homes as soon as they are identified". The judgement while stressing the need to keep the children from the red light areas and induct them into respectable and meaningful avocations and/or self-employment schemes ordered their integration in the social mainstream. The Court laid great emphasis on the right of these children to equality of opportunity dignity and care, protection and rehabilitation by the society to bring them into the mainstream of social life without pre-stigma fixed on them for no fault of theirs. The Judgement going a step further recalled the Fundamental Rights in Part III of the Constitution, Universal Declaration of Human Rights, the Directive Principles of the State Policy and desired that "they were equally made available and made meaningful instruments and means to ameliorate their conditions—social, educational, economic and cultural and bring them into social main stream by giving them the same opportunities as are available to other children."

Social activists who are working among the disadvantaged children are also convinced that unless the children of all the strata of the society grow up together and interact among themselves from the very beginning, the objective of an egalitarian society could not be achieved. The Constitution of India guarantees to all the citizens' equality of opportunity for their advancement. How can we ensure the enjoyment of this fundamental right by the disadvantaged children unless we provide them equal opportunity to grow from their very childhood on an equal footing with the children of other sections of the society? There would be denial of this constitutional guarantee to the disadvantaged children if they go to different schools with different norms and come out of these exclusive institutions stigmatised. Equality of opportunity implies that all the children have equal opportunity to grow as equals and then compete for life from an equally advantageous or disadvantageous platform. If the disadvantaged children are able to get the equality of opportunity it would instill the much desired sense of confidence among them and at the end of their school career they would find themselves empowered enough to face the challenges thrown by later life.

Exclusive schools for the children of the prostitutes after the age of five years would be injurious to them in the long-run. The children coming under one roof from one disadvantaged background would find it impossible to forget their social handicap and would grow up with the social stigma attached to them. Similarly when they pass out of the exclusive schools and they want to compete in life with children from other segments of the society their educational and school background would betray their social past and stigma and thereby deprive them of unbiased competition in life. On the other hand when they pass out of the mainstream schools where they attend the school with the children with diverse backgrounds their socially disadvantaged past would get dissolved and not haunt them. They would, mentally and psychologically, be more prepared to face the life after school, become useful members of the society, and be well-integrated in the mainstream of the national life.

It is likely that there may be a substantial number of children of the prostitutes who may have no aptitude for academic studies and if forced into academic institutions against their will, are likely to run away and resort to vagrancy. It would therefore be necessary to make sure that nothing was done which did not fit into their calibre and for which they did not have the required aptitude. Employment oriented vocational courses would suit such children better and efforts would have to be made for their placement in vocational institutions.

31
Domestic Violence

The air smelt of honey dew, the expanse of green tea gardens made one feel in total harmony with the creator ... the entire scenic beauty was so picturesque that it felt unreal. The little cottages tilted on the slopes of the holiday resort more a reminder of tranquility, peace and harmony. It was all so far and strange from the normal urban life... Children enjoying the magic shows, the excellent food and play grounds.

Shattering this silence suddenly came the repeated sounds of a whistle... unmistakably the sound of a pressure cooker — of course it could not come from the far away kitchen of the holiday resort ... hence I followed the trail of the whistling to cottage number two and to my utter disbelief I heard "Please finish cooking fast .. I have to eat and go for a walk. We have come here for a holiday and you must finish cooking early morning and don't forget to make my favourite sambar" ... I just could not believe this ... the poor wife was brought for a holiday and was expected to cook day and night ... and not only do cooking but also listen to the taunts of the husband. Wasn't this really harassment and domestic violence against women?

We never speak about "the citizenship of women". We are always looked upon as if to say that we are your sisters, therefore treat us equally. Its never taken into cognizance that we are human beings and if we are not treated equally then there is something wrong with the man!

Women's life experiences across the world and statistics and writing on women are testimony to the fact that violence against women is the gravest and most pervasive form of violation of human rights. This fact has been reiterated at several forums over the years, but its enormity and severe implications have begun to be recognized only in the last decade. To quote the Beijing Platform for Action, "VAW violates and impairs or nullifies the enjoyment by women of their human rights and fundamental freedoms". It is a blot on our collective conscience.

The Cry of Violence Continues

Little Gauri was 15 years old and was not paying any attention to what was happening in the class. She was losing weight steadily and her teacher felt concerned. After a great deal of counselling and confidence building Gauri confided to her teacher (in a very Prestigious School of Delhi) that her father was abusing her everyday. She said it all started when she was eight years old and had very high temperature and her father had got into her bed to console her and told her that if he had sexual relationship with her; her fever will subside. The case was brought to me and this is the time when I felt that a co-ordinated response towards all forms of violence was necessary. The police, the court, the witnesses, the investigator they all needed to converge and coordinate to tackle the problem in a holistic and integrated way. It also transpired that the father pressurised the mother and threatened divorce if the case was repeated to the police. The victim was in dire need of an entire range of crises intervention for her immediate protection like shelter, medical aid, treatment, counselling and lawyers.

It is little wonder children react the way they do. Unless someone actively intervenes, the cycle of violence continues. There is substantial evidence suggesting that offenders have grown up in violent homes —either being victims of abuse themselves or witnessing their fathers beating their mothers—leaving little doubt that violent behaviour is from family background.

Children from violent homes end up believing that:

- It is all right for husbands to hit wives.
- Violence is a way to win arguments.
- Big people have power they often misuse.
- Men are bullies who push women and children around.
- Women are victims and can't take care of themselves or their children.

Although the majority of wife assault victims have not grown up in violent homes, those that have experience much greater difficulty standing up for themselves and taking protective action leaving little doubt that victim behaviour is learned.

There is no safe territory left for women not even in their "mohallas". Not only are single women harassed but other women are being assaulted and raped before the eyes of their family members.

It is ironical that in a country where womanhood has been put on pedestal for worship, incidence of wife battering, molestation of women in various forms like rape, eve-teasing, abduction and bride burning among others keep on increasing year to year. Women find no security in the home, where they are ill-treated by husbands and in-laws, they have no security in streets and workplace, where they are vulnerable and fall prey to police, anti-socials, moneylenders, men colleagues, bosses and are subjected to innumerable indignities perhaps in higher frequency than in most of the civilized societies. Today the general perception among the people is that the crime against women has increased to such a great extent that women are not able to move freely and participate in the community.

The march of history towards the development in the field of Science and Technology has changed the life styles of the people and the man's lust for unattainable comforts at the cost of women's life has made the things worse. Adding fuel to the fire is the fact that in many of the incidents of dowry harassments while some women are being killed, few others commit suicide and many more prefer to leave the matrimonial house and becomes destitutes or liability on the parents. If at all in rarest of the rare circumstances a woman prefers to take recourse to police and judiciary the system is so cumbersome that she has to move from pillar to post and will get justice only after years. The most discouraging provision which makes women suffer rather than taking resource to the judiciary is the awarding of a meagre amount of Rs. 500/- as maintenance under the Code of Criminal Procedure after divorce. What a dismal picture; What then is the scenario? Will the Indian women have to suffer and die in the name of dowry even after 50 years of Independence? The answer is a clear no.

Taking into account the enormity of the situation I decided that there has to be quick coordinated action to save the girl from further trauma and harassment. We developed a very innovative method of speedy justice to women in a coordinated fashion. Idea of Parivarik

Mahila Lok Adalat is the result of all the anguish that I suffered because women in large numbers were left deserted and destitute. Many women could not bear the heavy cost of litigation with its accompanying cumbersome procedures which left women in a trauma–how to seek justice. Women could not be isolated from their families and therefore I looked around for a mechanism that could resolve family disputes and domestic violence.

The National Commission for Women has launched this movement with great success and has already conducted over 180 Parivarik Mahila Lok Adalats and it is expected that government or other agencies will pick up the idea and run it on a regular basis. This collective endeavour, contribution and service of the National Commission for Women, NGOs, Judges and legal service authority are vital to the success of this experiment.

While the counsellors prepare the contesting parties to come to settle their disputes, the cases are brought before the courts presided over by district and sub–ordinate judge and on any weekend. This concept of speedy justice at the doorsteps of women will surely have a multiplier effect and will be adapted by one and all.

Justice Ahmedi said about the Lok Adalats I quote "I am glad the National Commission for Women has launched a programme of holding Parivarik Mahila Lok Adalats in different parts of the country to resolve such matrimonial disputes and thereby bring about social harmony and domestic peace. I would commend every individual and institution to lend its helping hand to this laudable effort". One important role that we found could be played was by Family Courts.

1. The need for Family Courts geared momentum as it was felt that there were a large number of cases pending in the civil courts and if there was a Court which could exclusively serve as a conciliatory and coordinating body, then there would be less delay and adjournments would be fewer.
2. The functioning of the Family Courts in few cities and in some states where they have so far been established, the position does not appear to be happy. As I see it, at present the Presiding Officers of Family Courts are being drawn from the higher judiciary. The procedures and practices adopted in the regular courts are too formal in nature and judge has to follow strictly the rules of procedure and evidence as laid down in the procedural law.

Therefore, without proper orientation such judges may not adjust or adapt to the informal atmosphere of a Family Court. I, therefore, feel that it will be necessary that the Presiding Officers of Family Courts are given adequate training to suit the needs of the Family Courts. It will also be necessary to provide adequate training to Counsellors and Probation Officers attached to the Family Courts.

Some Pertinent Facts Regarding Dowry

Another very important violation of women's rights inside the house is dowry. Although giving and taking dowry is prohibited by the 1951 Dowry Act, a single day does not pass without newspapers headlines screaming, the most brutal incidents of dowry. Uttar Pradesh has a lead with an average of 1900 dowry deaths for the year. Out of the approximately 5000 dowry deaths reported of the entire nation.

1. Dowry is not a one shot affair. It continues throughout the span of married life. Expensive gifts are demanded from the bride's parents during festivals such as Diwali, Christmas and on other auspicious occasions such as the birth of a child.
2. Most people are vaguely, if at all aware of the law against dowry. Dowry seekers are, therefore, doubly careful in camouflaging their demands. They suggest that the bride's parents present a 'Honda or 'Maruti' car to the groom so that he can return home from work early enough to take his wife out in the evening!
3. Most brides suffer harassment in silence for many years. They do so for the following reasons:
   (a) They are conditioned to believe that after a girl's marriage her permanent place is with her husband and in-laws.
   (b) They are conditioned to suffer in silence.
   (c) They fear that their parents would have to suffer social ostracism. There have been incidents of young unmarried girls committing suicide to protect their parents from the burden of dowry. The first such case which caused a public outcry was that of three sisters at Kanpur, all educated, but helpless due to the dowry situation.
4. Men who do not take dowry are at times looked down upon in their community. Relatives, neighbours and others

believe that such men must surely be physically or mentally handicapped and therefore, agree to marry without dowry.

5. In dowry death cases (mostly due to burns) most women give a false dying declaration stating that the burns are due to an accident or that they have attempted suicide. This is due to their concern for their children, parents and themselves if they survive.

Wife beating is generally accepted as a cultural phenomenon. Most men take it upon themselves to beat their wives to 'improve them'. Women too accept it as a part of life. It is perceived as a token of the husband 's affection. The police too, especially of the lower ranks, all view it as a societal norm. The legislation against physical and mental torture (Section 498A) is of recent origin. Unfortunately, there are lapses in its implementation.

Mental torture of the wife is a covert phenomenon. It may be even more devastating than the physical assaults. Taunting the wife, insulting her in the presence of the children, guests and domestic help, ignoring her completely and cutting off communication with her are the common manifestations of mental torture. In a case of a retired senior civil servant harassing his daughter in-law, a home visit was paid by us in order to conduct a family interview. The civil servant would not allow his wife to participate in the interview, saying that she was stupid and that he was the spokesman of the family. He criticised our insistence on involving her in the interview by saying that 'Women libbers wreck families.' In another case of marital conflict the working wife stated that her husband locked up all the kitchen gadgets such as the mixer, peeler and pressure cooker so that she had to spend more time in the kitchen and consequently report late for work. This case has now been solved.

The harassed wives suffer in silence because of the following reasons:

1. They have been conditioned to obey their husbands.
2. Culturally it is assumed that the wife will silently bear the assaults.
3. She has no support as such. Her parental family and other relatives refuse to accept her back and bear the burden of supporting her and the children (if any) for the rest of her life.

4. She is usually ignorant of the provision in the law to safeguard her rights, as well as of shelter homes run by welfare organinsations and the government.
5. Assuming she has this information, that is, to resort to the police station, take a lawyer's advice or avail herself of facilities provided for harassed women, she is usually brainwashed to keep the Khandan ki Izzat' unblemished.
6. Children are used as Blackmailers.Rape by the husband is not as yet a cognisable offence in India. Women are conditioned to play a submissive role especially in the matter of sexual relations. Most husbands feel a sense of exclusive possession with regard to their wives. Hence in sexual relations, the wife's consent is rarely taken. Cases have been reported of deviant sexual behaviour of the husband, for example beating the wife prior to the sexual intercourse, burning her with cigarette butts or thrusting hard objects in her vagina. Refusal to give into the insatiable sexual desire of the husband is interpreted as the result of her extra marital relations. She is therefore 'doubly punished'.

There was a case of murder of a young housewife in Delhi some years ago. She had been married for two months. Her husband was impotent but this was not disclosed to her prior to her marriage. In his efforts to cure his impotency, the husband forced her to have sexual relations with his friends in his presence. Gradually her brother–in-law and father-in-law to began to rape her. On one occasion when she strongly resisted her father-in-law's advances, he strangled her and then threw her out of their sixteenth floor apartment. This case would have been registered as suicide because the in-laws made a statement to the police that the woman was mentally deranged. However, the timely intervention of a casual spectator, who happened to be a nurse, changed the entire complexion of their case. Cases of cruelty by the husband and her relatives have increased from 11603 in 1989 to 15949 in 1991 (Social Welfare, Vol. XXXIX, No. 11-12, Feb.-Mar. 1993).

Cases of domestic violence are usually, but not exclusively, associated with liquor consumption by the husband. Liquor, foreign and indigenous is freely available in most Indian states. Men drink with callousness and gay abandon. The hard earned money of both the husband and wife is devoured by alcohol. Consequently, the wives resort to taking up extra jobs and hiding their income. Deaths due to the consumption of alcohol are increasing but there is no statistical data available. It is estimated that the number of deaths due to spurious liquor exceeds the deaths due to communal riots. Many cases, however, are not reported .The death of the husband due to liquor consumption places heavy burden on the wife. She has to assume the entire responsibility of supporting her family if she has no grown-up children. At times, men have been blinded as a result of spurious liquor.This too equally cripples the family. (Extract from the book Women Against Violence, ed. by Shri Kudchedkar Sabiha Al-Issa, 1998)

Women's Reaction to Domestic Violence

During the early stage of violence the woman prefers to be silent, then sometimes she talks to her nearest relatives. She always reacts only through speech. She rarely reacts by resorting to violence herself. Rarely does she decide to take help from the police or the court. Immediate relief is what she looks for in the situation of violence, so she can be somewhat at ease. She always looks for help from her parental family. When she gets moral support, she feels that she is empowered and then she struggles against domestic violence.This attitude is mostly seen in labour class women, whereas middle or upper class women expect somebody else to fight for them. Mostly the women endure violence for the sake of their children. This attitude is common to all classes.Then again when we speak about relationships we always speak about women as the weaker sex, words such as "bechari", "pappam" (Tamil), "abala", stereotype jobs etc. But have we ever tried to institutionalize all our relationships within our family and outside with the NGO's, police, state etc.

Conclusion

We need a coordinated approach to change the general atmosphere in the country which would lead to greater accountability and it will be easier to change attitudes.

It is often felt that the police, judiciary, NGOs, counsellor should all meet together to solve the problems of victims. I am confident that this venture would give one window clearance to all her problems.

32

Imprisoned Women and Closed Society

In the past several years I have had the opportunity to visit 54 jails in the country and each time I visit a jail I come out with a feeling that many more women are suffering outside the jail because women-mothers-sisters-daughters have gone to prison. The way the society deals with women who break the law is simply an extension of what is considered best for men. I have often felt during my visits to the jails that the rules of imprisonment were created by men for men. Whatever policies are made for men need not necessarily be the same for women also. The policies which are prepared for men are usually disastrous for women. Hence a sound penal policy for women prisoners needs to be introduced and also followed.

Apart from man-made rules and policies most women in the prisons are also victims of men's actions one way or the other. They are either used by men to carry contraband for them or they are prostitutes because of man's actions or are provoked to fight by men over fellow women and last but not the least, most women retaliate in self defence to the frequent brutal assaults of their drunken husbands and the death occurs simply because of the circumstances. I was in Warangal jail where I met a few women who have been imprisoned as Naxalites. They were about 18 years old and I asked them if they knew about the philosophy of Naxalites? The answer was that they did not know about Naxalites. They simply obeyed the orders of their husbands. They were married at the age of fourteen and their husbands asked them to prepare lunch for some guests. During the course of the preparation of such they were raided and caught and since then these women have been in prison. Without any knowledge of their crime they are languishing in imprisonment. Similarly, 30 out of 100 women in all the jails told me that they killed their husbands. Hence they have been punished. Is it the fault of the women that they cannot take beatings, abuses of their drunken husbands? They also force women to have affairs with their friends. I do not find that using physical violence by women in such circumstances is a crime. Often they do not think about the likely result of the act which they have applied in self-defence. I have also noticed that many women steal in order to feed their children for whom the fathers are not providing and also many times in order to protect their husbands they take the crime on their heads. Their crime, therefore, cannot be treated out of context without realising the environment, the tradition etc. that exist in our country.

Many crimes are committed in circumstances where the strength of emotions, or the influence of drugs or alcohol, has overcome any rational approach. In fact, what stops friost people from committing crimes is not the fear of prison but internal controls, conscience, the "Policeman within". Prisons therefore are ineffective when used as a major plank in a policy to reduce crime.

Most women prisoners in reality fall in the category of poor and defenceless house wives, maids, slum dwellers. Relationship between poverty and imprisonment is very high. Their fate is often neglected and news about them are seldom published because such people constitute the "wretched of the earth".

In the Naini jail at Allahabad I met this young twenty three year old girl Meena. At the age of sixteen, Meena was orphaned and some one told her that if she has a bath on the 'Kumb Mela' occasion in the Ganga—her miseries would end. So this poor girl leaves her sari on the banks of the river and takes a dip. When she comes out of the water she does not find her sari and in order to cover her body quickly she picks up some other sari. Within minutes there is chaos and the police come beat her up because no one cares about a woman's bail or existence. She languishes in the prison.

It is said that most women in prisons are not legally represented at the trials. Often they are sent to jails without access to bail. They do not have the knowledge about the sections of law under which they have been imprisoned. Lawyers services are not available to women for a minimal defence. The endless delays by the police, by magistrates and lack of proper legal counsel together create a situation in which court proceedings constitute in themselves cruel and inhuman treatment for women. During many of my visits, women prisoners have narrated their horrifying experience of their being taken to courts which are at a long distance and the humiliation, molestation, rape etc. on the way by the escorts. Also, court proceedings are adjourned and dates after dates given without any final judgement thereby the under trials who are not guilty of the crime are already punished for the crime they have never committed.

During my Prothrapur Distt. Jail (Port blair) visit prisoner No. B/3012 Smt. Malancho, W/o. Late Shri Anil is undergoing imprisonment for life in the Distt. Jail, Prothrapur w.e.f.13.12.82. She was convicted by the Session Judge, Port Blair in Session Trial No. 2/82 for murdering her husband under Section 302 of the IPC. She was sentenced to suffer rigorous imprisonment for life. She served as an undertrial prisoner from 30.11.79 to 26.6.80 and from 10.1.81 to 12.12.82 that is for 2 years, 6 months and 2 days. She has undergone the actual sentence of 13 years, 5 months and 15 days as on today. Her character and conduct during the jail term has been found satisfactory. She has therefore, earned a remission of 5 years, 6 months and 1 day for her good conduct.

Under the law, there is provision for remission in terms of conviction on the basis of good conduct and other factors. Such remissions are more common in respect of convicts undergoing life imprisonment. I was told that remissions have been ordered mostly in cases of male convicts. The cases of female convicts have generally been ignored or overlooked.

During my visits to prisons I noticed that undertrials are also kept in the prisons for a large number of days without any facilities for training, education and even their food is brought from the male prisons. A general problem across all women prisons is that there is virtually no serious rehabilitation programme for them. Women waste most of the day doing usually nothing not because of policy, but largely through lack of resources and neglect.

I suggested during my Phulwari Sharif Jail (Patna) visit that the question of amendment to the Jail Manual should be taken up so that the undertrials also could be employed in gainful work. The undertrials, specially women should be given adequate training in stitching/rose budding, copy-making and book-binding etc. In connection with jail industries, I suggested that the old fashioned machines/tools be replaced with modern tools so that the productivity could be increased. I also suggested that some local voluntary organisations should be involved to look after the welfare of lady undertrials. The need for improvement of kitchen and sanitation in jail wards was also stressed by me. It was also understood that proper security was not available for women for being taken to hospital/court.

At the Sabarmati jail which ironically happens to be Mahatma Gandhi's jail a young girl told me that each time she has an attack of a seuere astama, she has to suffer silently or as many of her colleagues in the jail have died she would also die in the absence of no women police constable to take her to the hospital. I had lengthy discussions with the I.G. of Prisons and he assured me that he will take up with State Government the following proposals for implementation:

The jail manual may be amended to a authorise taking of gainful work from undertrials so that their time was better utilised and they may also earn in the process. The old tools and archaic machines in use in the jail industry should be replaced by technologically suitable machines/tools. The iron and aluminium utensils in use in jail kitchen as well as for eating by the undertrials/ prisoners should be replaced with stainless steel utensils in order to aviod health hazards. The lady undertrials should be given training for growing plants, rose budding, copy-making, book-binding, mushroom growing plants so that on return to their homes they could be economically self-supporting and acceptable to their families. The incentives being paid to workers in jail industry should be refashioned and increased.

"Not withstanding anything in the foregoing rules the cases of women prisoners may be considered after completing the period of 5 years including the period undergone during trial and remission earned. The earned remission shall not be less than 2 years in any case."

A good majority of women prisoners are quite aged. Because of social stigma attached as a result of their conviction, they remain ignored by the members of their family. This has led to their losing mental balance and in some cases prematured greying. One can imagine their plight when they come out of the jail after serving the sentence. There is human consideration involved to make them self-reliant so that they can earn their livelihood and spend remaining part of their life with self-respect. It is, therefore, of paramount importance to train them in different vocational activities like knitting, tailoring etc. In Bhagalpur jail, it was heartening to note that of late they have been engaged in growing vegetables. Apart from keeping them engaged, this has yielded financial benefits. Because of no work, some of he women prisoners go on brooding all the time. They always remain in pensive mood thinking over the past. This effects their physical and mental health. I came across a female prisoner who had an aged daughter of marriageable age. She was always apprehensive that the girl may elope. Such situations arise because the inmates do not have much work. They remain idle quite unlike male counterparts they cannot do hard work. They can, after training, be engaged in different trades like making uniforms for Police Department, Hospitals and various industrial establishments. I am told, TRYSEM scheme has been introduced in the jail with cooperation of Rural Development Department of Government of Bihar. But something more concrete is required. We may consider employment after initial training in candle making, making of jams and pickles, soap-making, making of Dons and Pattals of dried leaves etc. These products will have tremendous market. Bhagalpur is a prosperous commercial city. Besides, it is very well connected with different cities of Bihar as well as in West Bengal. The marketing of products made by the jail inmates may not pose a problem.

There is yet another problem of a wider nature that befalls the society at large as a result of female imprisonment. Studies have shown that women as partners or spouses tend to be more tolerant when the male partners are imprisoned. Such that if there was a marriage or a partnership, it will not easily come to an end if the husband or the partner is imprisoned. But if it is the female who is imprisoned she would finish her term of imprisonment only to come out and find that her male partner has long married another woman.

Social consequences of broken marriages are very obvious, especially where there are children. Women are the caretakers of families and once imprisoned, it is not only they who suffer but the children, the rich and the elderly who are dependent on their tender care. While the female convict undergoes the trauma of not being able to provide them with care, the dependents live in the uncertainty of not knowing what the future holds for them.

At Ganjam and Warangal districts of Andhra Pradesh, there were four children in prison, two of whom were male slightly above the age of two years. The children spent much of their time during the day with the male prisoners. The psychological damage done to such children has almost totally escaped the attention of many. "Prisoners in the Shadows", the Civil Liberties Organisation, had this to say:

"For children behind bars for no fault of theirs, life goes on in the prison. Other women take turns to nurse them, and life to the babies is basically what they observe around them. They have no knowledge of games, play, cars, men, schooling, etc. Life is simply waking up, bathing, eating and moving among women while prison life takes its effect on them. They may grow up to hate men, detest games, cars, or even commit crimes to put them back in the kind of life they are used to".

The net effect of all these is that the child is emotionally, physically, academically, socially and religiously deprived. He/she learns and grows up in a sub-culture that is quite unlike the structure. Right from the start, he is reared in an environment that will make it difficult for it to adapt to the mainstream environment. He might easily be groomed to be a deviant that will eventually end up in prison in the future.

The prisons which are attached to the local police stations are improvised temporary homes for custodial care. They are often dingy, foul smelling, small, scantily ventilated. Basic human needs like food, clothing and decent sleeping facilities are not adequate. In such circumstances the welfare of expectant inmates, and the well-being of infants becomes a problem. On average, there were 15 and 10 children in every jail I had visited. Children of prisoners are in effect prisoners of their own kind. Under the circumstances, they face restrictions with respect to the playing, space, freedom of association, choice of food, where to sleep, etc. For the pregnant prisoners who deliver in prison, there are no post-natal facilities including basics like clothing and bedding for the infant babies. Provisions for latrines and bathrooms are not available. These are the make shift short stay prisons' attached to police stations. The lack of female staff in many of their prisons have compelled women who are seriously ill to remain in the prisons without being taken to the nearest hospital for treatment and there are many cases where women have had to say good-bye to this world due to lack of timely medical treatment. Even the security for women is not guaranteed specially in Local Administration prisons where there have been reports of sexual assaults on female inmate by the male staff. An acute need is to provide more women attendants, supervisors, police officials to help women prisoners. The basic problem with prisons which are annexes of male prisons are that they are not environmentally or architecturlly meant for women. Hence the sanitation and other facilities which should be made available to women are lacking. Women's prisons are built on the basis of having to modify a system devised to incarcerate men, with a much smaller budget. The end result is typically a large, dilapidated building in an isolated place with virtually no facilities, tucked at the end of a male prison.

I feel that women in prison seem to be an after thought of the system run by man and consequently being accommodated in make shift circumstances that completely neglect the peculiar and unique nature of women. In India, a female prison in reality is only an annexe of the male prisons. Separate women prisons are very few. There are only 14 women's prisons in the country.

Due to the limited number of prisons with female sections, many women are detained in prisons which are far away from their homes. As a result, many of the women from the rural poor families, who constitute over ninety per cent of the prison population receive no visits by their relatives.

Imprisonment has also failed to prepare women for the eventual return to society. In most cases those on the verge of completing their sentences are not excited by the prospect of their pending release. They are instead faced with worries and anxiety about life is after prison. This is because imprisonment alienates them from their relatives, friends and neighbours. Some lose their jobs, for others marriages breakdown, and some lose their property. At the end, it is the society at large that suffers when a women is imprisoned.

In our country there is definately a need for political commitment and there is some evidence of it now to recognise women as special interest group in society at the administrative and legal levels. However, not much attention is being paid to women prisoners. While we recognise many other groups and confer special rights to promote their interests, the interest of women prisoners still remains a neglected area. Non-recognition of their special needs often lead to unfair and inhuman treatment by the criminal justice system. Some form of positive discrimination has to be adopted in the interest of fair and just treatment. My visits have confirmed my belief that women are less able then men to adapt to imprisonment and rigors of prison life. The positive discrimination policies have been neglected. Total separation from men in custodial institutions, supervision by female officers, exemption to pregnant women and mothers from capital punishment and provision of special accommodation, care and treatment for prenatal and post natal inmates re some of the just and reasonable provisions necessary for them.

I often wonder if we can really look forward to a plan of action where we could have a vision of an open jail system where families can live together.

These frightening experiences constitute a powerful argument for totally new procedures to protect women against imprisonment. The most cursory examination of what is taking place in women's prisons in India reveals that imprisonment of women, except in rare circumstances, is a costly, inappropriate and cruel form of punishment. Most of the women in prison should not in any case be there.

Although there will always be those women offenders for whom imprisonment mat be the only appropriate sentence, there is big number of female offenders for whom an alternative sentencing mechanism could be appropriate.

Information on women in prisons is scarce while projects looking into women's problems, aside from the recent attention on sexual abuse, domestic violence and the traditional focus on motherhood, are virtually non-existent. Problems faced by imprisoned women thus remain largely unknown.

The conclusion to be drawn from this picture is that a revolution in attitude to women's imprisonment is needed. Most women currently imprisoned should not be in prison. For the few who have to be incarcerated, we need a different system of very small, self-sufficient units with active programmes of training and considerable involvement from outside agencies especially women's organisations.

Our communities continue to harbour the traditional behef that a person who ends up in prison is "bad". There is an uphill task to change this perception in the case of women, to one which recognises them to be largely victims rather than criminals.

A change in attitudes in the community is the only basis for long-term improvements in prison conditions. If the community at large continues to believe that prisons are places to put people society wants to forget, then society is in the end going to require bigger and bigger prisons because as forgotten places they produce more and more criminals.

With respect to women, such an attitude also delays the possibility of the society ever realising that it is the very idea of having women's prisons which much be forgotten, not the prisoners in them.

This article may be criticised for appearing to argue that there is no such thing as a female criminal, or that females do not commit crimes. Women of course, do commit crimes and there are some women for whom imprisonment is justifiable. We believe, however, that this number of women is very small, and that the penal system should not be based on their cases. Imprisonment is not a reasonable punishment for the vast number of women who find themselves before the courts.

33
Women and Education

The emancipation of women in the western countries had its effect on the movement in India as it developed during the latter half of the nineteenth century and the early twentieth century. In India the feminist movement did not take the aggressive and militant form which it took in some European countries, for it did not meet with much opposition. In the latter half of the nineteenth century, the struggles and agitations carried on by women were purely reformist in nature and emphasized the needs of women of a particular class—the small class of the educated and privileged women. But the mass of women in the villages and the workers in the field and the factories suffered many disabilities which were legally removed only by the Constitution of the Indian Republic, adopted in January 1950.

Education has long been one of the most decisive of our life—choices, the key to equal opportunity and the ladder to advancement. Without education, and especially without equal educational opportunities or skills and qualifications, men and women alike of certain classes and social groups have over the years been condemned to inferior status, women specially in their personal development, in their choice of work, as citizens, and in their power to influence government, leadership, and decisions.

Widening access to education has been a major policy goal in most developing countries for the past three decades. This reflects a broad recognition that education is essential to economic and social development. The evidence is overwhelming that education improves health and productivity and that the poorest people gain the most. When schools open their doors wider to girls and women, as well as to boys and men, the benefits multiply. Indeed, failing to invest adequately in educating women can reduce the potential benefits of educating men. This failure exacts a high cost - in lost opportunities to raise productivity, to increase income, and to improve the quality of life. Yet women's education still lags far behind men's in most developing countries, with far-reaching adverse consequences for both individual and national well-being.

Several indicators - including measures of literacy, enrollment, and years in school, reveal important patterns and trends in women's education in developing countries. Each of these indicators leads to the same conclusions: the level of female education is low in the poorest countries, with just a handful of exceptions, and by any measure, the gender gap is largest in these countries.

Education, conceived as organised instruction is part of the development process. Theoretically, education must enable persons to acquire knowledge and necessary skills. This knowledge and skills should further enable them to compete for and acquire better occupational status or higher social status in life. Thus, education should lead to social and economic productivity of the individual and, as a corollary, of the society. These are some basic assumptions about education in an open and competitive society. Fair competition requires equality in the initial social status or situation affecting the person or one's community. Hence there is a need for protection or support by the State to those lacking such initial advantage or those who suffer from social and economic disabilities. It is universally recognised that "mother is the first school of the child", yet the formal educational system keeps her out of the school because of socio-economic reasons, foremost among them being the bias towards girls' education, primarily because of patriarchal attitudes. Thus, the society is deprived of 50 per cent of human power for human development. No doubt, in the course of history, the status of women in our country has changed for better in some spheres and for worse in some others. In particular, education has come to be considered more important for women than men at least in theory.

The University Education Commission (1949) remarked:

> There cannot be educated people without educated women. If general education had to be limited to men or to women, that opportunity should be given to women, for then it would more surely be passed on to the next generations.

As elsewhere, there is good deal of discrepancy between the idealistic notion of the Indian women and the actual life situation in which she finds herself.

As Linsay Mackie and Polly Pattalo pointed out:

> The education of women has ever been a matter of great debate. Opinions expressed about it have often been reactionary, sometimes absurd and occasionally extraordinarily insulting. It comes as no surprise that Dr. Johnson said that a man is better pleased when he has a good dinner upon his table than when his wife talks Greek.

In particular, the Working Group on higher education of Planning Commission for the Ninth Five Year Plan has specifically examined the issue relating to higher education of women. Dealing with access and equity, the Working Group observed:

The major issue concerning higher education is expansion versus consolidation, access and equity versus means to maintain quality of education. While the issue has been highlighted in plan after plan, it has not been addressed squarely. Hence, even the increased plan outlays have not made visible impact on expansion of programmes and the development of infrastructure with the large percentage increase in student enrolment. Unless, in the Ninth Plan, this is redressed, the system will continue to be paralysed by the sheer numbers entering it. Both conventional and non-conventional solutions will have to be addressed in the Ninth Plan. These would include a leap forward for open education, not only as separate institutions, but also within conventional universities offering the dual mode to both separate student populations as also to the same student.

There is also a need to be concerned about access and equity for groups in the system which remain marginalised. These are women who form almost half the country's population, the reserved categories, the minorities, and the differently disabled.

Social Inequity

In terms of horizontal segregation, women are concentrated in low-paying positions such as secretary, typist, beautician, nurse, caregiver and assembly-line worker. "Equal work but unequal pay" is still a common practice in India's private sector. Statistics have shown that in 1995 women on average received only 3 n.p. for every rupee earned by men.

If one analyses the women's education scenario, one would find that women's education is an area cluttered with contradictory complexes, opposing theories and tremendous emotions. In brief:

1. On the one hand, India has a large mass of people either disinterested in or ignorant of the problem of education for women; on the other hand, a few enlightened women alone express deep concern about the problem.
2. The area of education for women is at cross roads between intellectual rationality and social conservatism. It is often emotional and ends in negativism.
3. Some people believe that education cannot be different for males and females. Hence, men and women should have the same curriculum content. But, there is another school of thought which believes that there are inherent differences between girls and boys. Therefore, the content of education should also be different. However, there is consensus of the common general objectives of education, namely, character formation, personality development increasing employability competence and inculcation of civic sense.
4. Since education needs to be geared to the needs of individuals, one of its objectives for boys is employment, while the twin objectives of employment and home-making hold good for girls.

The women aspiring for higher education could broadly be classified into four categories:

(i) Employment oriented

(ii) Marriage oriented

(iii) Employment-cum-marriage oriented

(iv) Unspecified others

In taking up higher education and choosing a subject of specialisation girl students have in mind one or the other specific objectives. Where a professional subject has been chosen and then later on, in life they do not opt for a career of specialisation then, I need not emphasise, there is both waste of human resources and lack of national objectives. I have had occasions to discuss with experts about the non-availability of services of women agriculture graduates. After spending much time, energy and funds they do not utilise the knowledge they have acquired for the development of the society. Realising the importance of women's higher education vis a vis utilisation of their professional knowledge and skill NCW sponsored at the National Academy of Agriculture Research

Management. Hyderabad a Workshop on "Issues of Professional Women in Agriculture". The need is to evolve a system by which higher education resources are so channelised as would meet the demands of women, both in rural and urban settings. Women have generally been engaged in such traditional areas like teachers, nurses etc. A shift in a substantial manner, not in tokenism is needed.

The growth in the number of women students in higher education since independence has been phenomenal. While women constituted only 9.3 per cent of all students in institutions of higher education on the eve of independence the percentage of women students enrolled in all colleges and universities was 34.1 in 1995-96.

The pace of growth has been particularly faster in the last two decades, or so. The number of women enrolled, per hundred men, registered a four fold increase during the period 1950-51 to 1995-96.

A noteworthy factor of the general increase in trie number of girl students in higher education is the uniformity in their enrolment at all levels of education. Faculty-wise, Arts stream accounts for the highest, followed by Commerce, Science, Education, Law, Engineering and Technology.

The number of women's colleges in the country has recorded substantial increase. It increased from 780 in 1986-87 to 1146 in 1995-96. It is significant that the University Grants Commission has a programme for promoting women's studies wherein it gives assistance to universities for setting up Centres/Cells for women studies. As on 31st March 1996 the UGC had provided assistance to 33 Universities and Colleges for setting up such Centres/Cells (22 Centres and 11 Cells)

At the time of Independence in 1947 we had only 20 Universities and 500 Colleges. The number of students and teachers in higher education system was very small. At the beginning of 1996-97 we have 209 Universities and there is a tremendous increase in the number of colleges i.e. from 500 to 9278 in which the number of women colleges is 1146.

The annual report of the Ministry of Human Resources Development (1996-97) proclaims:

Women's education has always been a priority area and NEE envisages the entire educational system to work for women's education and empowerment. It has been emphasized that gender concerns must be built into all educational process. Emphasis has been laid on enrolment and retention of the girl child in formal and non formal schooling, recruitment of rural women as teachers and removal of gender bias in the curriculum.

One aspect of unequal relations of society, the world over and in our country, is the disadvantaged and marginalised position of women and girls in education, and specifically in higher education. While women form fifty percent of the population, in higher education they form only about 34 per cent in graduate and post-graduate studies and 26.6 percent in Diploma and Certificate Courses.

The issue is even more of social justice and gender equality. One of the main reasons for the majority of the girls not being able to take up higher education is the weak base i.e. at the school stage, particularly in the rural areas. Added to this are, economic deprivation, lack of motivation and strong patriarchal attitudes against girls education.

I would very much like to draw the attention of women's Universities to the needed flexibility in women's educational package. creativity has to be an inalienable part of the educational content; Innovation has to be encouraged. Literally adhering to the knowledge of the past may not hold good today and for tomorrow. A periodic review of educational packages is very important. Unless girls and women are enabled to identify their needs with the education offered, the purpose of education will not be achieved.

The Women Universities in the country (5), the number is very small could take a lead in this matter in association with the UGC and the women study centres. They could specifically examine the issues and recommend to the government and the Corporate Sector the needs of girl students, desiring and deserving, and to at least render financial and motivational assistance to those who go in for higher education.

34

Challenges — 21st Century

"Everyone carried in himself an image of woman derived from the mother, by this he is determined to revere women generally, or to hold them in low esteem, or to be generally indifferent to them."

Nietzsche

I feel proud to be a part of the process of transformation which is taking place not only in India but all over the world. During the past few years, I visited about 350 district in the country and when I ask "what do women want", the answer has always been "full and equal partnership with men in all aspects of governance and society". Needless to say that it is for all of us in our various capacities to decide how we will keep the doors of transformation open, to walk through them and to avail the opportunity with open mind, to work together to make appropriate changes or let things remain as they are. It is a continuing commitment to the difficult but crucial task of improving the lives of people everywhere and of course with special emphasis on women and children.

At the beginning of 21st century, the eyes of the world are turned towards India which is witnessing positive transformation in economic field as a result of the reforms initiated a few years back, with an unmatched diversity of political and social systems. Our efforts towards redressing gender inequality are more pronounced than many other countries.

We are now recognising that if women are healthy and educated their families do better. If they are free from violence their families do better. If they have the opportunity to earn and work as equal partners in societies those families do better. Needless to say when those families do better then the communities and nations of which they are a part also do better.

Institutionalised mechanisms in a democracy for gender equality would naturally include micro and macro level strategies and initiatives. At the micro level, India's record of initiating social legislations and positive discrimination through quota system in local self-government institutions are unparalleled. At the macro level, policy prescriptions for compulsory education, State policies on women, health policy, special dispensation for weaker social groups are too, well-known. It may be added that our national policy on women is yet to be officially adopted. Indeed, in a democracy impediments enroute to realising the goals of gender equality and gender justice could stem from the nature of Government, whether it is secular, whether it is truly representative, whether it is only party or coalition and so on. In this matter, we are fortunate in that we have a Government with wide representation of different shades of public opinion committed both by the constituent parties' election manifestos and through public pronouncements of leaders. Their adherence to empowerment of women is a significant aspect which cannot escape notice. It is a different matter that for some unclear internal differences of some constituents 84th Amendment Bill has some difficulties in being introduced.

In a democracy, the interests of women may not always get the protection needed because of legal impediments and/or absence of constitutional arrangements. In our Sovereign Socialist Secular Democratic Republic, justice and equality are guaranteed through specific provisions including positive discrimination in favour of women and certain social groups. As observed earlier, the legal support through various legislations to protect and promote the interests of women are reasonably adequate. It is a different matter that in our system where separation of powers between the legislature, the executive and the judiciary exist and where implementation is not keeping pace with the intention of such legal framework and changing times, the protection afforded to women has not been either commensurate with the needs or in proportion to the efforts put in. The remedy lies elsewhere.

One of the basic tenets of democracy is involvement of people in the governance of the country by which it is meant that the Government should, through a system of committees, commissions, expert groups, etc., continuously analyse, assess and implement measures for the well-being of the people. In our country, as is the case in many others, women's movement have had the benefit of the support of women's commission, women's council, women's board, etc. constituted by the Government, apart from those of the independent NGOs working in various fields. It should, however, be admitted that balanced and sustainable development is not a simple matter of Government alone. It is in this context that the relevance of various specialised Institutionalised arrangements rendering requisite imputs are recognised and appreciated.

I consider that the main challenge before all of us is the challenge to get empowered. When I say empowerment, I mean political, economic and social empowerment in its totality, not piecemeal. Empowerment can come about through awareness and education. We all know the disparity that exists between male and female educational levels. It is not necessary for me to quote statistics to assert female education has a long way to go before complete equality and cent per cent literacy can be had.

Then comes economic independence. We are aware, in our region women work harder and for long hours than men but their work is neither acknowledged nor compensated. There are a host of problems associated with women at work. Minimum wages, equal remuneration, harassment at workplace, etc. are too well-known to be needing any reiteration. There are more women in unorganised sector with no social security umbrella. They are not organised, to tackle the challenges. We have to recognise these handicaps and work towards their removal so as to ensure that women are empowered economically.

Next in order is the legal protection necessary to enforce a decent living with honour, dignity, safety and security. No day passes these days without the newspapers carrying extensive reports of heinous crimes committed on women—rape, gang rape, dowry deaths, trafficking in women and children, wife battering and so on. Notwithstanding manipulated statistics, any keen observer of current events could testify that in most countries violence against women is on the increase. The society, the Government and women's movement have to confront this atrocious demeanour with dedication, authority and effectiveness. We know that most of the countries have legislations to curb atrocities on women like rape, prostitution, trafficking, child marriage, dowry, desertion, wife battering, etc. The tragedy, however, is that the implementation of these Acts is woefully lacking. The NGOs have a very major role in this field. They could bring about a sea change in the situation with prompt reporting of such incidents, effective follow-up through police and judiciary, ensuring that the culprits get punished and the victims grievances are removed through counselling legal aid and rehabilitation packages.

An important issue before women is to get themselves adequately represented at all decision-making levels. World over, their representation in legislatures, bureaucracy, judiciary and other public services is negligible. For example, the figures are revealing in respect of seats held by women in Parliament, and those in administrative and managerial posts. (In Pakistan, it is 1.6%, South Korea 2 per cent, Japan per cent, India 8 per cent and Bangladesh 11 per cent in respect of women in Parliament and less than 10 per cent in all these countries in services).

Governance is a very broad based concept while democracy has very many shades. As somebody put it, democracy is like a hat which has almost entirely lost its original shape in the process of it having been worked by many. It has to be acknowledged that a working definition of democracy has to be that of a participatory system which provides adequate, unhindered, universal opportunity for all in the promotion of an equitable and sustainable social and economic order. For achieving optimum results in a democracy, there has to be a partnership accord between women and governance, ensuring as also safeguarding individual liberty and dignity and common interests. In almost all cases, the failure of democracy happens because of the failure of Government. In the words of Subhash C. Kashyap, it was mentioned that "governance has become a casuality of Government" with Government themselves more concerned with survival rather than attending to the needs of the people. Democracy thrives through democratic institutions. It is not an isolated and insulated phenomena. The effectiveness or usefulness of democracy would depend upon the structures supporting it. It will be agreed that what really matters is the quality of democracy by which it is meant that everyone, and especially the poor and the marginalised like backward social groups and women, have access to decision-making levels through inbuilt appropriate strategies so that their voices are heard and heeded. Further, as is the present case in our national government, democracy based on the principle of "consent" is more beneficial. The success of democracy, in so far as it concerns women would definitely be tested on the question of sensibility, sensitivity and suitability to answer to the needs of feminist concerns, though not divorced from society, nation and international interests.

I would submit that we are witnessing an enormous transformation in human history; that the changes in women's lives and voices are both cause and effect of larger processes at work. The world is becoming smaller and more interdependent.

From the experience world over, poverty has been considered to be an important women's issue, for poverty has a feminine face. In addition, everywhere women are the poorest of the poor with very limited livelihood resources or access to them. The Human Development Report, 1997 has this to say on the issue of poverty and women:

"Poverty affects women more severely. Already suffering from societal bias, they are more vulnerable than men and bear a heavier burden when poverty strikes. Poverty and gender are inextricably linked - gender inequality is strongly linked to human poverty.

Generally, the face of poverty is changing, but female poverty continues to remain a constant factor".

Tackling of poverty issue in a democracy is a ticklish problem not because of "a Government of the people, by the people, for the people". Here, in India as in most countries, women are severely underrepresented in decision-making levels. The efficacy of democracy for the good of the people, including women, in such a situation is doubtful. Look at our own planning process. In the early stages of our Plan era; women as a target group did not receive any specific cogent treatment. It took four Five-Year Plans to mount specific plan strategy to meet the minimum needs of the rural population in which female members of the family have high stakes. Rural poverty alleviation programmes by all counts constitute one of the largest segments of our development plan. A succinct account of the erosion of standards in administering development programmes and declining status of implementing structure in a vibrant democracy where fifty per cent of voters are women, is to be found in the report of the Task Force on Self-Managed Institutions for Integrated Development (Planning Commission, 1991). The Report states: "The entire poor of resources for development available in the country has been so allocated that they support proliferation of officialdom and bureaucracy. Little expenditure on priority areas of education, health, agriculture and energy is planned."

Women's place in every community is vital to the well-being of that society; without them both in the formal sector and in the family, most communities would not survive. It is now well recognised that enhancing women's status and enforcing their rights on an equal basis with men will do rnuch to achieve the objectives of Equality, Development and Peace adopted at the Fourth World Conference on Women held in Bejing in September 1995. These are the guide posts for nations and movements to take note of and act upon.

In conclusion, it may be said that for women, democracy is the best suited political system for it provides adequate space for accommodating women perspectives and gender concerns provided the system provides for women representation in all decision-making levels. However, equality and gender justice cannat be had through fragmented and routine approach. In the structure that supports democracy and governance women must be represented not merely by the fact of being females but by women of dedication, understanding and goodwill. It should not degenerate into a ritualistic phenomenon of filling "mali" "female" columns in a proforma.

35
Women and Peace

With nostalgia, I look back at the dawn of my life, at that aura of tranquility.... Chirping of birds jingling of bells, melody of religious chantings, fragrance of joss sticks... And the solemn figure of my grandmother praying in her tiny room full of idols. Our two-storyed home reverberated with holy chants and soft jingles of bells. And during that one hour each dawn, all of us remained absolutely silent as if spellbound.

Grand mother is no more. The dawn of my life has blossomed into noon. I do not remember when exactly I felt it but that childhood fascination of grandmother' early morning Puja (Prayers) still remains. That pious atmosphere of long ago is ingrained in me. I have reached a stage where religion is 'Peace and Purity' dating back to the fragrance that enveloped our home... the precious childhood memory still lingers and leads me on.

"O lord why have you not given woman the right to conquer her destiny—why does she have to wait head bowed by the roadside waiting with tired patience hoping for a miracle in the morrow" Rabindranath Tagore said this in the beginning of this milleninum. The millennium has drawn to a close—today we are not waiting for a miracle, the miracle is within us. We have the means to shape our destiny and that of our region, the courage of endeavor to stop the world from a mad roller coaster ride on the tracks of a weapon arsenal.

We wish to focus in a small way on women's strength that can and will shape peace of the millenium. After Beijing Plus Five nothing could, underestimate womenpower and the fact that the power had been dormant and suppressed, in India the five years have seen the growing awareness and assertion of women's rights. Through NGO advocacy, publications and seminars, there is an increasing awareness of the need for reservations for women in the parliament and in legislatures. But now with this kind of awareness it should only be a matter of time before reservation is a reality. Every political party in the last elections was forced to include it in the manifesto due to the strength of public opinion. It is due to the initiative taken by women's strong voice that the Bill was introduced on the 23rd of December 1999 We are confident that this Bill would be passed shortly.

Some more indicative changes as I see it have been the Supreme Court of India's judgement on the meaning, implications and consequences of sexual harassment at workplaces. As a fall out all organisations are to set up a committee well represented by NGO's, Counsellors and lawyers to look into cases of sexual harassment. Very recently was a Gujarat High Court's ruling on a custody case between a husband and wife which stated clearly that a husband cannot claim custody rights over a woman merely because she is his wife I quote "the practice of claiming custody over an adult human being is archaic". A wife is not a possession of a man.

Literacy level has increased to 39.4 per cent. All women police stations have been established. A rising number of women have opted for hitherto male bastions like the airforce and the army.

On the other hand violence against women has increased, gender based crimes are on the rise. India witnessed horrifying incidents of acid being thrown on the face of a girl who refused to cooperate with eveteasers. Upper caste men rape lower caste women. Women who refuse to two the patriarchal line are paraded naked. Sometime ago in a small village of Andhra Pradesh a woman was paraded naked as a consequence of an altercation at the village well. We have witnessed armed conflicts on the eastern and western parts of India, communal riots, cross-border terrorism all of which has left the women bereft of economic and social identity. It is very evident that peace was only a mirage in the region.

Peace in its narrowest sense would imply absence of war, terrorism and armed conflict In its broadest term, it implies the environment of just development and equality. A racial development that perpetuates the mechanics of patriarchal framework, the means of development in the hands of the very perpetrators giving rise to the distorted image of civilisation have together contributed to the absolutely unjust picture of progress as presented in the South Asian region.

There can be no peace in an environment of social imbalance —imbalances perpetuated either by traditional mindset, the very slow and limited permeation of educational process, or the forced compromise between the inferior and superior-either politically, socially or legally. Whatever the cause—the result is the same —a society that's a boiling cauldron of crime, violence, fundamentalism, and power tyranny. The greatest victim of this searing heat are the women—the second class citizens in all regions.

This broad sense of the absence of peace is interlinked inextricably with narrower implications of war. I will focus first on the broad meaning of peace being linked to equality and development.

Broad though the meaning be, peace roots itself in the smallest unit of the society the home. The two most telling indicators of the true state of affairs is the ever rising high incidence of domestic violence and the tailing ratio of women to men in the SAARC region. In India itself reported incidents of domestic violence have quadrupled over the last two years - short stay homes for battered women have mushroomed in ever}* major city of India so much so that the government feels the need to introduce a bill in the Parliament to curb domestic violence. The latest UNDP report states that 340 million women are not expected to survive to the age of 40. 1/4 to 2 of all women have suffered physical abuse by an intimate partner. All over the world the population of women is higher than that of men. In South Asian region the women fall short by 9.73 crores. In India the ratio is 929 to 1000 in the 1991 census. The reason for this fall—female foeticide, dowry deaths, missing women, the rising incidences of suicide among the middle class women, low health status etc. 68 per cent of pregnant women in Bangladesh are anaemic 30 per cent in Bhutan, 50 per cent in India.

Where is the Peace in the Home - Ironically called the Haven of Peace

The major contributing factor is the traditional mindset that's the result of centuries of gender prejudice. Why else would there be a dress code prescribed for widows—not for the widower? It is the basic streak of the human psyche to feed the ego by the humiliation of the other. It probably has got nothing to do with man or women. But because human society evolved broadly on patriarchal lines the male ego was always on the high.

The violence of the home spills into the society or vice versa. We are all aware of the rising incidence of sexual crime and gender based violence. Women are stoned to death, gangraped, paraded naked- everything to wound her body and, more horrifying, her psyche and soul The even more telling social injustice is the thread of economic dependence that is visible throughout in all the SAARC countries In India 62 per cent of all boys and men are in the workforce but only 19 per cent of women and girls. Bangladesh has shown a very heartening trend - from 5 per cent women in the workforce in 1965, 1995 shows 42 per cent . This has been important for the export growth since a large segment in the garment industry are women. But the catch is that women put 31 hours a week in unpaid work like cooking, collecting fuel, looking after children etc. On the other hand men put in 14 hours a week of unpaid labour.

How can Peace Survive as a Companion to Social and Economic Injustice?

Education, the major tool to progress, has permeated very slowly among the women. In India female adult literacy rate is 394 per cent in 1997 i.e., 39.4 point rise on the index of 1985. Nepal literacy rate is 20.7 per cent which is 104 point rise on the 1985 index. On the other hand, the rate in Mexico a developing nation the rate is 87.9 Venezuela is 91.6, Phillippine is 94.3. The very slow permeation of education keeps the women in ignorance of legal, social and economic rights. Unfortunately in her case ignorance has not given any bliss but only low self-esteem and to be a victim of socio economic tyranny.

Globalisation creates new opportunities. Paradoxically, it creates greater availability of the tools of crime. Gangsters use arms manufactured across the sea, terrorists use remote controlled bombs, women and girls are smuggled from South Asia and find their way to the sex shops of Europe. Chinese triads are in the restaurant trade in London and the Japanese Yakuza are financing pornography in

Netherlands. Illicit, trade in drugs, women, weapons and laundered money is contributing to the violence and crime that threaten all neighbourhoods. Organised crime estimated to gross 1.5 trillion dollars a year has the economic power to criminalise politics, business and police. Stop and think what this unbridled power can do to the most vulnerable sections of mankind today women and children.

Closely related to this is the rampant comodification of the human body—rather the women's body. Media stereotyping is probably the most visible culprit in reducing women to a commodity and a possession of man, Films perpetuating the image of women as a weakling and a silent puppet with no control of her destiny is familiar all my SAARC sisters. Compounding to this is the advertising that uses the women's curves to sell everything.

The commercialisation has snowballed to such an unwieldy size that you need a woman's body to sell anything. Where can there be respect for an object ?

Where can there be Peace for an Object to be Played and Dropped Therewith?

And finally in this broad term of peace is the lack of political identity and respect. The SAARC region has produced 4 women Prime Minister's in the last 5 decades. But the percentage of women in the Indian Parliament's Rajya Sablia is 12 per cent and the Lok Sabha is 7 per cent . Only 5.8 per cent women are in the government. Of this only 3.2 per cent are at ministerial level. The corresponding figures for Pakistan are 2.6 per cent of women in the government- in Bangladesh only 1.9 per cent and 5.3 per cent in Bhutan. Clearly indicative facts that women have still to take to political avenues to lobby for non-gender discriminated programmes. The cry of the woman as a victim of socio and economic tyranny is searing and powerful-but it never reaches the echelons of the government.

Lobby power is the vital weight that tilts the balance in favour. How strong is the woman's lobbying power?

Where then would there be Peace in the Silence of Victimisation?.

In the larger concept of peace as linked to development and equality the index of the SAARC countries is abysmally low. Are we to remain as Gertrude Mongella voices "as victims or witnesses"? Can we not be more than that when peace comes under threat? Yes of course women can and must be the ultimate initiators, builders and preservers of peace as linked to development and equality.

Empowerment begins first from within. The strength is within us, all we need is to unlock that vital force.

A woman in a small hamlet of Dubghunta in India having suffered the tyranny and violence of a drunk husband for years one day just decided she had had enough.

From there began the anti-arrack movement that fanned into such a flame that the state government was forced to introduce total prohibition in 1995. This woman was no social worker, she did not even know what empowerment meant. All she realised was that she had it in her to influence other victims to act. The first step is to stop thinking of ourselves as victims but as creators of our circumstances.

When women think of themselves as creators of environment, then only is there self-esteem. This self-esteem can change the mindset that society has been steeped in for centuries. Every woman has to respect herself before anticipating respect from others. From this arises the need for gender sensitised education—and compulsory education for all—particularly the women. Kerala in India which achieved literacy also clocked the lowest rate of heinous crimes against women. Compulsory education combined with gender sensitised curriculum would give the necessary awareness to assert her legal rights and be part of the economic mainstream. India has shown a steadily increasing female literacy level. Consequently women in the workforce have increased. But even then the women's economic activity rate is only 50.3 per cent of the male rate. In Pakistan it is 40.3 per cent Education goes hand in hand with legal and economic empowerment which alone makes her a identity instead of an marginalised non-entity.

In Bangladesh is the excellent example of the Grameen Bank—for rural micro credit. An illiterate woman wanted money to pound1 rice and earn a few rupees. That desire has pounded a way, to a great extent, of economic in dependence. The financial independence gave her the means to shape her life. Political education alongwith economic empowerment -the means to present her case and the tool to lobby for strength and finally the capability to ensure that the laws of the land don't discriminate. Indian women are now lobbying for the 33 per cent representation in the parliament - for a new political strength. The political awareness is there so also the knowledge of the pitfalls. Women in India cannot fall in the same quagmire of being represented by the incompetent and the incapable.

The narrow sense of peace is the absence of war, armed conflict and terrorism the SAARC region lias been beset with them. Where is the peace when pockets of the country are 5 decades backwards in terms of basic amenities, there is non-availability of adequate means of livelihood, and shrinking access to better standards of living? To every protest, uprising and revolt the bottomline and the topline is money—the lack of it and lack of means to make it, Governments cannot pay adequate attention to unrest that's brewing—because the political will is missing. Because the money to arrest the revolt is missing. Developing countries are caught in a debt trap. Money is borrowed to pay off more debts. The socio political framework gets fractured. The crack widens with every revolt that is fuelled by arms traders who make hay while guns boom. India, Pakistan and Sri Lanka have been witnesses to armed conflict.

In a region as closely knit as the SAARC every armed conflict will resound in the other countries either as cross border terrorism or as low intensity wars, When the cause of absence of peace is to a great extent economical, the solution must correspond. It is vital to insulate inter-country cooperation from political tensions. In this context the South Asian Preferential Trade Area and South Asian Free Trade Area assume great significance. This is the kind of cooperative effort that is likely to benefit all and have a direct impact on the people to whom the benefits accrue. This will, in turn, dispel doubts on interactive coopoeration. Surely patriotism must be fuelled by the war against non-development and inequitable distribution of resources.

Even as the rest of the world is moving towards freer regions of cooperation the SAARC region is very slow in dismantling barriers of suspicion and tension. The Group of Eminent persons report at the ninth SAARC summit meeting held at Male states that "the achievements have fallen short of the aspirations underlying the formation of SAARC. Through its programmes, the growth triangles and quadrangles, exchange of resources, SAARC can pave the way for peace. In this NGOs now face the call of the millenium sto become important pressure groups that can lobby for the humanisation of policies and projects. NGOs can provide the networking strength of the region to further help in insulating the people from political tensions. While inequality and warped development exist through non-empowerment of the marginalised sections, peace can at best be an aim alone and not an environment. Mahatma Gandhi once stated that women have the power to kick the atom bomb out like a football. Along with you I see that power–half awake certainly but awake nevertheless.

The ultimate power to bring about change rests with the people. It is not the power of weapons or economic strength which will determine the shape of the world beyond nuclear weapons. That will be determined in the minds and the hearts of thinking men and women around the world. For, as the Dhammapada of the Buddha teaches us:

"Our life is shaped by our mind:

We become what we think.

Suffering follows an evil thought

As the wheels of a cart fallow the oxen that draw it.

Joy follows a pure thought

Like a shadow that never leaves.

For hatred can never put an end to hatred;

Love alone can.

This is the unalterable law."

36

Dammed to be Doomed

It was in April 1998 when the phone suddenly rang. I heard crying, screaming in the background in pain and voices of many women asking me to come and intervene in the violence perpetuated by the police and the authorities. This was a call from 5000 tribal women who could not withstand the wrath of the bigwigs. We heard them in stunned silence, called a hurried meeting of the commission and decided to visit the site and enquire into the atrocities committed on thousands of tribals who had bravely withstood the onslaught of torture, terror and torment.

Dr. Hameed and myself had rushed to Indore where we were met by some citizens and delegation of men and women from affected areas who had been victims of violence. These people had definite visible physical injuries. I decided that we should do to the spot survey and investigate. Accompanied by Ms. Sandhya Vyas, District Women and Child Welfare Officer and Kalpana Mehta we went to Mandaleshwar town on the river of Narmada in Khargone district of M.P.

We found thousands of local people affected by the project whose land is either submerged or under threat of submergence protesting against the project for sometime.

As per government estimates 61 villages are expected to be partially or fully submerged involving loss of livelihood to 13000 people. According to Narmada Bachao Andolan these figures are a gross underestimate because they ignore the question of lives of landless and migrant labour who find abundant earning opportunities in the valley. The land in the area is extremely fertile and other than their own needs, people are able to cultivate a number of cash crops. Those without land can contract patches of riverbed land seasonally for cultivation, even the sand quarries provide livelihood for many.

Our conclusions and recommendations were as follows:

1. The investigation so far reveals that violence was used extensively against peaceful demonstrators on 22nd and 23rd April 1998 at the Maheshwar Hydel Project site. The violence was not provoked by self-defense or used as means to control an unruly mob. This violence was perpetrated against people who were protesting peacefully against the breach of promise by the government, which has gone back on its order to stay all construction till the report of the Task Force is complete.
2. This violence, accompanied by vulgar and sexual abuses, is a big blow to the empowerment of women who have, for the first time, come out of their homes to protect their right to life and livelihood. Their right to life cannot be equated with the financial losses, which may have ensued if there was any damage to the pits.
3. It is pertinent that the administrative circumstances under which the police have acted be investigated formally. This is not the first time that the NCW has been requested to step into investigating excesses by the State in the Khargone district. The last incident was just about seven months ago and comprised of large scale violence looting and displacement of tribal women. Even at that time the NCW had warned the Government that unless the method and the means to deal with the demands of the people were modified and their grievances handled in a just and fair manner there was every chance of creating massive discontent and unrest.
4. There is every need at this point to handle the review process in a just and fair manner. The government has to abide by its own promise to wait until the report of the Task Force is submitted. Even after the project gets a clearance, a genuine effort has to be made to rebuild the life of people. They should not be left exposed to blasting and lose free access to their fields, when construction starts again. Alternative arrangements have to be made before any displacement occurs. The government has to be proactive and not wait for struggles to be launched before taking cognizance. In the entire process the government should continue to involve the NBA.
5. Every effort needs to be made to repair the breach of confidence and to redress any injustices done. Doctors should be instructed

to examine anyone who comes to them with a complaint. Similarly the police must register complaints, no matter who complains.

6. The district administration should not be given the responsibility of maintaining law and order without being involved in decisions which are bound to create problems. It needs to be understood that cost and benefits of a project cannot be seen in isolation from sacrifices being demanded from some of the people.
7. These recommendtions are being made with a view to seeking a solution which prevents the recurrence of such events in the future. It must be recognised that unless status quo is restored with respect to staying all construction work pending the recommendations of the Task Force in this regard, violence will become a continuing reality in this otherwise peaceful valley.

Recommendations

1. That the State Government stops all construction of the safety wall, until the Task Force submits its report.
2. That People of Jalud must be provided with immediate access to their fields and to the river by dismantling the fencing.
3. That the State Government must institute a time-bound judicial inquiry and take action against those responsible for widespread violence against people.
4. That the State Government should investigate the circumstances under which people spent their time in jail and take action against those responsible for intimidating them and also against those responsible for making them provide bonds for their release.
5. That the State Government provides compensation to those who have suffered injuries and loss of jewellery and belongings. Jail and hospital records should be used as the basis for compensating people. An exgratia amount of Rs. 500/- should be paid to all those who were imprisoned, Rs. 5000/- should be paid to women who have reported a loss of jewellery and to those hospitalised. Cost of medical treatment should be reimbursed to those who have filed FIR's.
6. That the State Government should take action against those responsible for non delivery of release orders which lengthened the detention of hundreds of people.

7. The State Government should ensure that the presence of police at the dam site is there to protect people, the police should be prevented from becoming a private army working against people.

Today after nearly two and half years, the Supreme Court has given a judgement (judgement in annexure 1)

However as is well known justice P. Bharucha has also given his minority judgement (judgement in Annexure 2)

I was called upon to be a part of the jury on the 14th Nov. 2000. The other members of the jury were Jus. (Retd.) D.S. Tewatia, Jus. Jaspal Singh, Harubhai Mehta, U.R. Ananthamurthy, Ashis Nandy. The hearing conducted by Indian People' s Tribunal was held at the Parade Ground opposite the Red Fort and was attended by a large number of intellectuals, activists, NGO's and lawyers. Approximately 5000 people from the Narmada Valley were present at the hearing and deposed before a distinguished panel presided over by Jus. D.S. Tewatia, retired Chief Justice of the High Courts of Calcutta and Chandigarh.

The request to conduct a tribunal had come from the National Alliance of People's Movements (NAPM) in the wake of intense and extreme debates raging across the country over the Sardar Sarovar Project. Numerous reports and studies have raised the viability of the dam and questioned its environmental and social impact. Yet many questions dealing with rehabilitation, resettlement and the overall cost benefit analysis still needed to be answered. The day long public hearing sort to remove the veil from over some of these issues and present a glimpse of the ground realities.

The hearing was conducted on the following issues:

- Genesis of the Project.
- Costs and Benefits.
- Social Impacts.
- Environmental Impacts.
- The State, the Law and the people.
- Gujarat: The mirage of Benefits.
- Alternatives.
- Issues relating to other dams in the Narmada Valley.
- The Justification of the SSP.

Depositions

Depositions were made on the above issues by the people from the Valley, Vania, Dedlibai, Pratibha Shinde and Arundhati Dhuru from the Adivasi region, Kamla Yadav and Mansarambhai from the Nimad region along with Noorjibhai, Mukesh Bhai, Manglya, Dinkar Dave from Gujarat, Bablu Patwa, Guliabai and Urmila Patidar made depositions on their plight in the valley as a consequence of the Sardar Sarovar Project.

Representatives and leaders of the Narmada Bachao Andolan (NBA) deposed on technical issues and those related with the law, specially with those related to the acquisition of land, revenue surveys and settlement, the myth of rehabilitation and cost benefit analysis and the unviability of the SSP as a large dam. Shripad Dharmadhikari, Silvy, Alok Agarwal and Medha Patkar made depositions on behalf of the NBA.

1. While we respect the judgement of the Supreme Court but I know that 45 crore would be spent on this project. Cannot an alternative method be found for that much money to give drinking water to the thirsty villages today? This project only envisages the building of a dam which would not be complete for the next several years and water could not come to these villages till 2025. Are we expected to be without water after allocating 45 crore for 25 years? Their slogan was "Aaj pani chahiye, 2025 tak mar jayenge"
2. Once again I strongly feel that even if this electricity is produced from the Sardar Sarovar, would it really be given to the poor villages or be diverted totally to the rich industrialists.
3. According to an estimate in 25 years this electricity produced would be reduced to nil and bring us back to square one.
4. Today Vania, Dedlibhai and others have taken the courage to come all the way to Delhi. Each one confident using the mike calling out slogans and saying "why are the affected people not consulted"? time and again asking who benefits from the entire project.
5. When promises are made of giving alternate land where is the land? In the past those who are displace were given barren land. Arundhati Dhuru, Adivasi of the area said that she was totally self sufficient in her surroundings. She had only three

requirements to be bartered in the outside world—salt, iron weapons or utensils and clothes. She said all her requirements were met in her own tribal area. She went on to describe the inbuilt mechanism where there was no system of labour or wages and there was no need for clubs etc. She wanted to know in what mainstream were we wanting her to get in? Mansa Devi asked that you are wanting small family norms, micro development, small scale industries so on the other hand why are we propagating big dams? Couldn't development take place with small dams? For a tribal woman a small pathway is enough to reach the goal. It is only the urban car polluting man who needs big roads, big dams, big electricity. These simple Noorjibhai, Manglya, Guliabhai asked us what is right to life and livelihood? They said they know the concept of justice as a mother, as a sister and as a wife. They were afraid once the water comes through it will never reach them as in the name of tourism, water parks, golf courses, swimming pool would come up and their bare necessities would be neglected.

6. Today we have to sit up and think seriously if projects are more important than people and if the aspirations of the people would be trampled down.

7. After hearing this day long proceeding we at the panel arrived at some immediate interim findings and conclusions.

   (a) At no stage, the affected people were given a hearing either by the state authorities or the Narmada Tribunal.

   (b) The Government in the first instance launched the project and then thought of getting mandatory clearances which should have been done before start of the execution of construction work. And at every state confronted with *a fait acompli* the affected persons and authorities which had to accord clearances.

   (c) The engineers and the bureaucrats enticed the Government into undertaking the project with projecting costs which happen to be very wide of the mark and also projecting the benefits which too are appearing a mirage.

   (d) Such projects have very long gestation period. When ultimately benefits fall far short of projected benefits and costs had escalated many times of the initially estimated cost, there would be none the citizen can hold accountable for cheating at such a scale, because by then those who had been feeding on the fat funds not only may not be there in the government, they in fact by then may have (left for heaven or hell) quit the world. And this is the basic reason no effort is made to consider alternative schemes involving small money but holding out promise of at least equal benefits, if not more and without adverse impact on the environment, social and ecological as also without creating misery to citizens at a scale obtaining in the wake of the construction of the present Narmada Dam.

(e) It has been very strongly highlighted that whereas the scheme to rehabilitate should have actualized before they were about to be displaced, but here in the present case affected persons are being displaced and neither the scheme to rehabilitate not the land on which it was to take shape is there.

(f) Attention is invited to the fact that the citizens are treated as subjects if not as slaves. They have only such rights as the ruler in his magnanimity deems necessary and the Constitution is ignored with contempt as a scrap paper.

(g) The prescriptions for rehabilitation and resettlement that it should be completed well in advance before the actual submergence are observed in breach only. Rehabilitation and resettlement is utterly neglected by the authorities concerned. The project affected persons are not given any role in the process of rehabilitation and resettlement.

Interim Conclusions

From the evidence it is obvious that the Sardar Sarovar Project is primarily an enterprise of motivated politicians, bureaucrats and professionals. The project has little do with what people wish (nobody at any stage has asked them) or can do by themselves to solve their water problems (as can be seen by the small projects successfully implemented by many drought affected villages of Saurashtra and North Gujarat).

The cost escalation of the project, it seems from the evidence, is itself indicator of its main purpose - to benefit its sponsors. It has increased from Rs. 4,000 crore to Rs. 21,000 crore. Many expected it to go up to Rs. 45,000/ crore. This cost does not cover the irreversible costs of destruction of forests, the life support systems of the tribal forest dwellers, and the loss of their cultures and knowledge systems.

The project according to the evidence adduced, cannot and does not intend to meet the needs of the people of Gujarat, Madhya Pradesh and Maharashtra. Against all available data, the state governments (particularly the Gujarat government) have persisted with the project for reasons that have more to do with the vested interests of the enthusiasts than with the needs of the people. The callous attitude towards rehabilitation is an indicator of the amoral nature of the Project. An even better indicator is the way all dissent against the dam has been throttled. Even small meetings of protesters and even discussions of the issue have been systematically disrupted, and protesters physically assaulted by the hoodlums of the supporters of the dam or by the law enforcing agencies.

It is not out of place to mention here that former President and Human Right activist Nelson Mandela had submitted his report on big dams on 19 November 2000. After a detail study of various big dams all over the world the commission had concluded that the big dams are a danger to environment of the area, do not add to the enhancement of agricultural productions substantially and they add to the problems of rehabilitation of people affected in the area.

In all seriousness before launching a dam of such high magnitude, high costs of construction, time, and trampling on the aspirations of the common man, we should take lessons from such reports which are in abundance in several countries of the world.

The Narmada project is the ultimate symbol of the pathology of the developmental process in India. It reveals the psychopathic dimensions of our public life better than almost any other political or economic scam in the past fifty years.

These struggles of real people should not go in vain and without consulting those who are affected no project should be undertaken. Let every movement every struggle be a prayer to god.

Annexure 1

IN THE SUPREME COURT OF INDIA CIVIL ORIGINAL JURISDICTION WRIT PETITION (C) NO. 319 OF 1994

Narmada Bachao Andolan ....Petitioner

Versus

Union of India & Others ....Respondents

with

C.A. No. 6014/1994 W.P. (C) Nos. 345/94, 104/1997, S.L.P. (C) No. 3608/1985 & T.C. (C) No. 35 of 1995

JUDGEMENT

Kirpal, J.

Pages: 180-183

While issuing directions and disposing of this case, two conditions have to be kept in mind, (i) the completion of the project at the earliest and (ii) ensuring compliance with conditions on which clearance of the project was given including completion of relief and rehabilitation work and taking of ameliorative and compensatory measures for environmental protection in compliance with the scheme framed by the government thereby protecting the rights under Article 21 of the constitution. Keeping these principles in view, we issue the following directions:

1. Construction of the dam will continue as per the Award of the Tribunal.
2. As the Relief and Rehabilitation Sub-group has cleared the construction up to 90 metres, the same can be undertaken immediately. Further raising of the height will be only *pari passu* with the implementation of the relief and rehabilitation and on the clearance of further construction after consulting the three Grievances Redressal Authorities.
3. The Environment Sub-group under the Secretary, Ministry of Environment and Forests, Government of India will consider and give, at each stage of the construction of the dam, environment clearance before further construction beyond 90 metres can be undertaken.
4. The permission to raise the dam height beyond 90 metres will be given by the Narmada Control Authority, from time to time,

after it obtains the above-mentioned clearances from the Relief and Rehabilitation Sub-group and the Environment Sub-group.

5. The reports of the Grievances Redressal Authorities, and of Madhya Pradesh in particular, shows that there is a considerable slackness in the work of identification of land, acquisition of suitable land and the consequent steps necessary to be taken to rehabilitate the project oustees. We direct the State of Madhya Pradesh, Maharashtra and Gujarat to implement the Award and given relief and rehabilitation to the oustees in terms of the packages offered by them and these States shall comply with any direction in this regard which is given either by the NCA or the Review Committee or the Grievances Redressal Authorities.

6. Even though there has been substantial compliance with the conditions imposed under the environment clearance the NCA and the Environment Sub-group will continue to monitor and ensure that all steps are taken not only to protect but to restore and improve the environment.

7. The NCA will within four weeks from today draw up an Action Plan in relation to further construction and the relief and rehabilitation work to be undertaken. Such as Action Plan will fix a time frame so as to ensure relief and rehabilitation *pari passu* with the increase in the height of the dam. Each state shall abide by the terms of the action plan so prepared by the NCA and in the event of any dispute or difficulty arising, representation may be made to the Review Committee. However, each state shall be bound to comply with the directions of the NCA with regard to the acquisition of land for the purpose of relief and rehabilitation to the extent and within the period specified by the NCA.

8. The Review Committee shall meet whenever required to do so in the event of there being any unresolved dispute on an issue which is before the NCA. In any event the Review Committee shall meet at least once in three months so as to oversee the progress of construction of the dam and implementation of the R and R programmes.

9. The Grievances Redressal Authorities will be at liberty, in case the need arises, to issue appropriate directions to the respective

States for due implementation of its directions, the GRAs will be at liberty to approach the Review Committee for appropriate orders.

10. Every endeavour shall be made to see that the project is completed as expeditiously as possible.

This and connected petitions are disposed off in the aforesaid terms.

...............CJI

(A.S. ANAND)

..................J

(B.N. KIRPAL)

New Delhi, October 18, 2000

Annexure 2

IN THE SUPREME COURT OF INDIA
CIVIL ORIGINAL JURISDICTION
WRIT PETITION (C) NO. 319 OF 1994

Narmada Bachao Andolan ....Petitioner

Versus

Union of India & Others ....Respondents

with

C.A. No. 6014/1994 W.P. (C) Nos. 345/94, 104/1997, S.L.P. (C) No. 3608/1985 & T.C. (C) No. 35 of 1995

JUDGEMENT

Bharuch, J., Pages: 30-32

I should not be deemed to have agreed to anything stated in Brother Kirpal's judgement for the reason that I have not traversed it in the course of what I have stated.

In the premises,

1. The Environment Impact Agency of the Ministry of Environment and Forests of the Union of India shall forthwith appoint a Committee of Experts in the fields mentioned in Schedule III of the notification dated 27th January 1994, called the Environmental Impact assessment Notification, 1994.
2. The Committee of Experts shall gather all necessary data on the environmental impact of the project. They shall be free

to commission or carry out such surveys and studies and the like as they deem necessary. They shall also consider such surveys and studies as have already been carried out.

3. Upon such data, the Committee of Experts shall assess the environmental impact of the Project and decide if environmental clearance to the Project can be given and, if it can, what environmental safeguard measures must be adopted, and their cost.

4. In so doing, the Committee of Experts shall take into consideration the fact that the construction of the dam and other work on the Project has already commenced.

5. Until environmental clearance to the Project is accorded by the Committee of Experts as aforesaid, further construction work on the dam shall cease.

6. The Grievance Redressal Authorities of the States of Gujarat, Madhya Pradesh and Maharashtra shall ensure that those ousted by reason of the Project are given relief and rehabilitation in due measure.

7. When the Project obtains environmental clearance, assuming that it does, each of the Grievance Redressal Authorities of the States of Gujarat, Madhya Pradesh and Maharashtra shall, after such inspection, certify, before work on the further construction of the dam can begin, that all those ousted by reason of the increase in height of the dam by 5 metres from its present level have already been satisfactorily rehabilitated and also that suitable vacant land for rehabilitating all those who will be ousted by the increase in the height of the dam by another 5 metres is already in the possession of the respective States.

8. This process shall be repeated for every successive proposed 5 meter increase in the dam height.

9. If for any reason the work on the project, now or at any time in the future, cannot proceed and the Project is not completed, all oustees who have been rehabilitated shall have the option to continue to reside where they have been rehabilitated or to return to where they were ousted from, provided such place remains habitable, and they shall not be made at all liable in monetary or other terms on this account.

The writ petition is allowed in the aforementioned terms. The connected matters are disposed of in the same terms. No orders as to costs.

....

(S.P. Bharucha)

New Delhi, October 18, 2000

37

Binding and Bonding

Many among friends and relations tried to dissuade us against this journey of bonding in the land of Chinar and lakes, saints and sages but we had become converts to the cause of peace and did not heed any warning bells. Before launching the journey to Jammu and Kashmir I made efforts to contact as many people as possible to acquaint myself with the history of Kashmir.

Before we could find any solutions it was important to know what was Kashmir, how did the people live, who were its saints, who were its poets Therefore WIPSA which rhymed with the Sanskrit word "Vishesh Ichha" (Special Desire) had to learn about the past glory of Kashmir Our Vishesh Iccha went far beyond the surface in Kashmir. It did succeed in touching the core of Kashmiriyat.

The name Kashmir I found nearly as old as civilization and mentions *of* Kashmir had been made in the Hindu texts like "Nilamat Purana" and Pannis Ashtadhyay. I discovered that women's initiatives were there and references to it were found in Mahabharat, Purana's and Braht Samhitta. The name Kashmir existed and could be traced back by an unbroken chain of documents for more than 23 centuries. The region was known as Kashperia and the valley is situated to North of the Pir Panjal range of mountains in the North India. It is of an irregular oval shape lying north west and south east. The valley is perched securely among the Himalayas at the average height of 6000 ft above sea level.

The valley is about 84 miles in length and 20-25 miles in breadth. According to the legends and old Hindu scnptures like Nilamat Purana and traditional accounts confirmed by modern Geologists a huge lake called "Satisaras lake of Sati (Durga)" occupied the place of pride in the Valley of Kashmir. I was quit impressed and hoped now the women's initiative for peace in that region would resound with the ripples in the water of Sati Saras lake

Kaihana Pandit in his historical narration ot Kashmir in Rajatarangini mentions that from the beginning of Kalpa ceycle of creation) Kashyap Muni was perhaps residing in that region. It is interesting to note that Kashmir is perhaps the only region in India which besides legends can claim the distinction of possessing an uninterrupted series of written records of its history between 8" and 12th century which has been covered in a scientific manner by Rajatarangi in and is today the most direct source of information on that early period of the Hindu Kings of Kashmir. Huen Tsang and many other historians have corroborated the fact that Kashmiris have always period themselves on the country's safety from foreign invasions due to the strength of natural defences, force of soldiers and efficient defensive system.

As I moved from Srinagar to Anantnag to Baramullah to Doda to Nowpora Distt. Budgam etc. I wondered where did that safety, security and serenity of natural defences, independence and strong organisation vanish?

History pointed out to women's power even as far back as 980-1003 AD when Queen Dida ruled Kashmir and her masterful, dynamic personality dominated the politics of Kashmir for nearly half a century. My initiative for peace was inspired by listening and acknowledging the feats of this remarkable and beautiful woman. She built Didapura and Hindu, Muslim "Math" known as Didavar.

M.A. Troyar said Dida was the Messalina *of* Kashmir The Kashmir valley with its region of lakes, springs and wealth of shrines, resorts and legends is the abode of fascinating saints and sages that lend credibility to its very foundations. One of the greatest Yoginis of Kashmir was called Lalleshwan or Lal Dev the 14th century Shaiva Vedanta poetess of Kashmir, the first woman who really launched the women's initiative for peace, one in whose footsteps we now walked. She lived dunng Shah Hamdams period in 1335 AD. Once again my mission of bringing peace and harmony in that region was inspired by this great reformer of peace of that period. Her poetry till today resounds in the valley. She said I am like a shop in the middle of the marketplace without a lock. At the mercy of carpenters who cannot even fashion a lock.

Meaning that the society had already become incompetent and without any restrictions. She brought forth a series of reforms for Hindu and Islamic culture and to her religion meant faith in the highest. purity of heart, absence of false ego equality among all. I was doing nothing new in bringing forth the message of WIPSA to that already inspired community. Lalleshwari preached non-injury and non-violence. Today the trouble torn valley of Kashmir needs to look at Lalleshwari's philosophy whose peace and reforms movement can be classed among the great reforms of India of the 14 century with Kabir, Nanak and Ramanand. If her preaching of the Hindu. Muslim unity and tolerance could be relevant then, why can't we adopt the same today?

Dawn of 1589 saw Akbar the Great bring in another era of peace and prosperity to the poor and harassed. He instituted many missions for the rehabilitation of Kashmiri people. He proclaimed religious tolerance and abolished "Jazia and Begar" (Bonded Labour). During his period Todar Mal was sent to make a settlement of Kashmir. However, Abdul Majid was the first to make a settlement in Kashmir but even in those days the settlement of Kashmir was arbitrarily and badly made which led to rebellion. Akbar had to visit Kashmir 3 times and each time he had to stay for a long time in the valley. After Mughals in 1753 to 1819 Maharaja Ranjit Singh came to power and Kashmir was ruled by them for some time. Afhaan King's also ruled Kashmir for some time. Then after nearly 400 years in 1753 Sukhjewan Mal had the distinction of becoming the first Hindu ruler.

Turmoil and turbulence was the story of the valley of Kashmir from 1819 to 1846 when Kashmir was granted by the English to Raja Gulab Singh. The tale of Kashmir during the Sikh rule was just a little better than the previous Pathan rule. During the treaty of Amritsar 1846 Raja Gulab Singh appeared as a mediator between the English and the Lahore Darbar. After a great deal of mediation it transpired in the end that Maharaja Gulab Singh acknowledged the supremacy of the British Government. Remission of Rs. 25 lakh was made by the British in lieu of some areas Lahore, Kulu and Chhamb. Gulab Singh and his successor became the rulers of Jammu and Kashmir and the Frontier districts of Ladhak, Skardu and Gilgit. Treaty of Amritsar thus marks the commencement of history of Jammu and Kashmir as a political unity. Ironically it also marks the beginning of the British/ulterior motive' to become the de facto rulers of the state.

Till 1931 throughout the history of the state communal violence was unknown. The local Hindus and Muslim people of that period not only lived in harmony and affection but shared each others joys, sorrows and sufferings. The reason behind the harmony was that racially, culturally and linguistically Hindus and Muslims were practically one. With a few exceptions majority of the Muslims of Kashmir came from the same Aryan stock as the Pandit. Only their religion was different.

Jammu and Kashmir has its own Acquisition and Requisition Act. The state legislature headed by Sheikh Abdullah acquired the land and properties of the State Citizens in 1952 without paying any compensation. The then legislature, called Constituent Assembly, abolished the authority of the king who remained head of the state till the said Act was passed in September 1952. More interestingly monarchy was abolished under the seal and the signatures of Yuvraj Karan Singh in his capacity as the Regent appointed by his father, Maharaja Hari Singh in March 1949 when the latter moved to Bombay on health grounds. Yuvraj Karan Singh was elected Sadar-e-Riyasat in the same year (1952) by the Legislative Assembly and continued in that capacity till 1965 when the Legislative Assembly with all its wisdom and commitment to democracy amended the State Constitution by changing the nomenclature of the prime minister to chief minister and status of Sadar-e-Riyasat was replaced by the governer to be appointed by the President of India in accordance with the procedure adopted in respect of any other state of the Union. Dr. Karan Singh thus became the first governor.

There have been eight Legislative Assemblies since then which were duly constituted including the present one in accordance with the provisions of the Constitution of Jammu and Kashmir. Several Central Laws and Acts were introduced in the State Constitution by the respective State Legislatures after adoption of due procedure and thorough discussions and debates inside each legislature. The present Constitution of Jammu and Kashmir which was initiated by Sheikh Abdullah was finally promulgated on January 1, 1957 under the leadership of the most popular Kashmiri Prime Minister Bakshi Gulam Mohammed. This Constitution was based on the Jammu and Kashmir Constitution Act, 1939 which was introduced under the command of Maharaja Hari Singh. The autocratic Constitution of 1939 introduced the parliamentary system as well as a right to seek redress against the State through writ petitions.

After India's victory over Pakistan in 1971 the Government of India initiated a dialogue with the leadership of Kashmir which brought Sheikh Abdullah to power as an undisputed leader. Sheikh Saheb had in the past four decades before 1971 become an unchallenged leader for the aspirations and hopes of the Kashmiri people. However the Kashmir problem has been a cancer to the Kashmiri people and the Government of India. Sheikh Abdullah's stature and his Muslim leadership was extremely valuable during the Bangladesh liberation.

I searched the beautiful valley for answers and solutions in the paradise of lakes, land of mountains, but now torn and tormented and terrorized. I hope to find answers for this valley of Gods.

We, Women's Initiative for Peace in South Asia (WIPSA) visited Jammu and Kashmir from 24th June to 3rd July 2000. We had chalked out a programme for ourselves as the second step in our effort to create Women's intervention for peace in the region. WIPSA's first initiative was launched with a bus journey to Pakistan undertaken by 42 women and the impact of our message of peace went through the corridors of power and by-lanes of the poor in Pakistan and a return journey was planned by the Pakistani women to India one month after our journey. During deliberations between the Indian delegates and the Pakistani women delegates we had also planned out that each of our delegations would visit Kashmir. They would visit Pakistan Occupied Kashmir and we would visit Srinagar. Our plan was to mobilise women for building Peace in South Asia. Our delegation was headed by the renowned Gandhian Ms. Nirmala Deshpande and apart from me, Dr. Syeda Hameed, Kumkum Chaddha, Suman Yadav, Suman Gupta, Shakuntala Joshi, Ram Mohan Roy were the delegates.

Our second step was to identify and find out the facts relating to Kashmir and to create an environment of peace. We had a very comprehensive programme of interaction with various stratas of community in the region.

Our first stop was Jammu. At the railway station itself we were greeted by hundreds of women and men who had come to express solidarity for our cause since peace was the most important agenda. From the station itself we went in a cavalcade of cars for a rally for peace at the Gol Chakkar.

The state chapter of WIPSA was launched and we were told that WIPSA in Hindi meant "vishesh ichha". We all stressed the need for peace in the region and greater involvement of women from all walks of life to make this movement a success. The meeting was attended by many displaced women. Their faces still bore the marks of tragedy that had struck them. There were about 60°o Hindu displaced and 30 per cent Muslim displaced women. Ms. Nirmala Deshpande introduced WIPSA to the gathering and said that Jammu and Kashmir region had been suffering the most due to hostility and tensions between India and Pakistan and lasting peace in South Asia was imperative. We had a spontaneous outpouring of voices to help us achieve our objectives. They all promised to fulfill our dreams and aspirations. The women told us that it is difficult for them to explain the devastation that had occurred in Jammu and Kashmir and survival had become difficult. Hindu women longed for the Kashmir that they had left behind. Both communities expressed the need for living in harmony and togetherness.

Dr. Hameed and we emphasised the need to build bridges and see that violence has no place in civil society. We emphasised that men have failed so far in the efforts of peace and it was time for women to take up the challenge. We felt and thought that women with all their sincerity and dedication could establish peace in the region.

We emphasised the need for extension of jurisdiction of the National Commission for Women to Jammu and Kashmir also. I recalled the various recommendations that were made pertaining to Jammu and Kashmir and to pursue their implementation with the Governments. While launching the WIPSA, we also emphasised the need to open a day care centre, vocational centre for widows.

The youth in the region of Jammu and Kashmir were indeed very active and to packed audiences they explained the condition of unemployment and the problems of widows. Violence was a theme that all spoke about, however they all agreed that violence was not only from the militants but the security forces as well. During our visit to Ranbir Singh Pura known as R.A. Pura in the village of Muralia which was on the border of Pakistan our interaction with 40 nomadic tribes known as Gujjars and Bakarwals and who lived six months of the year in the mountains of Kukernag, Pahalgam. Aishmaqam, Bhadarwah and Sanasar was very meaningful.

They narrated to us their desire to live and let live. They all complained about firing from across the border and how many of them had lost their near and dear ones. These Bakarwals and Gujjars had no schools for their children, no health facilities and WTPSA promised Razia, Rehana, Savitri, Reshma who were singing and dancing that we would open up schools and health centres for them. In the troubled land of Kashmir we had to build bridges and see that alongside peace initiatives development was also initiated

We went to many refugee camps where, huddled together, thousands of men and women lived. They all narrated how they lived in spacious houses with ventilation and today they were bereft of their home, hearth, property and privacy. They had neither jobs nor any occupation and the very trauma of facing a new dawn was making them ill and restless. Be it Hindus, Muslims or Sikhs the tragedy of conflict and insurgency had struck each one and the conch of peace resounded more and more from all of them.

At Srinagar also we faced similar situation like in Jammu. The day we reached Srinagar there was a total strike there against custodial killings of the Kashmiris. Once again warning signals were given to us before leaving Jammu but we were the soldiers for peace and despite all warnings we reached Srinagar. Despite the call for the Bandh we were received with flowers at the airport by several admirers of Nirmala Deshpande.

After having interacted with several groups of militants, peace lovers, chief minister and groups of ordinary people, leader of the All Party Hurriyat Conference, Abdul Ghani Lone of People's Conference, Mr. Yaseen Mallick of JKLF and Mr. Gillani several media people, several advocates etc. we came to the conclusion that the common, cry was "Aman" Peace.

I was in Kunzer on my way to Tillburg to see the families of the homeless and hapless victims of communal violence. In a village I asked a group of women "How are you" and the prompt answer that I got was " What a stupid question to a sk". When we get up in the morning we do not know whether we will be all right in the evening and you are asking us how are you?" I visited the Valley of Jammu and Kashmir nearly after 3 years and to my utter dismay I found women, children, caged in the grip of fear and traumatized beyond words. The faces of the displaced women still bore the marks of tragedy that had hit them.

We have already entered the 21st century and the above past history I narrated seems like a dream. Every corner of Kashmir that

I visited without exception had only the cry of AMAN. Today when we have crossed the frontiers of space are we really denying ten million brothers and sisters their basic human rights? These are the people who are suffering untold miseries silently and have no option but want freedom and peace.

Our mission was to listen patiently to the Hurriyat leaders of JKLF, Farooq Abdullah, and the public particularly women. We had to sit back and listen to each one of them in order to even understand and fathom to what was happening. We discovered that time had not really changed the psyche of the subcontinent intellectually or politically. The tensions that had been witnessed in ancient times between centre and state relations existed even today. Age old diversity and competition to transcend and confront still existed. Anarchy, *arajakta* of the old century still existed. The damage to the psyche of the Kashmiri people after 1986 will have to be rebuilt, repaired and confidence measures to be taken before any initiative can succeed there.

Women's Initiative for Peace in South Asia is concerned about the deeply hurt psyche of the people of Jammu and Kashmir. We feel that the effort of the state and the civil society to understand what is happening to the people particularly to the women has so far been superficial. The cases of human rights violations that we saw were grains of sand in vast deserts of such occurrences. We found no explanations for incidents such as a girl child taken in police custody in the middle of the night. Despite the fact that we raised the question before people in authority we found that there was no effort to probe the incident and pin the responsibility. We sadly found absence of initiatives by government, political parties and civil society (barring a few excellent human rights and social activists) to provide succour to the hapless people, in particular the women who are the hardest hit of all.

WIPSA in its role of trying to bring peace to the region feels that the first and foremost need is to listen to the people. This is one way of applying salve to their wounds. The second is to open dialogue; 'goli nahin boli' is the one and only way. Our recommendations based on our personal experiences and observation are addressed to the State of Jammu and Kashmir, the Government of India and the Civil Society.

To the State of Jammu and Kashmir and the Goverment of India

Without reminding the Government of India of the international human rights instruments to which it is signatory, WIPSA would like the following action from the central and state governments:

1. Impartial investigations to be commenced immediately on the human rights violations that occur in the state. Such investigations should be entrusted to responsible members of the civil society; teams to include men as well as women. Since the rural areas, where people are alleged to suffer the most, are generally hidden from the public eye, it is recommended that such citizens' teams be created not only at the district but at the block and the village level as well. The State Human Rights Commission and the newly created State Commission for Women should be involved in this process. Necessary facilities to be placed at the disposal of citizens committees for conducting investigations.
2. The recommendations of these Civil Society Tribunals should be binding on the State and the Government of India. This is to ensure that bodies thus created become effective instruments for providing relief to affected people.
3. All political parties to give their immediate attention for initiating a process of healing and reconciliation with the people of Kashmir

To the Civil Society

The ignorance about Jammu and Kashmir, which prevails in the rest of the country is truly abysmal. Although people in the rest of the country are anxious to know about the prevailing conditions in the state. Capping it all is the disinformation that is fed to common people by certain sections. One routine example is the scare given to people who express a desire to visit Kashmir. Such deterrence creates a vicious cycle, which prevents people from finding out for themselves, thus widening the gap between that region and the rest of the country. Given these conditions, WIPSA recommends the following:

1. In any peace process which begins as a result of years of efforts by manv individuals and groups, it be made compulsory that women's group's from the state of Jammu and Kashmir

and other parts of the country should play a major role. Peace should not be left to men; women who have major stakes in peace should be invited to play a major role in bringing it about.

2 That more and more civil society groups, particularly women, should visit Jammu and Kashmir on their own initiative and thereby forge personal links with the people. There is no substitute, we feel, for people to people understanding, and in this endeavour women must play a dominant role

3. That the business community should make a concerted effort to treat Kashmir as it does other parts of the country insofar as putting up industries and thereby providing employment opportunities to the youth of the state.

4. That the state of Jammu and Kashmir being replete with stories of amity between the two communities, particularly among the women, it is imperative that efforts are made to publicize them in the rest of the country so that instead of talks of bifurcation and trifurcation people to people bonding may be created.

5. That NGOs should come into the state and set up facilities for displaced migrant and widowed women. These should include legal literacy centres, micro credit schemes and training-cum-production centres for those affected by the conditions that have been prevalent for over a decade.

38

Trafficking in Women and Children

While I go round the country I hear people talking about earthquakes and natural calamities, about border conflicts, match fixing and in between glaring ads of beauty contests, vulgar display of not only a woman's body but her unequal status in society. No one really talks about how the dreams of young girls are shattered, how many deaths does a little trafficked girl undergo? What is poverty and economic deprivation? Do our little girls have enough to eat? Why are men so brutal to take away a little angel and sell her? Why is this little bundle of joy who is physically, mentally defenceless pushed into the flesh trade? We have symposiums, seminars, street plays, get togethers but my mind searches for solutions. It is an impossible task that I seek to reach my goal. I have several obstacles. Abuse of these little children is the most heinous crime that I can think about.

Who is the purchaser of the girl's virginity? Who is the highest bidder to have the right to spend the first night with a small girl? Who is it who wants the company of women while travelling, or while staying alone in a city? Who are those people who come with false promises of marriages and jobs? Who are the people who sell their little daughters for economic reasons? Aren't they all really our uncles, our brothers, our fathers.... All of them men?

Commercial sexual exploitation of children is an all pervasive obnoxious global problem. At present it is one of the major flourishing trades. No civilised society should tolerate this form of violence on innocent young vulnerable children who is a potential national human resource. Today, it is a universally recognised fact that child abuse constitutes a gross violation of the child's right to protection and healthy development. It is also a flourishing industry operating worldwide that capitalises on the sale and trafficking of children through Internet and other means. Hence it is of serious concern to multidisciplinarians. This is a multifaceted problem which needs well planned multipronged strategies for its eradication. However, all these global and national efforts need a microlevel understanding of the situation in different regions if they are to succeed.

India, with 28,000 kms of spanning dimension and a rich tradition of civilisation, inhabited by people of diverse economic levels and cultural attainments, speaking a variety of languages, is a country which presents a distinct flavour of the high and the low, the ugly and the beautiful. These contradictions are nowhere more manifest than in the case of prostitution owing to the steady increase in the levels of income, different levels of affluence as a result of international trade, economic liberalisation and the green and white revolutions. The scene is indeed pathetic when we discuss child prostitution!

We find ourselves today at a particular historical juncture, where progress and development in human society has created two contradictions. On the one hand, there is modernity with the improved quality of life while on the other, the same change threatens many aspects of community life, such as the loss of ethics and moral values to the corrupting influence of modernity itself.

We have a growing population of children and young people exposed not only to the seduction of capitalism, but also to the economic pressures of survival. The social conditions emerging out of this phenomenon become fertile ground for the easy recruitment of innocent victims into the vicious market of human flesh.

In many areas of the country women are forced into prostitution or flesh trade in the name of religion and culture. The induction of adolescent girls into the sex trade takes place with the full knowledge and even the connivance of family members. The practice of this 'contemporary form of slavery' needs to be brought to the foreground of development concerns, and eliminated. This is an intolerable form of child labour and abuse of the child. In India sexual exploitation of children has its roots in traditional practices, beliefs and gender discrimination. The problem of child prostitution in India is more complicated than in other Third World countries where it is directly related to sex tourism.

Like child labour, child prostitution is almost everywhere. It runs the sordid gamut from incest and sexual abuse by friends and family members to the systematic commercial plundering of children and young teenagers in lucrative prostitution and pornography markets.

The very basis of the child sex industry—designation of a child as a commodity for sale and purchase—demeans and dehumanises the child. It also serves the sexual drive of sexually immature men who seek emotional release by exploiting a completely powerless slave child.

Sexual abuse of children is a matter of grave concern. Trafficking of children has national and international dimensions. Of late, the problem of children in prostitution has assumed serious proportions. Identification and enumeration of factors conducive to child prostitution is in a way difficult because it has roots deep in the fabric of society. Ratification of the convention of the rights of the child in 1992 by India signifies the nation's commitment to the well being of the children. Creating safe, secure and harmonious environment for children in society is the onerous task of the family, the community, and the government. It cannot be denied that for effective implementation of any social legislation, public support is necessary.

It was heart rending to visit various jails in India and identify little children who are found at bus stops, railway stations and rescued from many brothels living in the unhealthy unnatural jail environment. Each child told me how when they were four years, six years, eight years, old they were kidnapped and brought to India either from Bangladesh or from Pakistan or from villages of India and how they ran away or were rescued from the trafficker. We were able to identify 500 such small children at that time belonging to Bangladesh and got them taken back to their parents in Bangladesh.

The little girl in a choked voice calls out and says "Ma I have not done anything, please let them not punish me". Time and again the victim is looked upon as a criminal. It is critical that laws should not be used against the victim but against the exploiters. On the one hand child traffickers force the children to offer their bodies and, on the other, the police lock them up in exploitative institutions in the name of rehabilitation. These homes are not a positive affirmation of the child's growth rather, the way the child is often treated here is as if it did something wrong is only a reaffirmation of the wrong doing. The police only attack the symptom of the problem and not the cause.

Certain recommendations have been formulated for the trafficked children.

- The child who is a victim of sexual abuse or exploitation is under great stress and trauma. To add to the child's problem, he/she is repeatedly exposed to the exploiter for sake of identification. It is grossly unfair for the child because just the sight of the exploiter is enough to trigger the mind back to the trauma she had passed through. The sight of the exploiter is sufficient for the child to destabilise her mind. Therefore, we strongly recommend that the information from the victim should be elicited in a closed room in the presence of a child psychologist, counsellors, social workers and above all the camera. All the proceedings should be recorded. At the same time speedy justice should be provided to the victims. It is often seen that the cases lie pending in the court, the children and the women are kept in remand homes or short stay shelters where these people are unable to mould their life into any channel because of the uncertainty of the future. At times they go out on bail and are again caught in the vicious circle. The opportunity to rehabilitate them or prepare them to join the mainstream is lost, especially in the case of children who had been inducted into the trade recently.
- Many a time it is observed that police personnels refuse to register the FIR as the complaint of the victim is not supported with a medical report, etc. it is recommended that FIRs should be immediately registered without waiting for any formalities. Further, cases of rape or sexual assault of an individual should not be judged solely on the criteria of medical examination. Sexual exploitation of a child in the name of custom, tradition and culture should be declared a punishable crime.
- Education should be made free and compulsory for both boys and girls as literacy spreads general awareness, strength, economic empowerment as well as a sense of judgement to differentiate between the right and the wrong. As no schools admit children of prostitutes it is strongly recommended that child prostitutes and children of prostitutes should be admitted

in schools on the lines of Navodaya Vidyalayas. Adult education programmes should also include destitute women. This particular section of women and children need to be approached with lot of sincerity, compassion, kindness and lots and lots of patience. First, their mindset should be changed, then there is a need to break their routine as their body is temporarily conditioned to have sex for above 8-10 hours each day. The parents should be provided incentives to send their children to school.

- It is often seen that when girls are married at an early age, if they are deserted by their spouse or if they become widowed or get separated from their husband, these young girls, most probably teenage mothers of small children are unable to stand on their own feet and support themselves and their children. Such women come under high risk group as they are easy targets for traffickers. This is the group of women which opts for the most loathsome profession voluntarily out of sheer desperation. At a young age these girls are uneducated and untrained for skills. As a result to earn their livelihood, they may have little choice and may become either domestic servants, daily-wage labourers, etc. or prostitutes. If we are able to prevent entry of this group into the profession it will reduce the number of women in prostitution quite significantly. One of the preventive measures could be compulsory registration of all marriages like birth and death, among all religions alike. This step could prevent child marriages as well as discourage fake marriages. The second solution is education and mass awareness.
- Though networking of traffickers is very well established yet it the remains hidden from the police. Various trafficking routes, supply, transit centre/countries should be identified by the police by working in close coordination with national and international agencies. At the same time there is need to establish strong networking among the police, NGOs, village panchayats and State administration in order to build an information data base in conjunction with Interpol and CBI.
- As one of the preventive measures, the police should keep a close eyes on all those foreigners who stay for long periods without any apparent occupation; who visit the same place

repeatedly as tourists; who display any abnormal behaviour or look suspicious.

- For rescue, rehabilitation and prevention beside the government, police and state a major role would be played by the community and grassroots bodies such as village panchayats, teachers, anganwadi workers, etc. The active participation of community at large is a must to prevent recruitment of new girls into this system. Though the Act regarding Devadasi system was passed long time back but is implementation lies in the hands of community. Then, the tribals who had been practicing prostitution as their only occupation should be discouraged. They practise this trade near the roadside in dhabas, as "floating prostitutes" and of course in brothels. Thereby, in a way they spread wrong signals to the men seeking sex that all girls seen alone are available for their perverse desires. This practice needs to be stopped by providing these people alternate means of livelihood, education, etc. the community should be empowered through specific mechanisms such as representatives and responsible bodies. At the village level these bodies should include panchayats, women's group, NGOs, school teachers, community leaders and stock holders.
- There is need to have a monitoring agency with the specific task of liaisaing with various agencies to look after the welfare of society, to prevent induction of new girls into the trade and to stop trafficking. The dedicated fit into this role best. NGOs are the best grassroots bodies who could play a significant role in rescue and rehabilitation. They have the privilege to reach out to remote villagers as well as to the administrative bodies alike. They could play an instrumental role in spreading awareness among the most vulnerable group regarding the modus operandi used by traffickers and pimps to recruit new young and innocent girls.
- NGOs could collate all the laws relating to prostitution and document success stories of rehabilitation to the potential candidates while imparting counselling to them. They can also run schools, vocational training centres and can also help the women to collect together and form cooperatives or self-help groups so as to generate income and enable these women to be financially independent. The products prepared by these

girls and women should be marked with assistance from various industries and State governments. NGOs could also arrange health camps for these women periodically and keep these women abreast of their latest health status—such camps will spread general health awareness beside enabling the women to guard themselves from various STDs, HIV, AIDS and other health problems.

- The efforts of government, community and NGOs if assisted by media can reach far in a short period. Media is the best and most effective way to mobilise people at grassroots level with latest technology and if by portable mediums the remotest corner of earth is approachable then why not the remotest village which is the target group of traffickers and resource of new victims. Media should spread awareness against child prostitution and trafficking by constantly displaying visuals with simple but clear messages but at the same time they should be careful not to portray children in compromising, illegal or pornographic situations. Media should campaign to demolish myths on sex with children. It can help in revealing trafficking operations for public through news, plays, skits etc. as often as possible and should publicise the follow up actions in similar manner. It should highlight that it is always not "easy money" in this trade but it cost one's social life, health status, and carries a curse for one's children all through life.
- When any person presents himself/ herself as parent/ guardian of the abused child to seek her/ his custody from the police or court the child should not be handed over to them without proper verification. Many NGOs have reported that brothel keepers and traffickers present themselves as parentsguardians. When the child is asked to verify them, they do what they are told to as the very sight of them is enough for the child to think back to the miserable time she/he had gone through. It is suggested that in case of parents at least, simple forensic tests could be performed like blood group tests, dermataglyphic tests, etc, so as to establish the relationship between the two. In case of guardian proper verification should be done.
- It is also recommended that whenever the rehabilitative programmes are being formulated they should not be bound by time as it affects the efficiency of the programmes.

- Trafficking has become an international nuisance. It is strongly recommended that the Indian Government should negotiate with SAARC countries particularly Nepal, Bangladesh and Sri Lanka to effectively prevent the migration or transport of children for sexual abuse in India. Each country should enact legislations whereby their citizens are punishable for the offences, related to sexual abuse and trafficking they have committed in another country.
- There is need to identify the risk groups and their data should be compiled, kept updated and information shared internationally on a regular basis. State and national level representatives of international organisations such as the World Tourism Organisation, International Union of Food, and hotel management organisations should be urged to take necessary actions.
- To curb trafficking and paedophilia, sex tourism should be curbed by close association of the government, municipal councils, village panchayats, educational and religious institutions. Prevention of child trafficking entails proper safeguards, including independent monitoring and follow-up. For children to be returned to their country of origin, they should not be treated as illegal immigrants by the receiving countries but dealt with humanely as special cases of humanitarian concern upon the children's return, the countries of origin should treat them with respect in accordance with international human rights principles.

Thus it is imperative that all stakeholders—government, NGOs, the media and the communities pay more attention to strengthen response mechanisms; to reorient cultural attitudes and social values to be more sensitive to the child; to increase advocacy for children's right; and to work towards a more active participation of children in all matters affecting their lives.

I know the path is not at all smooth, I know there is no easy way to solutions. There is no magic wand which can be twirled to remove this blot. I know, too that no matter how many conferences we have, how many laws we make, the truth is that we cannot wipe off the tears from the face of every girl who has been hurt, abused and traumatised. There are no choices. A bold beginning has to be made. We are far from achieving our goals, but for as long as we keep the struggle alive, we can continue to give hope to our children, and vindicate all those who perished as victims.

However, while we delibeorate like this and go back to our homes we might set into action some forces which will work towards the total eradication of this ill from our society.

39

Human Rights and Women

Millions of women in our hamlets know what unemployment means. Give them access to economic activities and they will have access to power and self-confidence to which they hitherto have been strangers.

Mahatma Gandhi

It is Said that Justice is that Justice does

Women in India are tightly wedged between laws, in laws, and their fundamental rights are often infringed. When she resists these sociolegal laws she is often branded as an outlaw!

In the course of my thirty years of interaction with women I have found that there is a constant struggle for the women to confront the mammoth law of gender bias ready to engulf her every second. In order to help her in her struggle for equality, equity and gender justice the International Human Rights Movement, the National Commission for Women and the National Human Rights commission have spelt out and interpreted Fundamental Rights and Directive Principles of the Constitution.

Very often when I go to the villages and speak with my grassroot brothers and sisters they often ask me "ma what is this new human rights?" They often tell me that sharing, caring, giving, taking and treating each other with respect and dignity have always formed a part of their culture. Then I ask them why is it that your wives live in purdah?, why is it that she has not gone to school?, why is woman's world restricted to the kitchen? How come that a woman toils the whole day, works harder than the man and yet she is the last to eat and least to eat. I explain to them that all the violence that is perpetuated by society, rape, dowry is infringing upon the woman's fundamental rights. I tell them that because we are human beings all our rights and obligations flow from our human needs and because these are the foundations of humanity and that because they must be protected they are known as fundamental rights.

Human Rights as an expression may have a modern ring to it, but as a concern it is as ancient as Plato and Aristotle when "humanity" literally started gaining grounds. Scholars like them taught the then rulers that people weren't subjects who are exclusively made to bow but also were "human beings" who needed to be looked after - both physically and emotionally. Even after so many years we still feel the need for good governance and participation of civil society. Unfortunately even today the bureaucracy and government expect us to bow to their will! Looking into modern times, there is a possibility that the study of human rights deals with humanity itself! On the practical side of it, a large number of human right organisations have now been established all over the world to watch and protect rights and their violation.

All human rights are without question women's rights and have real application and relevance to every single citizen. There is a misconception that all these human rights are the responsibility of the Parliament, the courts and other authorities but I propose that such issues cannot be the concern of only the Parliament, judiciary etc. but a concern of the family, society, community, international community etc. too. It is increasingly apparent that all these human rights are vital to the peace and prosperity of every society and play a critical part in the quest to achieve a just and fair society.

Women's place in every community is vital to the well-being of th.it society; without their work, both in the formal sector and in the family, most communities would not survive. It is now recognised that enhancing women's status and enforcing their rights on an equal basis with men will do much to achieve the objectives of Equality, Development and Peace adopted at the Fourth World Conference on Women held in Beijing in September 1995.

In 1993 the World Conference on Human Rights concluded that: "the human rights of women and of the girl-child are an inalienable, integral and indivisible part of universal human rights. The full and equal participation of women in political, civil, economic, social and cultural life at the national, regional and international levels, and the eradication of all forms of discrimination on grounds of sex are priority objectives of the international community. The world conference on human rights urged governments, institutions, inter-governmental and non-governmental organisation to intensify their efforts for the protection and promotion of human rights of women and the girl-child".

During the World Conference on Human Rights two significant issues were stressed: first, the Universality of human rights described: "the common language of all humanity" and secondly the importance of including and emphasising the particular nature of women's human rights.

Successive United Nations Conferences and regional meetings have concluded that issues critical to the future well-being of the world's people, such as resource development coupled with protection of the environment, the pursuit of peace and the improvement of basic human rights such as health and education are all heavily dependent on an improvement in the status of women. And this improvement is needed urgently in all nations, not only in the developing nations and those nations which are torn by years of war and civil disruption. For it is now well-known that although most nations promise equality of opportunity for women, few come close to delivering it and that failure has a huge impact on the ability of half the world's population to contribute fully to the economic and social, civil and political spheres of the community's activities.

In all nations women earn less from paid employment than men; they have less likelihood of inheriting land and other assets than their brothers; they are more likely to be physically assaulted regularly by members of their own families; they are less likely to serve in governments in senior positions and they are likely to be the sole bread-winner for something approaching one-third of the world's families. And now they are being infected with the HIV/AIDS virus at a faster rate than men simply because they lack the information with which to protect themselves, or the right or ability to refuse intimate relationships whether with their own husband or with the rapist.

These barriers to attainment of equality apply as much in a small and wealthy country as they do in our country with its enormously diverse population. The barriers which women must overcome, if they are not to remain disproportionately represented amongst the world's poorest with all the resulting health problems and lack of community and political participation are not to be found only in a reform of the law but also in the reform of attitudes, traditions and beliefs.

Many violations of human rights take place in jails. Upon a visit to the Naini jail I found Kala sitting in a corner and crying. She looked in her mid-twenties and upon my questioning her she said that ten yeas ago she had gone with her parents to the Kumbh Mela at Allahabad. Leaving her clothes behind on the shore she went for bath and on coining out of water she could not find her clothes. In order to clothe herself from nakedness she picked up some saree that was lying on the shore. The police immediately caught her on charges of theft and put her in Naini jail. It has now been ten years. She was still an undertrial at the Naini jail. Human rights violations are rampant in jails.

Judges and the Courts have an important role to play in the protection of v omen's rights. Few women however would think first of the court as a means of changing the structural factors which are the real barriers to achieving equality with men. In fact, it is in the making of policy, or in the work of government agencies such as the police that women's human rights will be implemented or frustrated. The courts therefore have the responsibility to respond appropriately to issues which will assist them in this task.

The judiciary and members of the legal profession have a role to play in ensuring that women are treated with dignity, that they have equal access to justice, and that the outcome for them is one of true equality. This necessarily requires that judges adopt a role which is less than passive. Leadership is required from the judiciary. It is expected that they will show the way in identifying and refusing to condone violations of human rights and inequality of treatment. If judges are not aware of the gender nature of many of our institutions then it is less likely that the legal profession will actively promote measures which will assist women in their objectives of obtaining justice and equality with men. There are many issues in which an approach which recognises women's disadvantage at law or before the Courts can be actively pursued.

It is the empowerment strategy which is today emerging as an unique Indian response to the challenges of gender justice, sustainable development and human rights guarantees. If women are to be empowered, it is necessary to provide support services. If women are to be economically empowered, they are to be provided with additional channels of credit, training, employment, management skills and social security. If women are to be politically empowered, the imperative is to resort to different forms of affirmative discrimination, such as quotas of reservation in various political apparatus, to enable them to participate in decision making process. Women have to be given access to knowledge, power and resources. If women are to be persons in their own right, they must be in control of their own bodies. In India we have moved a long way in all these fronts and the results are not disappointing. A strong women's movement supported by NGOs and national machinery keeps a vigil to ensure gender equality and justice.

What is needed is action from concerned persons, optimism and collective wisdom if we are to bequeath a happy peaceful world to our next generation. Dynamic leadership, dedicated entrepreneurs, continued and concerted efforts for sustainable development oriented services for rational and pragmatic attainments are the variables to be utilised for common goals and aspirations and that requires endless cycle of learning from past, understanding present and planning for future to pass from a "Stormy Today" to a "Better Tomorrow".

Establishment of National Commission for Women was an important step for human rights. The Commission is concerned with the rights of women; matters of inequality and discrimination against women. It is concerned with the representation of women in public life; employment, equity; and the problems of violence and abuse against women. It is concerned with the empowerment of women.

Given the present scenario in India will the rural people, poorer class and women be able to make their voice heard? Will they be able to come up with holistic concept of development for the country? Till now NGOs have been plyaing a compartively free run through the stranglehold of age old bureaucracy and intricate rules and regulations of various government programmes. Power sharing is a must and the measure of our success for sustainable development can be better appreciated if all the sectors/segments are harnessed to extract the best out of them and to do all that is possible for them.

Equal protection of law, equal reasonable opportunities to access to the course of law otherwise justice remains a myth. I often hear from clients that "Justice is always advantageous to the rich". One of the pre—requisite of development is the achievement of equality and equity not only between men but also among men and women. Our goal is universal and shared aspiration of all people. Wishful thinking alone is useless. Of course, man's spiritual growth should not lag behind his material advance. Major imbalance in progress often causes conflict among people and thereby increases unhappiness.

A deep concern with the status of women and the recognition that the progress of the nation is integrally linked with the advancement of women, have under-pinned Indian approach to planned development since Independence. Mahatma Gandhi was a champion of women's rights. He emphasised that, "subjugation and exploitation of women was a product of men's interested teachings and women's acceptance of them". The leaders of the nation recognized that freedom gained without the active involvement of women would be a hollow and fragile freedom.

The time has come to reconsider our development strategy. Development has to come from within not from outside and there must be realisation that community participation is a must to checkmate the evil force within society, to reconcile the constitutional ideals of public justice with novel social condition to enlist the support of benefactors to attain economic freedom.

Political participation by women is a must for the progress of a nation. The low numbers of women occupying positions of influence in public and political life has retrogative effect on the health of the political life of a country.

While we talk about women and their awareness it is strange that even today thousands of women are made to tonsure their heads when they become widows and are sent to Vrindavan or Varanasi. This violation of human rights has been perpetuated since time immemorial. Hence if we have legal literacy, education, perhaps this violation will be reduced.

The low level of literacy among women particularly in countries like India is against the interests of their human rights. Women or men who are illiterate or have a poor education are more likely to have large families because they are less able to have access to family planning advice. This has an impact on the environment, on the health of the population, and on a nation's economic status. Women who are educated are better able to provide for their children in a world where around 25 per cent of the families are totally supported by women, (although in Asia the percentage is likely to be less than 20 per cent). Women who are educated and literate can access public information concerning health and justice to name but two. A women who cannot read may not know that certain crimes perpetrated against her are forbidden by law; nor will she know that she may have the same rights as men to housing and jobs and nor will she have access to nutrition advice or advice on how to avoid the terrible disease of HIV/AIDS. A literate woman is less likely to figure in the very high maternal mortality figures for this part of the world. In a national such as India where female illiteracy outnumbers male illiteracy and where providing access to education for the whole population is fraught with almost insuperable difficulty, what limited sources we have ought to be applied vigorously to women's education. Studies of reports to CEDAW demonstrate that in nations where women are educated to a reasonable standard, the birth rate decreases, the health of families improves and environment and the economy benefits and their human rights are asserted and better protected.

Realising that legal literacy is of critical importance if women are to know their rights and obligation and how to exercise them. The work done by National Commission for Women through its "intensive and extensive legal literacy campaign" is an invaluable contribution to the goal of ensuring that women have access to justice.

It is my intention to persuade people that human rights of women relate not just to their status in society, but have a very real and serious bearing on the general health and well-being of the whole community.

40

Transforming Approaches to Conflict Resolution

"If only the women of the World came together they could display such heroic non-violence as to kick away the Atom Bomb like a mere ball. If the Women of Asia wake up they will dazzle the world. My experiment in non-violence would be instantly successful if I could secure Women's help."

Mahatma Gandhiji

We are meeting at crucial point in the history of the sub-continent. Torn by communal strife, destructive tornado of fundamentalism, and blatant terrorism, the conditions of the sub-continent tear the fabric of world peace. The need of the hour is vital. The endeavour is to be made now, so that in the millennium humanity can reach the zenith of social and human progress.

The building of peace is a constructive activity. There is nothing passive about either the concept or the state of peace. From time immemorial India has been a harbinger of peace to the world. We feel that it is only within the framework of peace women's fullest potential can be realized and it is primarily the women who can usher in an era of peace in the 21st century. There is a need to gather on one platform women who are in decision-making, in order to discuss their overarching image of a culture of peace. This would include the hindrances to women's role in peace, such as family and societal violence interstate trafficking in women and children; as well as the strategies for the removal of political and social hindrances, economic empowerment and education of women.

Women have made and will continue to make significant contribution towards building a culture of peace. It has been known that women are largely responsible for nurturing positive cultural practices as alternatives to the patriarchal symbols and practices that separate people alienate one culture from another, and human beings from the natural order; in short they offer non-violence as the alternative to violence and strife.

Women focus on actions, which have a transformative potential. This is manifested in four areas:

1. Cross-cultural dialogue and exchanges.
2. Creativity not bound by the limits of ethnic and political differences. It brings to mind the examples of women writers who have been hounded after expressing their views through the written medium.
3. Social stratification and stereotyped gender roles. Some media projections of the socially prevalent role of women as sex symbols or as weak personalities ignorant of their strength and resources have to be changed in the new millennium.
4. Positive interaction among different groups leading to social bonding and consequential non-violence.
5. Conflict prevention and resolution. Paradoxically the fact that woman has been away from the theatre of war gives the vital edge to her personality, to fight for the cause of conflict resolution.

   A national meeting was held in New Delhi, which brought out various instruments and negotiations for peace building in South Asia. Some of the major recommendations that emerged are:

To International Agencies

- Create a network to disseminate all peace efforts at various levels - locally, nationally and internationally.
- Lobbying with international organizations and sensitization of NGOs/women's groups belonging to other countries of the world, on issues pertaining to total nuclear disarmament, the restriction of arm sales from industrialized nations, increase of aid and equitable trade to create the environment within which peace can flourish.
- Women's initiative in the international institutions should be encouraged specially for making policies regarding matters relating to peace-keeping, preventive diplomacy and in all stages of peace mediation and negotiations.

- Encouragement of exchange of experiences in peace initiatives, inter-country visits and peace studies.

To the Government

- Lobbying strategies should be for formulated with the Government for the purpose of furthering peace and equality in the sub-continent and also for conflict resolution.
- A national policy be framed to promote secular values, and constructive nation building attitudes among the citizens and an ethos of peace by strengthening the family as the basic unit.
- Enact and enforce legislation against the perpetrators of practices and acts of violence, particularly those on women and children and give support to the efforts of NGOs and community organizations to control practices.
- Provide access to information on peace treaties and defense budgeting.
- Ensure women's participation in all international and national committees set up to deal with armed conflict, peace resolution and security matters.
- A peace bus be used to ride to peace which will ply between Delhi-Lahore and Dhaka-Calcutta consisting of women and men from both countries committed to peace.

To Civil Society

- Promote a strong network of groups and organizations working to ensure peace.
- All human rights and social organizations must campaign to awaken people to the dangers that communalism, racism, cross-border conflict etc. pose for the struggle for equality and social justice.
- Equality, partnership between women and men and respect for human dignity must permeate all stages of the socialization process.

To Educational Institutions

- Ensure that all curriculum and textbooks are free of communal, racial bias, prejudice, refrain from stereotyping and propagate a culture of gender equality.

- Ensure that the culture of violence does not begin in the early years itself through toys and children's literature.
- Drawing from all spirituality and Gandhian principles to promote literature and other media that will help in developing better understanding among people different countries, races and religions, thus removing misconceptions, distressed and suspicion.

To the Media

- Strong action against those indulging in printing and publishing inflammatory literature and preventing misuse of media for unsecular and anti-people purpose.
- Distorted images of women and the marginalised in media communications should change. Media in most countries does not provide a balanced picture of people's diverse lives and their contribution to society in a changing world. Violent and biased media products negatively affect the relationships of people and under the ongoing trend of consumerism, people are primarily portrayed as consumers only.
- Create a forum to lobby against and educate public opinion of the negative consequences of the objectification/ commodification of the human body and psyche.

To the Family

- Emphasizing on women's role as the providers and peace-makers both in normal and crisis situations.
- Promotion of egalitarian attitudes in the family and to promote democratic family relations in place of authoritative, male dominated relations.
- Values of equality, peace and justice should be included in the family. Family as unit be strengthened highlighting the values of respect, dignity and interdependence.
- The relationship within the family should be governed by the principle of justice wherein the rights and responsibilities of its individual members are properly understood and safeguarded.

In order to take our initiative to the SAARC countries we went to Dhaka where not only did we interact with the delegates of the

SAARC countries but also pledged to work in our own areas towards peace. It was felt that conflicts arise only when cultural differences are not respected.

Our initiative was further carried on 6th of August 1999 when the whole country was not only reliving on T.V. camera's the battle field of Kargil in every home.

It was in that atmosphere that the women's initiative for peace in South Asia a small group of Delhi based women activists met to share their grief and to think of ways they could takes as an initiative to refocus public attention on the critical need for peace. A statement was issued which was signed by millions of women wanting peace in the subcontinent.

The women's Peace Initiative resulted in a substantial breakthrough in the stranglehold of the prevailing atmosphere. More than 150 activists from over 45 organizations of civil society, including some from Pakistan and Bangladesh, expressed solidarity with the statement, which was released on 6th August.

This unique programme was planned on 6th of August 1999. Simultaneously several such programmes were organized on the 6th of August from Kashmir to Kanyakumari and peace marches were held everywhere.

In Dhaka-Bangladesh 400 women and men met in a rally at the Central Shahid Minar in Dhaka and expressed solidarity with the peace movement in the subcontinent.

In Kathmandu Nepal Stri Shakti organized a meeting where everyone lit candles, recited poems and sang songs for peace and non-violence.

In Pakistan also a number of events were held to mark the 6 August, Hiroshima Day, and to use the occasion to speak out for peace. In Islamabad, the citizens Peace Committee organized a silent demonstration. In Lahore, several organizations took out processions, which included a very large number of women.

In Karachi, the Pakistan Peace Coalition rallied people from various walks of life-trade unions, professional bodies, voluntary organisations, women's and youth organisations—outside the Karachi press Club, despite a ban on assembling. They demanded a halt to ongoing arms race in India and Pakistan and initiation of concrete measures for the elimination of nuclear weapons. Active participants of the Peace Coalition were the Action Committee Against Arms Race; Pakistan India People's Forum for Peace and Democracy: Association of the Peoples of Asia. The demonstrators included a good number of women holding placards in English and Urdu stating. "No Nuclear Weapons. No to Nuclear War! War of Peace—Peace for All. Peace is a Human Right".

The Women's Initiative for Peace in South Asia has been a spontaneous coming together of women and men in the cause of peace and non-violence. It needed no external funds or support to demonstrate the strength of ordinary people to speak out for what they believe in and what is right. But peace goes beyond cross-border conflicts. It extends to the congenial environment in which woman can develop her full potential. After Beijing Plus Five nothing could underestimate women-power and the fact that the power had been dormant and suppressed. In India the five years have seen the growing awareness and assertion of women's rights. Through NGO advocacy, publications and seminars, there is an increasing awareness of the need for reservations for women in the Parliament and in legislatures. But now with this kind of awareness it should only be a matter of time before reservation is a reality. Every political party in the last elections was forced to include it in the manifesto due to the strength of public opinion. It is due to the initiative taken by women's strong voice that the Bill was introduced on the 23rd of December 1999. We are confident that this Bill would be passed shortly.

Some more indicative changes as I see it has been the Supreme Court of India's judgement on the meaning, implications and consequences of sexual harassment at workplaces. As a fall out all organizations are to set up a committee well represented by NGO's, counsellors and lawyers to look into cases of sexual harassment. literacy level has increased to 39.4 per cent. All women police stations have been established. A rising number of women have opted for hitherto male bastions like the airforce and the army.

When women think of themselves as creators of environment, then only is their self-esteem around. This self-esteem can change the mindset that society has been steeped in for centuries. Every woman has to respect herself before anticipating respect from others. From this arises the need for gender sensitized education—and compulsory education for all-—particularly the women.

A woman in a small hamlet of Dubghunta in India having suffered the tyranny and violence of a drunken husband for years one day just decided she had had enough. From there began the anti-arrack movement that fanned into such a flame that the state government was forced to introduce total prohibition in 1995. This woman was no social worker, she did not even know what empowerment meant. All she realized was that she had it in her to influence other victims to act. The first step is to stop thinking of ourselves as victims but think of ourselves as creators of our circumstances.

In Bangladesh ourself is the excellent example of the Grameen Bank for rural micro credit. An illiterate woman wanted money to pound rice and earns a few rupees. That desire has pounded away a great extent economic dependence. The financial independence gave her the means to shape her life. Political education alongwith economic empowerment—the means to present her case and the tool to lobby for strength and finally the capability to ensure that the laws of the land don't discriminate.

In a region as closely knit as the SAARC every armed conflict will resound in the other countries either as cross border terrorism or as low intensity wars. When the cause of absence of peace is to a great extent economical, the solution must correspond. It is vital to insulate inter-country cooperation from political tensions. In this context the South Asian Preferential Trade Area and South Asian Free Trade Area assumes great significance. This is the kind of cooperative effort that is likely to benefit all and have a direct impact on the people to whom the benefits accrue. This will in turn dispel doubts on interactive cooperation. Surely patriotism must be fuelled by the war against non-development and inequitable distribution of resources.

"O lord why have you not given woman the right to conquer her destiny—why does she have to wait head bowed by the roadside waiting with tired patience hoping for a miracl in the morrow" Rabindranath Tagore said this in the beginning of this millennium. The millennium has drawn to a close—today we are not waiting for a miracle, the miracle is within us.

There shall be peace on Earth
But not until—
Each child shall daily eat his fill
Go warmly clad against the winter wind
And learn his lessons with a tranquil mind
And thus released from hunger, fear and need
Regardless of his colour race or creed
Look upwards smiling to the skies
His faith in man
Reflected in his eyes
Then there shall be peace

41

Women's Initiatives for Peace in South Asia

As a young thirty year old, my heart used to swell with pride when I saw our brave Jawans marching in step as my father-in-law took the salute. I was proud of our great standing Army considered to be among the best in the world and our victories on the battlefield.

But my mind saw a sea change in '1971. I was still proud of our brave soldiers but tempered with a realization on the futility of war. A young twenty-two years old soldier died in my lap begging me to take care of his eighteen year old wife and unborn child. With the rest of the nation, I was given the responsibility of taking care of thousands of lives darkened by missiles and deadened by the roar of tanks. Is this civilization? Is this progress? What kind of nationalism is this which boasts of victory that is coloured by the blood of soldiers and the lives of orphans? Surely nationalism has a greater stake in the permanence of peace? Surely patriotism means the war against poverty and not war against another section of humanity.

For me peace was a personal agenda too, since as Founder President of the War Widows Association of India, I had seen agony at its most searing intensity. And since governments are deaf to the women's cry for peace and systematically keep them away from decision-making when it comes to deciding on conflicts, I had to approach the Almighty alone, hoping He would hear our cries. This led to our observing Interfaith Peace Prayer every year since the past 20 years at Amar Jawan Jyoti.

A century ago, there were only 16 billion people on earth. Currently, there are 6.3 billion people. Over the past century, humankind has experienced two world wars, more than 30 regional wars and 150 plus internal wars. War can only bring death and destruction. By no means can it create happiness nor solve problems. History tells us that those who instigate war will eat their own evil fruits.

Power itself tends to be arrogant and encroaching. Yet, love urges and leads those who possess power not to harm others. Science and technology are powerful, but it is love that makes those skilled in technology humane. By contrast, without love, it would be merciless and ruthless.

I was convinced that as women and children are the worst victims of war, we had to take initiative for Peace in our hands.

A bloody partition, fifty-three years of hostilities, three wars and innumerable border skirmishes between India and Pakistan were occurrences which people of both countries had learnt to bear with patience in the hope that the next year or next month will bring this nightmare to an end. But the nuclearization of both countries, each claiming to have outdone the other, has brought this proverbial patience to an end. The realization has taken root that in this game of one-upmanship between both governments, the people have been forgotten. Inexorable fact such as, it is people who make countries, people who chalk destinies and people who install governments have become embedded in the popular imagination. Centrality of people can never be overlooked or undermined; people are at the heart of decisions concerning the countries which they inhabit. Consequently, the argument that political decisions should be detached from public sentiment is flawed logic that needs to be expunged.

In the summer of 1999, when the guns boomed on the Kargil front and war rhetoric was at its highest pitch, many women, in their separate spaces, found themselves increasingly disturbed. The naked aggression and untold suffering on both sides was unnerving. Through the lens of television cameras, they saw it all; smoking guns, body bags, grieving mothers and wives—foregrounding the drum-rolls and bugles of valour and victory. A few women came together with their shared, yet unspoken grief. From this event was born the Women's Initiative for Peace in South Asia.

The year 1999 saw the culmination of three programmes on Peace involving WIPSA. All of them exemplified women's intervention and initiative in creating peace. On August 6th the day Hiroshima exploded peace gatherings were held at many places in South Asia.

In India several hundred women and men gathered at Gandhi Smriti, where Gandhiji, the universal symbol of peace, fell to an assassin's bullets. At dusk, each one, holding a lit candle and a flower, pledged to work for peace.

On August, 10th a cross-section of women met in a one-day conference "Women's Vision" "A culture of peace". The conference facilitated by UNIFEM focussed on women's initiative in peace and built consensus on several key issues which were identified during the course of the day. The idea of a "Bus of Peace to Lahore" originated at the conference.

On December, 19th women and men were mobilized all over India and in several countries of South Asia to form human chains for peace. Their slogan was "Peace for Empowerment and Empowerment for peace". The purpose of this initiative was to demand a war free and nuclear free South Asia and indeed, a nuclear free and war free world.

People to People Initiative

It was very evident that women of South Asia were not just making a call for peace. They were endeavouring to realize it. Since Indo-Pak relations were at the lowest ebb the people to people contact began with Lahore.

— On March 25th, 2000 41 women comprising a section of activists, lawyers, writers, teachers, artists etc. boarded the bus for Lahore. At Lahore and Islamabad they met, talked and listened to intellectuals, human right activists, politicians, common people finally the CEO of Pakistan Gen. Parvez Musharraf. It was a journey of discovery of commonalties, of differences, of issues that hint on solutions in sight.

— As a part of the ongoing process towards a planned strategy to build the pressure of public opinion a delegation of 64 women from Pakistan visited Delhi, Agra and Jaipur to interact with women's educational institutes, Women's Study Centre, minority groups and members of the government.

— The spontaneity with which people of both Pakistan and India responded to the people to people contact now charted the course for an action oriented strategy. This called for channelising political sensitivity in both countries.

— As a part of careful strategy to comprehend ground realities that obstruct peace, WIPSA India visited Jammu and Kashmir. This comprehension called for an informative campaign which would dispel the ignorance about Kashmir and political parties were called upon to initiate the healing process in Kashmir while citizens teams should independently examine the alleged atrocities in the State.

— The 4th initiative of WIPSA widened the people to people contact to comprise academics, professors, teachers, readers of the universities. This aim was to enhance opportunities for youth to youth exchange so that future relationship can be built on pillars of authentic information about each other.

The Learnings

— People to people contact is the surest way to build a pressure of public opinion for peace which no government can afford to ignore.

— Women though not part of the decision process when it comes to war or foreign relations are an integral part of the decision for peace. In fact for the first time women initiated a peace process which is now snow balling at such a swift pace.

— Historical, cultural and social commonalties ensure that a direct link of understanding can be built.

— Kashmir is an issue that troubles the peace process. But the optimism is high that a pragmatic process of compromises can solve the problem.

— The pragmatic view that half a century old distrust must be put behind.

— The approach that India as a vibrant democracy with an industrial, educational and commercial infrastructure has much to offer other South Asian countries.

— The vital need to build a cohesive South Asian identity that will ensure a greater negotiating muscle on the global stage.

— Above all the realization that despite what successive Governments in Pakistan have reiterated India has no hegemonistic design on Pakistan.

— The vital realization that peace in South Asia is no longer a choice but the only reality left for survival.

In order to facilitate the formation of a common world culture to be shared by all human beings, it is necessary to find common threads of universal values that are embedded in the existing civilizations. If found, threads of these common and universal values will enable people to live in peace, to avoid conflicts, and to promote mutual respect and cooperation among various cultures.

The Outcome

(I). The women's peace initiative has given an impetus to the process of peace. The warm welcome that the initiative has received bears witness to the fact that most women on both sides are committed to peace and reject the prejudices which have partly been state sponsored.

(II). There is the vital realisation that both Governments of India and Pakistan must end the rhetoric of violence and aggression.

(III). Responsible media must continue its effort in promoting peace and urges those who have glorified war and violence to play a positive role for the healthy survival of this region. We will strive to form networks of responsible media. WIPSA noted with concern that this propaganda of violence has also infected popular media such as film and television serials. In this regard the language used in the electronic media to communicate news and information has become incomprehensible and should be made intelligible to the people it addresses.

(IV). We demand an end to violence against women, be it on cultural, political or economic grounds.

(V). There should be a free exchange of newspapers, magazines and books in the region.

(VI). We are convinced that in order to restore the peace of mind of the people there is an urgent need for confidence building among the governments and among the peoples of both countries. To achieve this, several steps need to be taken. Among them are:

   (a) Intolerant militant forces of the region have to be marginalised and particularly the Governments of Pakistan and India urged to remove all Government patronage to such forces.

(b) The arms race and nuclearisation of the subcontinent must come to an end. There are misplaced priorities in a region where injustice, illiteracy, hunger, disease, child and maternal mortality is a rule rather than an exception.

(c) All educational curricula must be purged of inaccuracies, biases and prejudices. Our future generations should be educated primarily to recognise themselves as citizens of the world in order to promote peace among all human beings regardless of nationality, religious belief, caste, class or sex.

Who can take responsibility for today's world? Can the military or the politicians? Can businessmen or people with new technology?

I strongly feel that if women take the initiatives many issues can be resolved, because women communicate as women not as nationalities—as women with the greatest stake in the security of their progeny.

The truth is the more chaotic the world becomes as days go by, the more mankind thirsts for peace.

Then, how can peace the achieved? In today's world, orderliness has been destroyed. Therefore, to establish peace means to restore that order. To restore, subjects must find their positions and establish mutual, unified relations.

World peace has not come even through the worldwide efforts of the League of Nations and the United Nations, established to prevent further conflict following the First and Second World Wars. Nor through the efforts of religious organisations has a world of happiness been realized. The ideals of international communism and the dreams of fascism have likewise failed to bring about an ideal world. Even the highest levels of technical skill and political effort have not been able to bring peace and happiness to humankind.

Even now, tragic conflicts rage in many areas of the globe.... Peace and human happiness depend on the moral and spiritual development of people. This is because world peace, or a peaceful nation, is composed of individuals and families. Science and technical skill can be used for good-for the improvement of human life—when they are utilized by good people.

Peace is not desired on the world level alone, but also on the level of nations, societies, and families as well. Even individuals yearn for peace between their minds and bodies.

Of those various levels of peace, which level should be established first? It is easy to think that if world peace were established first, then on that basis the peace of nations, societies, families, and eventually individuals would also be established.

It is actually the reverse of the sequence necessary to establish peace. Individual peace must first be realised. Then family peace can soon follow, and only on that foundation can the peace of societies, nations, and the world be expected. This is because individuals are the basic units of families, and families are the basic units of societies and nations.

People have continued to pursue peace and happiness in many ways. However, they have not found satisfaction.

Throughout history, the saints and great teachers have devoted themselves to guiding families, societies and nations towards a peaceful and happy world.

In order to take on the challenges of the twenty-first century, we need true parents of human-kind, true teachers, and who can raise impeccable leaders on the basis of morality and spirituality.

In a developing country as India, the lifeline of progress is peace. Only in an economy capable of higher rate of social spending can women have access to education, better health facilities and viable economic opportunities. The empowerment that comes from within us needs the avenues of education, health, political and economic opportunities to sustain it. When woman endeavours for peace, it is not just for the security of her family or for care of her progeny - but ever more so for the security of her personhood.

42

The Unsung Brave

Kargil has been cleared—so the press tells us. It has been a great victory for India - so the government tells us. But in war there are no winners. There are only losers—loss of property, resources and precious human lives. The soldiers have made their ultimate sacrifice leaving behind bereaved families. The war has just begun for them - war against deprivation, poverty and loneliness. They are the unsung brave. It goes to the credit of the government that once the first shell shock had worn off, they quickly got their act together for aid and succour to the bereaved families. The Hon'ble Defence Minister convened a committee to put forth certain recommendations which the government accepted. The broad gist of the rehabilitation measures are:

- Fast Track procedure for speedy payment of ex-gratia compensation. Controller General of Defence accounts to settle all cases within 48 hours from date of receipt of claims.
- Ex-gratia lumpsum compensation payable increased from Rs. 2 lakh to Rs. 7.5 lakh along with family pension equal to last monthly salary drawn by the deceased soldier.
- In addition to ex-gratia payment of Rs. 7.5 lakh in case of death and Rs. 6 lakh in case of injury Rs. 5 lakh would be given to families to acquire - dwelling with an out of turn basis by housing projects or state housing boards.
- Rs. 2 lakhs additionally would be deposited in long term fixed deposits—the interest would go towards education of children.
- 500 petrol pumps and LPG dealership have been reserved for the bereaved families.

It is certainly a laudable effort on the part of the government to incorporate the families into the mainstream of life. But the problem has so many ramifications and there are so many slips and red tapes between the policy and the execution, that the families are never able to fully reap the benefits of the government's rehabilitation measures. Pushpa Rawat widow of Kripal Singh Rawat (4055826) of 18 Garhwal Rifles, mother of 5, lives in a rented house in Karbala, New Delhi. The landlord threatens to evict her from her house. When will the Rs. 5 lakh set aside for her dwelling reach her? For pregnant Mukesh widow of L/NK Satbir Singh (2886165) of 2nd Rashtriya Rifles, a separate dwelling unit away from her in-laws is a must since her life is threatened by them. At the moment she has got a reprieve on life because the sonagraph showed that she was carrying a son. The wheels of the government may move too late for Mukesh. The government needs to fix a time limit for disbursal of the money for a dwelling unit.

Available Options

On a personal interaction with the bereaved families it was clear that only 2 options existed with the widows:

- To continue staying with in-laws or parents.
- To stay in an independent unit.

The advantages of the first option are the continued relationship with the husband's family and a possibility of the children getting a share in the property. Of course in-laws and parents could provide the emotional support if—only if they are not blinded by greed for the compensation. On the other hand in the first option the widow trades away her financial independence for the shelter provided. She is also likely to be swindled of her money - as is the case with Vimlesh widow of L/NK Ravi Karan. Mother of 2 children, she is caught between the devil and the deep sea. Vimlesh on the one hand faces the jealousy of her in-laws since the total compensation is in her name. On the other hand she faces the greedy pressure from her parents, 2 unemployed brothers, and an unmarried sister. Most of these widows particularly in the states of Rajasthan, Haryana, Punjab and parts of Uttar Pradesh are pressurized to marry their brothers-in-law. Manoj Devi widow of Sepoy Naresh Muskoh (3179697) of 17 Jat will almost certainly be married off to her brother-in-law. After all her mother-in-law a 16 year old widow of 1971 aggression was married off to her brother-in-law!

Many of the widows prefer the second option of staying in 2 room tenements provided by the government in Regimental centres or cantonments nearest to their villages. Even though she would be away from relatives, she would not be beholden to anyone for her shelter. The financial independence is secure. Vocational training, educational opportunities, employment facilities are facilitated by this arrangement. The support system provided by other sisters in her plight would lessen the emotional trauma.

Role of Big Brother

What has clearly emerged from a detailed study of the bereaved family is that the armed forces would have to take an even more proactive role in the case of the families. If in individual regimental centres or cantonments, 2 room tenements can be provided, the forces would have at one place the families needing their care. One of the major obstacles in the disbursal of aid, and the follow-up on rehabilitation measures is the sheer distances. A congregated community would make investment guidance, educational opportunities, vocational training, employment facilities, counselling etc. practical and viable. The forces could make use of the services of retired officers, JCO's and the welfare centres to facilitate this role of a guardian. Reema Begum widow of L/NK Hussain Als (2690297), with only a coolie father-in-law for support can turn to the armed forces alone for support, guidance and care.

Financial Fall Outs

The compensation given is certainly generous and the government is making every attempt to ensure that she is not swindled of her right, by depositing the cheque in the name of the widow. But the money itself divides her away from her in-laws. For those who adopt the options of staying with the in-laws, some part of the compensation must be made available to them. The compensation attracts the greed of relatives and an illiterate widow is very easy to dupe. Illiterate Malhori Devi widow of L/NK Kharak Singh (3180920) does not even know-how many zeroes are there in Rs. 7.5 lakh. The welfare institutions of the armed forces, NGOs, Banks and financial institutions must ensure that proper and viable investment guidance is made available to them.

The complete expense incurred by injured soldiers in any private institution is borne by the government. Often children of deceased soldiers require specialized treatment which sometimes the army hospitals may not be able to provide. Kamlesh widow of Naik Soran Singh of Rajputana Rifles has a 6 year old son with a hole in the heart. He needs specilized treatment. Possibly the government/armed forces could provide special medical cards to the bereaved families which could obtain treatment for them in any private hospital or institution.

The Armed forces must with all firmness work out a system by which marriages are registered in their own records, and this should be accepted by the civil authorities too. Ideally still, dual registration both with the armed forces and civil authorities must be compulsory and immediate nominations too should be made simultaneously. Many widows share the plight of 18 year old Sunita, widow of Sepoy Gajpal Singh (3189532) of 17 Jat who has still to get her compensation as her name had not been nominated in the official papers.

The government while granting compensation must make the tax status clear. This alone can prevent petty officials from making a profit from ignorance. Finanally all ex-gratia payments must be uniform for all states. The soldiers were Indians fighting for India. Why should there be a distinction between a soldier from UP and one from Rajasthan?

Zilla Sainik Boards

These boards certainly need to be rejuvenated to take a more proactive role. The very composition needs to change. These male dominated Zilla Sainik boards, with a strong gender bias can hardly be a focus of emotional counselling for the widows. How would these gunghat clad women ever confide in them? More often than not, these boards want to settle matters quickly by joining hands with the family in pressurizing the widow to marry her brother-in-law. As Geeta widow of L/Nk Rishi Pal is being pressurized in village Sonali Khend, Panipat. There must be a woman member in the Zilla Sainik Board - ideally an educated war widow from that region and an NGO representative. The Boards have to take on the role of counsellors. Kalpana widow of L/NK Naresh (3185589) of 4 Jat received the mutilated, tortured body of her husband. Yogendra Singh's (2893507) parents too received the mutilated body of their son. Their agony is difficult to fathom. Tremendous and consistent emotional counselling is needed to exorcise their grief and rage.

New Paradigms

The governmental perspective of the rehabilitation measures must undergo a qualitative change - to make the package more viable, more in keeping with the demands of the new millennium. The attitude earlier was to see the widows as beneficiaries. They must be seen as primary authors and actors of their own development. The strategy should not be to just provide services, but to empower and mobilize self reliant action by providing an enabling environment. The rehabilitation package must seek with the help of NGOs and Armed Forces to make the war widow a self-supporting entitity. Aid should not be seen as a one time availability. Care of the bereaved families is a continuous process as the Armed Forces have realized. Most of the widows are between the ages of 18-25. Any programme created for them has to be long-sighted keeping future options in view. This alone is the dignity that we can accord to the unsung brave.

43
Sustainable Development

"Poverty anywhere constitutes danger to prosperity everywhere". Economic disturbance and imbalance m one area are bound to create repercussions in other areas also. We can only achieve peace and progress if the population and general masses share the fruits of prosperity. Hence it is essential that we have sustainable development so that the fruits of progress are enjoyed by one and all a like. It is also essential for the whole world to unite and work in close cooperation with one another and maintain balance. When we look at the maintenance of this balance of cooperation we must try and understand that poverty in India is a concern of not only Indians but the world at large. Hence as the late Mr. Jenks, Director General of ILO put it "let us tackle together the problem of population, poverty and productivity". Needless to say this was the overriding concern as reflected in the preamble *to the United Nations charter.*

In order to achieve sustainable development in *the* world a progressive agricultural, political, social and cultural climate is necessary. Social security of the masses is the basis of a healthy and sound democratic structure which we are endeavouring to build up and each one of us should plunge into effective action and create a new social order of contentment, happiness and prosperity. We need "Development that meets the needs of the present without compromising the ability of future generations to meet their own needs".

Mr. V.V. Giri in his monograph: "Towards Solving Poverty and Unemployment" has concluded his study with the pertinent observation that politicians, economists, industrialists, educationists, social workers and all others should come together to wage a crusade against poverty and want.

I would like *to* consider a few specific points that we need to consider at the World Summit for Sustainable Development. Role of women in sustainable development has to be emphasized and to note that while women continue to perform their traditional domestic roles, more and more women are now involved in also earning livelihoods. It should be noticed that there are several female headed households, where women are the sole bread winners and the conference at Johannesburg must have a major thirust at policy level to ensure equity and justice to them.

There are three million elected representatives in India (0.8 million women and 6 million dalits) at all levels and I feel now women in India and more and more people are being involved at the grassroot democracy that is Panchayati Raj. This figure represents more than 240,000 gram panchayats, about 6000 intermediate level tiers and more than 500 district panchayats. These panchayats cover more than 580,000 villages and nearly 99.6 per cent of the rural population. Planning policies and economic programmes have to be activated at the Panchayat level. The activisation of the panchayats in the country can be brought about only through adding of schedules of economic services as part of a well knit programme for fully involving these women at the grassroots.

A massive effort has to be made towards capacity building of panchayati women. Women, while continuing to perform their traditional domestic roles are increasingly involved in earning livelihoods. In many poor households they are often the principal or the sole bread winner. A major thrust at the policy level is necessary to ensure equality and justice for them. Literacy and basic education are essential for enabling the poor to access the benefits offered by development initiatives and market opportunities. Basic education is therefore a precondition for sustainable development.

While I am talking about female headed households, panchayats and education, I would like to mention the role of women vis a vis water. It is not unknown to most of us the involvement of women for this prime natural resource and the basic human need. Women's role should not be belittled in managing water when and where it is required.

I have just come back from Narmada valley where I met thousands of tribal people still living in the 18th century or 17th century yet they all spoke about the water, floods, protecting the ecosystem and food security. They spoke about forests being preserved in order to have proper social, economic and environmental values of water. It is indeed very important to reflect the links between surface and groundwater and those between inland and coastal water keeping in mind the growing urbanization and the need to maintain ecosystem. Women need rights over land, forest and water management.

It would not be out of place here to also mention the role of women and democratic governance. I dream of a governance that can promote and support sustainable development. To have this dream fulfilled we need a political leadership and bureaucracy that is well informed. We need transparency and accountability in institutions. Focus should be on poverty eradication, protection of environment. To get a greater share for women at the participatory decision-making level and insist for 33 per cent reservation for women, we need legislation for this.

Two-thirds of the Indian population depends on agriculture as means of livelihood and yet we very often hear about drought and hunger death and suicides by fanners. Agriculture is an integrated part of the general development system. I would be very happy if the food distribution system is put into the hands of women. That will make it possible for people to have easy access to good quality and quantity of food. I would once again like to mention that to remove hunger and malnutrition we need not just think about food, it is linked to acute poverty that women face and the reproductive rights and slowing down of the population growth.

Every village, every panchayat should have food banks at the grassroot level. This would empower women to organize themselves in several ways and also give them gender justice.

These are some of my stray thoughts on the need to incorporate women so that 50 per cent of the population can also lead a healthy, sound democratic life and create a new social order.

Take the case of India, where the shameful paradox of plenty fails to move the government to wage a war against hunger and malnutrition. And that too in a country, which alone has a third of the world's estimated 800 million hungry and tragically over 65 million tones of food stocks rotting in the open.

Let us not forget the single women who are intertwined into the fabric of the country. Here I would like to give speciai emphasis on the widows and war widows who are neglected, torn by war and conflict and left to fend for themselves. They have thes right to earn their livelihood. I call upon the policy-makers to initiate a sustainable development programme for these unfortunate women so they can lead their lives in dignity.

44

Participatory Democracy

Much has been said about the need and the needlesness of reservation for women in the Parliament. A nation is a living pulsating entity - changing and throwing up new aspirations and challenges. A visionary Parliament, as our founding fathers hoped it to be, will constantly evolve devolve and evolve again new combinations and permutations keeping the changing economic, social, legal and political factors in view. Socio-economic framework is changing rapidly to bring women into the lives of employed millions. Either as a housewife or as a professional she contributes towards nation building. And then the lawmakers of the nation turn around and say that we can reserve seats for the backward, the deprived the marginalized. But despite being violated despite the sexual, psychological and physical assault on you, despite economic dependence and deprivation, despite a heavily patriarchal legal code, despite a plethora of social tradition meant to supress you.......you are not marginalized enough, not discriminated against enough, not deprived enough, not weak enough to merit reservation in the Parliament.

The demand for a reservation is not new to our country. If I may recall in 1920 Ms. Sarojini Naidu and Margaret Cousins had led a small delegation of women demanding similar rights of representation as men. This was at that time when women in most western countries had no right to vote. Later in 1931, the Karachi session of the Indian National Congress had committed itself to political equality of women regardless of their status and qualifications in response to women organisations memorandum demanding complete adult franchise.

Formerly women's participation in politics or their presence in this area was not considered essential. We know that there are two major methods of political participation, one as voter, and the other as elective office for representation in legislature and government. Women's presence is visibly lacking. Despite persistent efforts women continue to be marginalized due to the patriarchal mindset of the society.

A major hurdle is really getting women into politics. It is not just a matter of finding women willing to stand for election but getting women to show that first vital interest in participating, which is registering to vote. Around the country women are being mobilised by the Women's movement and local female politicians - to take more interest in politics.

The campaign for women's reservation in the Lok Sabha and the Legislative Assemblies has been going on since the past five years. This initiative is without question to establish political equality which is guaranteed in our Constitution. The campaign that has been carried on by the NCW and the women's movement has created sustained public interest from grassroots onwards to assert the rights of women. The campaign without question signifies the social and political space created by women's movement and the NCW in India for building up an effective initiative for the rights of women. We have been striving hard to pave the networking and alliance with different groups of women activists all over the country trying to evolve the identity of women as one political constituency in India.

The Bill was introduced in the Lok Sabha on 13th September, 1996. 1 hope the number 13 does not elude us from 33 per cent! The Bill that was supposed to be passed on the very same day is still a far cry towards reality. All political parties had reached a consensus that 33 per cent reservation for women should be made in the Legislature. The highlights of the bill are:

1. There should not be less than l/3rd seats reserved for women in Lok Sabha and Legislative Assemblies.

2. The reservations are for indefinite period.

3. The reserved constituencies are to be determined through a draw of lots because for SCs and STS, constituencies are reserved on the basis of the proportion of the population. Constituencies with a high SC/ST population are supposed to be delimited after some years. Since the population of women

is unevenly spread through out the country, this formula cannot be applied to them. The draw of lots systems mean every time a new set of constituencies will be declared as reserved for women.

4. There is also a provision for parallel reservations for SCs and STs, which is to say women belonging to SCs and STs will be getting one-third of seats reserved for people of that category, that is quota within a quota.

5. The Bill leaves out of its purview reservations in the Rajya Sabha and Legislative Council.

The denial of rightful share of political power to women who constitute half of the total population is a global phenomenon. Today the world is watching us to see if we would be able to gain this historical step towards equality. In a polity where money, feudalism and muscle power dominate, women's political participation is not only difficult because of the patriarchal structure of the parties but virtually impossible. We have noticed that women were denied their rightful share in the power by a virtual monopolisation of party tickets by men.

Most of the women MPs confided to me that they continued to be elected, because, they say that they are known for their track records which speak well for them. To be elected, a woman needs to join a political party. The potential candidate must go through a selection process by applying to and being endorsed by their party, then campaigning, usually with the other endorsed candidates, to convince the electorate of their credibility and ability.

Several women's organisations have shown that solidarity among women can fight even powerful vested interest lobbies and today if all of us come together we will be able not only to give good governance but set up good parliamentary democracy.

I also feel that women have a special place in politics and that "we are better organisers and leaders. Men sometimes overlook issues that women can see clearly. We can dig in our heels and give the men something to think about."

I have explored the possibility that women coalitions identify potential women candidates to be fielded. When we ask women about fielding women we are told "We are getting the support of the ladies in the town," they said. "I don't think we will have a problem reaching our target if we field the candidates. "Things are changing and now women are aware of their rights. They can vote for who they like and don't have to be bullied by their husbands to vote for their preferred candidates and how they can also be prospective candidates."

Some women said that women who were already known as social workers made good candidates. "They are known and are easy to contact so constituents, particularly women can air their problems" they said. "Aspiring candidates should stay in their own area, where they are known, and look for an issue they can speak on such as the drinking water, environment, health, schooling etc." Being female is important, it is not the main criteria for election.

"People see you as a familiar face, someone they can come back to with a problem that needs sorting out".

They also deal with many of the women's issues that come before the public. "Women should be more active and more vocal, of course they have their roles as citizens and part of that role is in local government." Training aims to give women the opportunity to have a greater say, show they can be heard at all levels, so that their particular viewpoints are taken into consideration at the decision making levels".

Common people and women at the grassroot level are all clamouring for the smooth passing of this Bill. Hence opposition of this Bill if any is not from the common people of our country but from male politicians who are reluctant to give 1/3 seats of power.

Party Democracy: Rationale

Contrary to what has often been said, democracy in India marginalises women. But, humanity is composed of two, women and men. The concept of "parity" ensues from this reality - as a recognition of the fact that both women and men have something to bring to society. No real democracy is possible in India if the question of equality between women and men is not regarded as one of the constitutive elements of the political system, as well as universal suffrage, the separation of powers and accountability. A real democracy will therefore necessarily be a "parity" democracy, which will integrate not merely half of humanity but humanity as a whole, and thus, every member of the community. In order to achieve this objective, the strategy of parity should consist of measures which will ensure full participation of women at all levels and in all aspects of the functioning of a democratic society, on an equal footing with men.

Parity is, in the end, the best way to guarantee that women have the right to defend their own interests, as it is clear that, until now, men have not wanted or not been able to defend the interests of their whole electorate, especially the interests of women. They have not been capable of ensuring the respect of equality of rights and opportunities for each and everyone. The injustice lies also in the face that men, thanks to their over-representation, have been able to put forward the diverse interests that different groups of men can have, whereas women, whose interests are just as diverse as those of men, have not been able to do so. Because of their very low number in political and public life, women who have been elected are always expected to defend "Women's interests", as if women were a homogeneous group or an interest group, having only common interests.

In the prevailing social context, women have been confined to the private sphere as if they were the only ones entrusted with the reproduction and care of the human species, and all the social structures have functioned in relation to the masculine norm. If democracy is considered as having to integrate all social forces, it is obvious that such a relegation can no longer be tolerated in a democratic society, whatever the structure of that society a new perspective and mindset needs to be inculcated in society.

Who says that tokenism is not the order of the day. Men, women all have the temptation to overwhelming play to the gallery. When we talk about reservation men look surprised and say—wasn't Indira Gandhi the Prime Minister of this country? worse they quote the South Asian countries being headed by women presidents and prime ministers. Then they quote several hundred laws favouring women. Some of them cynically observe various untouchability. Isn't the president of India a member of the lower caste. One could go on like this, but the problem of tokenism cannot be solved. Heated discussions ensued in the Parliament on the 23rd of Dec. 1999 and the Lok Sabha was thrown into a turmoil once the reservation bill.

Thanks to the ingenuity of the Union Law Minister Mr. Ram Jethmalani the Government was able to introduce the bill after having failed three times before, first in 1996, then in 1997 and last in 1998. Amid pandemonium the speaker Mr. Balayogi asked for voice vote which though inaudible was announced loudly. The Samajbadi Party leader Mr. Mulayam Singh Yadav refused to accept the verdict and Mr. Vajpayee the Prime Minister was heard saying that he had never in his 40 years as a parliamentarian experienced such incident in the Lok Sabha. The bill seeks to reserve one-third seats to the Lok Sabha, the Legislative Assemblies of the states and the National Capital Territory of Delhi for a period of 15 years.

Swami Vivekananda once stated "No nation can be great if half of its population is degraded and discriminated against. Women constitute half of India's teeming billion. Political participation is a vital link towards total empowerment of women. With that empowerment she, as many of my brothers seem to fear, is not a threat to men but a partner in progress the effective participant—the true Bhagidhari.

Appendices

Incidence of Crime Committed Against Women during 2001-2004 (Source: National Crime Record Bureau)

	2001	*2002*	*2003*	*2004*
Rape	16,075	16,373	15,847	15,618
Kidnapping	14,645	14,506	13,296	13,893
Dowry Death	6,851	6,822	6,208	6,540
Cruelty by Husband/Relatives	49,170	49,237	50,703	47,565
Molestation	34,124	33,943	32,939	31,181
Sexual Harassment	9,746	10,155	12,325	NA
Importing of Girls	114	76	46	112
Eve-teasing	NA	NA	NA	13,202
ITPA	8,796	6,598	5,510	4,990
Indecent Representation of Women Prohibition Act	1,052	2,508	1,043	3,088
Dowry Prohibition Act	3,222	2,816	2,684	2,534
Total	**1,43,795**	**1,43,034**	**1,40,601**	**1,38,723**

Percentage of Crimes Against Women in the Year 2005

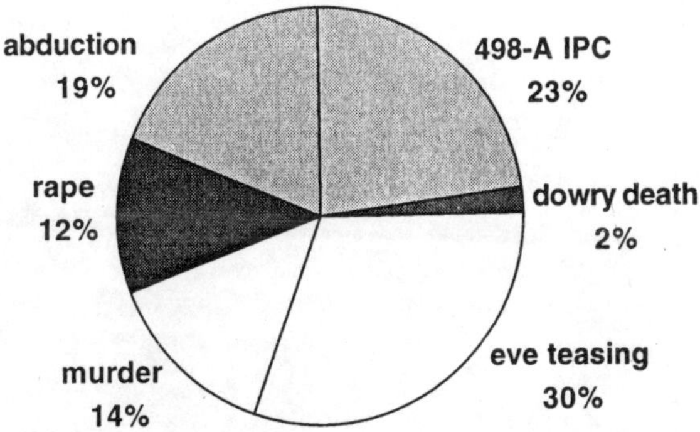

Statistics of Rapes in New Delhi (Statistics Compiled by the Delhi Police for the year 2005)

2004 total **540** **2005** total **642** 19% increase

% of dropouts who were illiterates dropouts or matriculates **95.5**

% of dropouts who were aged between 12 – 18 years **61.2**

Raped by a Stranger

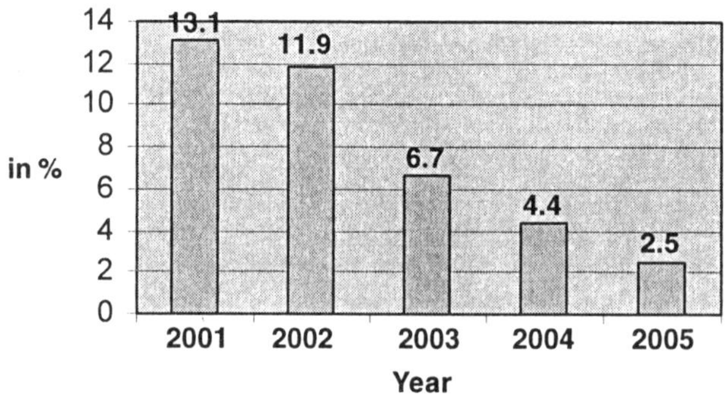

Number of Girls per 1000 Boys in India (aged 0 – 6 years)
(Source: Lancet Medical Journal)

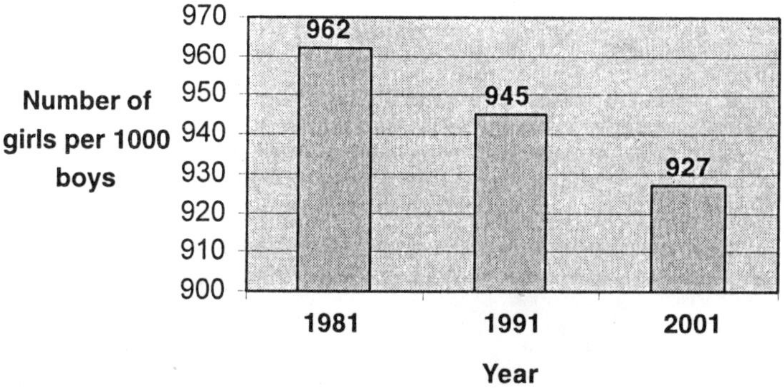

There are **0 – 5 million** missing female births per year.

Indicating **10 million** female fetuses have been aborted in the past 2 decades.

Crime Chart (Statistics Compiled by the Delhi Police for the year 2005)

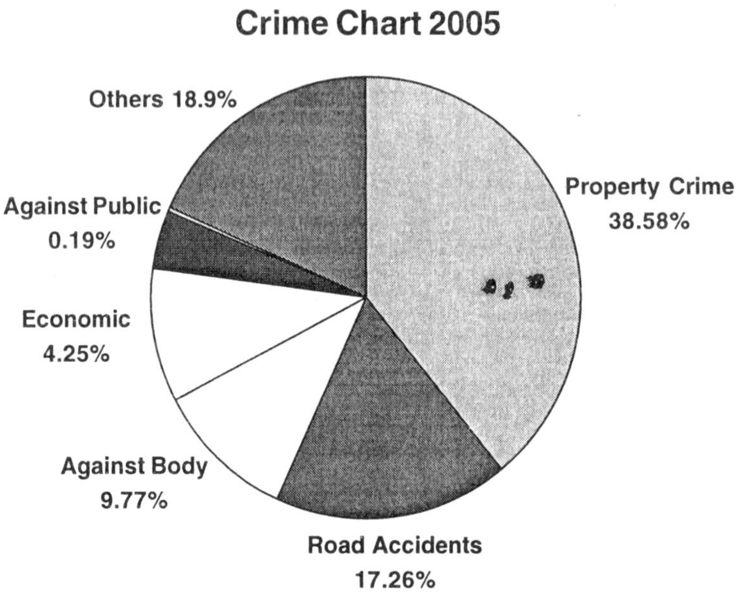

Table 5. Incidence of IPC Crimes against Body during 2003

Sl. No.	State/Ut	Murder	Attempt to Commit Murder	C.H. Not Amounting to murder	Kidnapping & Abduction	Hurt	Causing Death by Negligence	Total IPC Crimes Against Body	Percentage share	Crime Rate	Percentage To Total IPC Cog-Crimes
(1)	(2)	(3)	(4)	(5)	(6)	(7)	(8)	(9)	(10)	(11)	(12)
	States:										
1.	Andhra Pradesh	2667	1678	147	1485	41545	8515	56037	13.84	71.86	35.70
2.	Arunachal Pradesh	77	20	3	68	427	0	595	.15	52.65	28.87
3.	Assam	1191	485	48	1628	4952	2086	10390	2.57	37.48	27.20
4.	Bihar	3771	3540	398	2427	8884	2574	21494	5.31	24.77	23.30
5.	Chhattisgarh	776	513	51	177	3653	1158	6328	1.56	29.13	16.46
6.	Goa	34	25	6	14	198	164	441	.11	30.95	19.65
7.	Gujarat	1114	478	29	1044	12611	3536	18812	4.65	35.74	.88
8.	Haryana	702	446	76	388	4153	971	6736	1.66	30.56	17.45
9.	H. P.	125	74	5	113	1385	463	2165	.53	34.65	18.03
10.	Jammu & Kashmir	929	1216	29	712	310	378	3574	.88	33.30	16.33
11.	Jharkhand	1482	957	109	487	3062	642	6739	1.66	24.07	20.93
12.	Karnataka	1506	1241	58	531	21913	172	25421	6.28	46.76	22.62
13.	Kerala	435	448	343	189	17696	35	19146	4.73	58.69	19.37
14.	M. P.	2227	2413	203	887	29358	3778	38866	9.60	61.34	20.34
15.	Maharashtra	2772	1412	113	926	29205	9378	43806	10.82	43.67	26.66
16.	Manipur	150	199	6	120	324	4	803	.20	32.41	31.65
17.	Meghalaya	175	60	17	49	106	41	448	.11	18.74	26.84
18.	Mizoram	46	36	3	8	142	11	246	.06	26.65	7.12
19.	Nagaland	91	34	8	38	48	41	260	.06	12.53	26.64

(1)	(2)	(3)	(4)	(5)	(6)	(7)	(8)	(9)	(10)	(11)	(12)
20.	Orissa	1044	1214	188	477	4759	2497	10179	2.51	26.91	21.53
21.	Punjab	731	644	89	464	4124	2226	8278	2.04	32.96	28.79
22.	Rajasthan	1262	1977	61	2238	26173	5074	36785	9.09	62.00	25.27
23.	Sikkim	14	7	3	0	56	18	98	0.2	17.47	22.12
24.	Tamil Nadu	1591	1843	28	879	30228	9112	43681	10.79	68.69	27.79
25.	Tripura	254	87	0	146	534	109	1130	.28	34.30	32.16
26.	Uttar Pradesh	5284	3793	1525	2208	7760	4428	24998	6.18	14.34	26.29
27.	Uttaranchal	268	236	31	171	687	362	1755	.43	19.89	22.15
28.	West Bengal	1425	400	484	902	4172	2300	9683	2.39	11.69	15.83
	Total (States)	**32143**	**25476**	**3961**	**18776**	**258465**	**60073**	**398894**	**98.54**	**37.97**	**24.03**
	Union Territories										
29.	A & N Islands	21	4	1	2	110	0	138	.03	37.00	21.43
30.	Chandigarh	21	15	2	32	71	8	149	.04	15.60	5.31
31.	D & N Haveli	11	5	0	7	22	1	46	.01	19.74	13.61
32.	Daman & Diu	6	3	0	1	14	6	30	.01	17.86	11.15
33.	Delhi	485	407	65	1156	1708	402	4223	1.04	28.48	8.91
34.	Lakshdweep	0	0	0	0	1	0	1	.00	1.59	3.23
35.	Pondicherry	29	32	0	18	1053	182	1314	.32	130.75	29.09
	Total (Uts)	**573**	**466**	**68**	**1216**	**2979**	**599**	**5901**	**1.46**	**33.48**	**10.54**
	Total (All India)	**32716**	**25942**	**4029**	**19992**	**261444**	**60672**	**404795**	**100.00**	**37.89**	**23.59**

Table 6. Incidence and Rate of Crime Committed Against Women In States, UTs and Cities During 2003

Sl. No.	*State/Ut*	*Incidence*	*Percentage Contribution to All-India Total*	*Estimated Mid-Year Population (In Lakhs)*	*Rate of Total Cognizable Crimes*	*Rank **	*Rank ***
(1)	(2)	(3)	(4)	(5)	(6)	(7)	(8)
	States:						
1.	Andhra Pradesh	18382	13.1	778.7	23.6	1	1
2.	Arunachal Pradesh	139	0.1	11.3	12.3	15	15
3.	Assam	5312	3.8	277.3	19.2	6	12
4.	Bihar	5900	4.2	867.7	6.8	27	8
5.	Chhattisgarh	3336	2.4	217.2	15.4	12	15
6.	Goa	121	0.1	14.3	8.5	25	28
7.	Gujarat	5735	4.1	526.4	10.9	19	10
8.	Haryana	4170	3.0	220.4	18.9	7	14
9.	Himachal Pradesh	729	0.5	62.5	11.7	17	21
10.	Jammu & Kashmir	2164	1.5	107.3	20.2	4	19
11.	Jharkhand	2488	1.8	280.0	8.9	24	17
12.	Karnataka	5834	4.1	543.7	10.7	20	9
13.	Kerala	5653	4.0	326.2	17.3	8	11
14.	Madhya Pradesh	14547	10.3	633.7	23.0	2	2
15.	Maharashtra	11273	8.0	1003.1	11.2	18	5
16.	Manipur	137	0.1	24.8	5.5	33	26
17.	Meghalaya	69	0.0	23.9	2.9	34	29
18.	Mizoram	147	0.1	9.2	15.9	11	24
19.	Nagaland	25	0.0	20.8	1.2	35	31
20.	Orrisa	4946	3.5	378.2	13.1	14	13
21.	Punjab	2375	1.7	251.1	9.5	23	18
22.	Rajasthan	11812	8.4	593.3	19.9	5	4

(1)	(2)	(3)	(4)	(5)	(6)	(7)	(8)
23.	Sikkim	37	0.0	5.6	6.6	28	30
24.	Tamil Nadu	8888	6.3	635.9	14.0	13	6
25.	Tripura	537	0.4	32.9	16.3	10	22
26.	Uttar Pradesh	12840	9.1	1743.8	7.4	26	3
27.	Uttaranchal	886	0.6	88.3	10.0	22	20
28.	West Bengal	8508	6.1	828.3	10.3	21	7
	Total (States)	**136990**	**97.4**	**10505.9**	**13.0**		
Union Territories							
29.	A & N Islands	22	0.0	3.7	5.9	31	32
30.	Chandigarh	159	0.1	9.6	16.6	9	23
31.	D & N Haveli	13	0.0	2.3	5.6	32	33
32.	Daman & Diu	10	0.0	1.7	6.0	30	34
33.	Delhi	3282	2.3	148.3	22.1	3	16
34.	Lakshdweep	4	0.0	0.6	6.3	29	35
35.	Ponidcherry	121	0.1	10.1	12.0	16	27
	Total (Uts)	**3611**	**2.6**	**176.35**	**20.5**		
	Total (All- India)	**140601**	**100.0**	**10682.1**	**13.2**		

Table 6 A

Sl. No.	State/Ut	Incidence	Percentage Contribution to All-India Total	Population (In Lakhs)@	Rate of Total Cognizable Crimes	Rank *	Rank **
(1)	(2)	(3)	(4)	(5)	(6)	(7)	(8)
	Cities:						
36.	Agra	308	1.6	13.2	23.3	11	19
37.	Ahmedabad	815	4.2	45.2	18.0	19	8
38.	Allahbad	86	0.4	10.5	8.2	32	34
39.	Amritsar	103	0.5	10.1	10.2	29	32
40.	Asansol	171	0.9	10.9	15.7	21	30
41.	Bangalore	1227	6.3	56.9	21.6	15	4
42.	Bhopal	425	2.2	14.6	29.2	8	15
43.	Chennai	895	4.6	64.3	13.9	23	6
44.	Coimbatore	285	1.5	14.5	19.7	16	20
45.	Delhi (City)	2888	14.8	127.9	22.6	12	1
46.	Dhanbad	84	0.4	10.6	7.9	33	35
47.	Faridabad	916	4.7	10.6	86.8	2	5
48.	Hyderabad	1945	9.9	55.3	35.1	4	2
49.	Indore	555	2.8	16.4	33.9	5	12
50.	Jabalpur	412	2.1	11.2	36.9	3	17
51.	Jaipur	634	3.2	23.2	27.3	9	10
52.	Jamshedpur	211	1.1	11.0	19.1	17	26
53.	Kanpur	445	2.3	26.9	16.5	20	13
54.	Kochi	160	0.8	13.6	11.8	26	31
55.	Kolkata	725	3.7	132.2	5.5	34	9
56.	Lucknow	603	3.1	22.7	26.6	10	11
57.	Ludhiana	428	2.2	14.0	30.7	7	14
58.	Madurai	258	1.3	12.0	21.6	14	23

(1)	(2)	(3)	(4)	(5)	(6)	(7)	(8)
59.	Meerut	363	1.9	11.7	31.1	6	18
60.	Mumbai	881	4.5	163.7	5.4	35	7
61.	Nagpur	270	1.4	21.2	12.7	25	22
62.	Nasik	178	0.9	11.5	15.5	22	29
63.	Patna	196	1.0	17.1	11.5	27	28
64.	Pune	413	2.1	37.6	11.0	28	16
65.	Rajkot	221	1.1	10.0	22.1	13	25
66.	Surat	277	1.4	28.1	9.9	30	21
67.	Vadodara	201	1.0	14.9	13.5	24	27
68.	Varanasi	101	0.5	12.1	8.3	31	33
69.	Vijaywada	1651	8.4	10.1	163.3	1	3
70.	Vishakhapatnam	242	1.2	13.3	18.2	18	24
	Total (Cities)	**19573**	**100.0**	**1078.80**	**18.1**		

1. * Rank on the basis of Rate of total cognizable crimes (Col. 6)
2. ** Rank on the basis of Percentage share (Col. 4)
3. @ based on actual census of 2001

Table 7. City-Wise Incidence of Cognizable Crimes (IPC) During 2003

Sl. No.	State/ City	Murder	Attempt to Commit Murder	Culpable Homicide Not Amounting to Murder	Rape						Dacoity
					Total	Custodial	Others	Total	Women & Girls	Others	
(1)	(2)	(3)	(4)	(5)	(6)	(7)	(8)	(9)	(10)	(11)	(12)
	Andhra Pradesh										
1.	Cyberabad	155	101	4	31	0	31	102	62	40	14
2.	Hyderabad	124	132	5	57	0	57	155	64	91	18
3.	Vijayawada	34	58	0	27	0	27	63	45	18	5
4.	Vishakhapatnam	19	21	0	9	0	9	30	20	10	4
	Assam										
1.	Guwahati	50	29	3	38	0	38	216	184	32	36
	Bihar										
1.	Patna	260	384	25	15	0	15	150	11	139	59
	Chhattisgarh										
1.	Durg	36	24	0	24	0	24	10	9	1	1
2.	Raipur	18	38	2	36	0	36	22	16	6	1
	Gujarat										
1.	Ahmedabad	90	68	3	18	0	18	157	96	61	31
2.	Bhavnagar	16	12	0	3	0	3	22	13	9	5
3.	Rajkot	37	12	1	5	0	5	34	30	4	7
4.	Surat	75	16	5	25	0	25	62	40	22	16
5.	Vadodra	38	28	1	8	0	8	36	31	5	6
	Haryana										
1.	Faridabad	29	14	1	15	0	15	41	34	7	2
	Jharkhand										
1.	Dhanbad	36	10	2	21	0	21	25	22	3	14
2.	Jamshedpur	71	112	2	48	0	48	43	40	3	21

(1)	(2)	(3)	(4)	(5)	(6)	(7)	(8)	(9)	(10)	(11)	
	Karnataka										
1.	Bangalore	216	280	1	34	0	34	132	11	121	46
2.	Belgaum	12	11	1	1	0	1	9	4	5	3
3.	Gulbarga	7	9	0	3	0	3	10	6	4	1
4.	Hubli Dharwad	23	18	0	3	0	3	11	4	7	4
5.	Mysore	26	22	0	8	0	8	9	7	2	3
	Kerala										
1.	Kochi	21	28	7	11	0	11	11	5	6	26
2.	Kozhikode	14	14	18	10	0	10	7	3	4	4
3.	Thiruvanathpuram	10	53	16	17	0	17	14	7	7	14
	Maharashtra										
1.	Amravati	31	25	2	26	0	26	15	12	3	6
2.	Aurangabad	28	26	1	8	0	8	19	13	6	17
3.	Mumbai	242	115	8	133	0	133	150	85	65	30
4.	Nagpur	104	40	0	26	0	26	36	29	7	16
5.	Nasik	27	20	1	11	0	11	14	12	2	13
6.	Navi Mumbai	50	19	0	16	0	16	17	7	10	10
7.	Pune	110	54	4	40	0	40	46	27	19	11
8.	Solapur	22	15	2	15	0	15	15	8	7	9
9.	Thane	111	63	4	51	0	51	58	35	23	23

Table 7 A. City-Wise Incidence of Cognizable Crimes (IPC) During 2003

Sl. No.	State/ City	Prepration and Assembly for Dacoity	Robbery	Burglary	Theft			Riots	Criminal Breach of Trust	Cheating	Counter-feiting
					Total	Auto Theft	Others Theft				
(1)	(2)	(3)	(4)	(5)	(6)	(7)	(8)	(9)	(10)	(11)	(12)
	Andhra Pradesh										
1.	Cyberabad	0	56	1041	1489	291	1198	49	67	691	8
2.	Hyderabad	1	91	1875	6574	2195	4379	231	158	2093	21
3.	Vijayawada	0	61	876	3417	351	3066	17	54	816	27
4.	Vishakhapatnam	0	5	281	532	174	358	1	81	290	24
	Assam										
1.	Guwahati	2	100	606	1157	248	909	415	168	213	7
	Bihar										
1.	Patna	25	594	377	1367	654	713	127	150	312	23
	Chhattisgarh										
1.	Durg	3	27	326	402	184	218	17	5	58	3
2.	Raipur	0	24	311	618	331	287	21	10	107	4
	Gujarat										
1.	Ahmedabad	6	365	959	5377	2287	3090	212	294	394	6
2.	Bhavnagar	0	21	121	330	182	148	46	22	56	5
3.	Rajkot	0	51	350	1525	655	870	98	38	77	10
4.	Surat	3	57	388	1749	1192	557	64	54	239	21
5.	Vadodra	0	44	434	1385	692	693	195	97	197	2
	Haryana										
1.	Faridabad	12	5	189	498	356	142	48	74	30	5
	Jharkhand										
1.	Dhanbad	3	21	82	231	28	203	102	2	32	0
2.	Jamshedpur	4	47	157	553	122	431	145	25	91	0

(1)	(2)	(3)	(4)	(5)	(6)	(7)	(8)	(9)	(10)	(11)	(12)
	Karnataka										
1.	Bangalore	46	311	1713	7123	2682	4441	273	241	1780	87
2.	Belgaum	2	32	84	139	62	77	35	13	65	2
3.	Gulbarga	2	14	77	92	36	56	31	1	34	0
4.	Hubli Dharwad	1	16	126	288	118	170	80	6	81	0
5.	Mysore	1	49	132	324	127	197	47	17	43	3
	Kerala										
1.	Kochi	0	66	304	486	145	341	220	19	290	1
2.	Kozhikode	0	23	494	335	145	190	399	17	233	2
3.	Thiruvanathpuram	0	113	334	442	185	257	311	19	277	8
	Maharashtra										
1.	Amravati	3	35	316	948	157	791	85	21	38	5
2.	Aurangabad	5	49	234	506	167	339	126	16	111	4
3.	Mumbai	53	239	2550	9793	2883	6910	131	392	1178	73
4.	Nagpur	37	172	1079	2022	722	1300	165	46	151	16
5.	Nasik	3	31	375	705	241	464	86	25	101	2
6.	Navi Mumbai	19	49	318	782	330	452	67	52	145	4
7.	Pune	8	97	868	2740	1568	1172	531	63	462	7
8.	Solapur	1	45	160	351	104	247	66	19	116	2
9.	Thane	20	148	929	1872	650	1222	238	76	570	20

Table 7 B. City-Wise Incidence of Cognizable Crimes (IPC) During 2003

Sl. No.	State/ City	Arson	Hurt	Dowry Death	Molestation	Sexual Harassment	Cruelty by Husband & Relatives	Importation of girls	Causing Death by Negligence	Other IPC Crimes	Total Cog-Crimes Under IPC
(1)	(2)	(3)	(4)	(5)	(6)	(7)	(8)	(9)	(10)	(11)	(12)
	Andhra Pradesh										
1.	Cyberabad	45	1203	25	96	78	543	1	787	3719	10305
2.	Hyderabad	68	4595	42	165	296	1082	0	489	1980	20252
3.	Vijayawada	21	2101	7	170	146	1208	0	249	727	10084
4.	Vishakhapatnam	3	362	3	11	30	146	0	195	1214	3261
	Assam										
1.	Guwahati	7	527	4	52	0	135	0	171	1664	5590
	Bihar										
1.	Patna	31	173	35	31	0	80	0	148	2179	6545
	Chhattisgarh										
1.	Durg	12	267	10	90	15	16	1	0	2321	3668
2.	Raipur	51	331	2	52	6	69	0	115	1828	3620
	Gujarat										
1.	Ahmedabad	10	1371	3	50	30	595	0	173	5987	16199
2.	Bhavnagar	4	0	0	1	7	18	0	0	836	1525
3.	Rajkot	16	357	5	8	13	158	0	87	1913	4802
4.	Surat	7	428	19	17	2	126	0	234	794	4401
5.	Vadodra	20	366	0	17	5	136	0	123	2574	5712
	Haryana										
1.	Faridabad	0	123	4	7	778	76	0	6	2030	3987
	Jharkhand										
1.	Dhanbad	0	307	11	5	0	2	0	0	1023	1929
2.	Jamshedpur	3	352	16	27	0	73	0	153	607	2550

(1)	(2)	(3)	(4)	(5)	(6)	(7)	(8)	(9)	(10)	(11)	(12)
	Karnataka										
1.	Bangalore	0	3487	34	213	39	213	0	84	12547	29260
2.	Belgaum	5	90	0	8	4	3	0	1	367	887
3.	Gulbarga	10	127	0	17	0	36	0	1	315	787
4.	Hubli Dharwad	0	183	3	3	9	28	0	4	906	1793
5.	Mysore	0	361	5	14	0	44	0	0	711	1819
	Kerala										
1.	Kochi	15	531	0	77	7	54	0	1	4654	6829
2.	Kozhikode	15	546	2	50	5	157	0	0	2372	4717
3.	Thiruvanathpuram	13	893	2	114	5	82	0	0	2452	5189
	Maharashtra										
1.	Amravati	20	435	3	45	19	77	0	71	760	2986
2.	Aurangabad	11	339	4	25	10	130	0	102	515	2286
3.	Mumbai	7	3562	8	282	44	199	0	632	5865	25686
4.	Nagpur	14	783	4	36	36	136	0	224	2214	7357
5.	Nasik	4	233	4	18	14	116	0	153	586	2542
6.	Navi Mumbai	1	319	6	28	7	55	0	291	606	2861
7.	Pune	7	983	2	61	92	166	0	368	2093	8813
8.	Solapur	10	197	4	19	3	72	0	76	463	1682
9.	Thane	10	1378	4	66	29	153	0	241	644	6708

Table 7 D

Sl. No.	State/City	Murder	Attempt to Commit Murder	Culpable Homicide Not Amounting to Murder	Total	Rape Custodial	Others	Kidnapping & Abduction Total	Women & Girls	Others	Dacoity
(1)	(2)	(3)	(4)	(5)	(6)	(7)	(8)	(9)	(10)	(11)	(12)
	Punjab										
1.	Amritsar	41	22	3	11	0	11	32	29	3	0
2.	Jalandhar	20	47	8	22	0	22	52	35	17	3
3.	Ludhiana	58	58	5	33	0	33	80	46	34	1
	Rajasthan										
1.	Ajmer	14	22	1	13	0	13	34	33	1	0
2.	Bharatpur	9	15	1	6	0	6	24	16	11	0
3.	Bikaner	20	43	0	7	0	7	19	19	0	0
4.	Jaipur	50	88	7	35	0	35	158	137	21	2
5.	Jodhpur	18	40	4	8	0	8	70	47	23	0
6.	Kota	23	137	0	13	0	13	96	80	16	0
7.	Udaipur	13	33	0	3	0	3	28	17	11	1
	Tamil Nadu										
1.	Chennai	71	279	4	38	1	37	34	0	34	6
2.	Coimbatore	22	17	0	4	0	4	6	1	5	3
3.	Madurai	27	39	1	7	0	7	24	16	8	5
4.	Salem	15	18	0	11	0	11	9	8	1	3
5.	Thirunelveli	12	38	0	4	0	4	10	10	0	1
6.	Trichy	17	11	0	6	0	6	14	7	7	1
	Uttar Pradesh										
1.	Agra	61	53	19	11	0	11	65	53	12	16
2.	Aligarh	62	56	16	5	0	5	51	31	20	1
3.	Allahabad	49	39	7	2	0	2	21	18	3	8

(1)	(2)	(3)	(4)	(5)	(6)	(7)	(8)	(9)	(10)	(11)	(12)
4.	Bareli	58	70	16	11	0	11	22	18	4	3
5.	Gorakhpur	24	42	13	6	0	6	13	0	13	0
6.	Kanpur	187	107	38	24	0	24	84	58	26	7
7.	Lucknow	103	69	18	20	0	20	81	64	17	5
8.	Meerut	74	58	3	14	0	14	46	28	18	4
9.	Moradabad	49	47	12	8	0	8	27	16	11	1
10.	Varanasi	49	36	11	4	0	4	14	6	8	3
	West Bengal										
1.	Asansol	28	5	5	8	0	8	11	11	0	2
2.	Howrah	18	5	12	6	0	6	12	7	5	5
3.	Kolkata	52	123	13	36	0	36	108	85	23	33
	Delhi										
1.	Delhi (City)	401	320	50	406	0	406	968	673	295	22

Table 7 E

Sl. No.	State/City	Murder	Attempt to Commit Murder	Culpable Homicide Not Amounting to Murder	Rape			Riots	Criminal Breach of Trust	Cheating	Dacoity
					Total	Custodial	Others				
(1)	(2)	(3)	(4)	(5)	(6)	(7)	(8)	(9)	(10)	(11)	(12)
	Punjab										
1.	Amritsar	5	14	126	144	81	63	2	19	144	4
2.	Jalandhar	2	4	190	215	120	95	0	6	323	1
3.	Ludhiana	18	12	336	722	358	364	0	45	330	8
	Rajasthan										
1.	Ajmer	1	14	147	250	129	121	15	20	103	2
2.	Bharatpur	0	8	36	192	93	99	1	11	122	0
3.	Bikaner	1	6	73	187	89	98	0	15	66	0
4.	Jaipur	1	42	675	2553	1213	1340	918	192	1147	17
5.	Jodhpur	2	16	208	804	456	348	60	53	399	1
6.	Kota	0	35	220	743	433	310	27	28	295	2
7.	Udaipur	1	23	104	246	132	114	72	18	229	1
	Tamil Nadu										
1.	Chennai	0	74	649	3779	959	2820	43	19	927	8
2.	Coimbatore	0	29	173	993	374	619	106	27	69	3
3.	Madurai	0	12	83	468	82	386	64	5	115	2
4.	Salem	2	2	51	337	144	193	14	1	25	1
5.	Thirunelveli	0	9	39	124	14	110	40	6	14	0
6.	Trichy	0	5	62	449	99	350	10	1	51	2
	Uttar Pradesh										
1.	Agra	0	30	149	582	375	207	83	58	94	21
2.	Aligarh	6	24	50	269	139	130	50	28	43	2

(1)	(2)	(3)	(4)	(5)	(6)	(7)	(8)	(9)	(10)	(11)	(12)
3.	Allahabad	0	20	70	232	151	81	27	28	71	4
4.	Bareli	0	22	74	176	85	91	26	26	59	1
5.	Gorakhpur	0	18	42	162	52	110	49	27	49	0
6.	Kanpur	3	67	167	830	588	242	61	71	119	5
7.	Lucknow	1	93	301	962	118	844	77	144	266	11
8.	Meerut	10	42	116	485	274	211	36	42	71	11
9.	Moradabad	0	13	28	155	69	86	14	28	43	3
10.	Varanasi	2	19	61	303	215	88	26	35	27	19
	West Bengal										
1.	Asansol	73	9	8	75	15	60	37	1	20	1
2.	Howrah	89	21	2	275	87	188	29	18	63	2
3.	Kolkata	60	173	144	3684	929	2755	200	222	990	95
	Delhi										
1.	Delhi (City)	102	372	1566	14322	6886	7436	59	389	1962	43

Table 7 F

Sl. No.	State/City	Murder	Attempt to Commit Murder	Culpable Homicide Not Amounting to Murder	Total	Rape Custodial	Others	Riots	Criminal Breach of Trust	Cheating	Dacoity
(1)	(2)	(3)	(4)	(5)	(6)	(7)	(8)	(9)	(10)	(11)	(12)
	Punjab										
1.	Amritsar	1	139	3	7	4	43	0	30	349	1143
2.	Jalandhar	0	196	5	15	0	80	0	102	735	2026
3.	Ludhiana	9	260	5	70	159	111	0	173	1763	4256
	Rajasthan										
1.	Ajmer	0	114	7	19	0	154	0	66	904	1900
2.	Bharatpur	5	3	2	6	0	24	0	36	976	1480
3.	Bikaner	3	187	8	5	0	65	0	54	590	1349
4.	Jaipur	18	862	14	95	0	347	0	344	4014	11579
5.	Jodhpur	6	884	4	34	4	208	0	104	948	3875
6.	Kota	7	253	8	46	1	188	0	80	1527	3729
7.	Udaipur	4	328	0	8	0	1	0	64	570	1747
	Tamil Nadu										
1.	Chennai	1	749	18	90	212	159	0	547	1173	8580
2.	Coimbatore	1	115	1	18	6	24	0	159	1411	3187
3.	Madurai	6	224	10	29	49	35	0	84	1964	3253
4.	Salem	2	149	3	11	13	13	0	110	1280	2070
5.	Thirunelveli	4	68	0	11	18	21	0	68	578	1065
6.	Trichy	3	86	0	5	41	44	0	131	1531	2470
	Uttar Pradesh										
1.	Agra	1	213	26	30	44	140	0	30	501	2227
2.	Aligarh	33	86	9	16	6	63	0	61	190	1127
3.	Allahabad	3	31	8	3	14	37	0	66	332	1072

(1)	(2)	(3)	(4)	(5)	(6)	(7)	(8)	(9)	(10)	(11)	(12)
4.	Bareli	0	108	9	6	51	56	0	75	446	1315
5.	Gorakhpur	0	55	6	4	21	23	0	34	1105	1690
6.	Kanpur	7	328	43	39	144	106	0	260	921	3618
7.	Lucknow	6	48	19	36	267	194	0	233	1323	4277
8.	Meerut	1	19	10	13	153	141	0	159	133	1641
9.	Moradabad	1	23	11	15	77	56	0	30	221	862
10.	Varanasi	0	63	10	2	58	14	0	69	321	1146
	West Bengal										
1.	Asansol	0	100	4	19	1	128	0	64	728	1327
2.	Howrah	1	101	5	11	1	65	0	0	676	1417
3.	Kolkata	0	1225	16	185	57	222	0	447	2629	10714
	Delhi										
1.	Delhi (City)	54	495	100	406	81	1163	0	348	17322	41961

Index

A

Abdul Majid, 271
Abdul-Bahai, 18
Acquisition and Requisition Act, 272
Action Committee Against Arms Race, 302
Adi Shankaracharya, 15
Adult Literacy Programme, 119
Africa, 60, 61, 63
African Traditions, 64
Agiary Temple, 13
Agra Summit, 148
Agricultural Ancestral Property, 19
- Workers, 22-23

AIDS, 60
AIDS, HIV, STD, 285
Akbar the Great, 155, 271
All Party Hurriyat Conference, 275
Amar Jawan Jyoti, 305
Amazonian Society, 189
Amnesty International, 113
Anant Nag, 270
Andhra Pradesh, 144, 204
Anganwadi Programme, 119
Anti-Arrak Agitation (Nellore—AP), 75, 182
Anti-Dowry Movement, 162
Anti-Poverty Measures, 128
Armed Forces, 125-126, 131-33, 317
Arunachal Pradesh, 144
Asma Jehangir, 122
Ayodhya, 185
Azerbaijan and Bulgaria, 112

B

Babri Masjid, 188
Backward Social Groups, 243
Bahai Religion, 18
Bakshi Gulam Mohammed, 272
Balyogi, 328
Bangladesh, 68-69, 249, 251-52, 281, 303
- Liberation, 273
- War, 117

Baramullah, 270
Beijing
- Conference, 66
- Platform for Action, 87, 181, 216
- Plus Five, 247, 302

Bhagawat Gita, 16
Bhawri Devi case, 32
Bhopal Declaration, 28
Bhutan, 69, 249
Bible, 16
Bihar, 25
Bihar and UP, 95
Bihar—UP, 192
Bonded Labour (Labourers), 22, 24, 26, 32
Border Conflicts, 279

Bride Burning, 181, 217
British Empire, 155, 174
Buddha, 154, 253
Buddhism, 154
Budgam, 270

C

Capital Punishment, 107-08, 111, 230
Caste and Customs, 38
- Oppression, 24
- System, 27
- Violence, 189

CEDAW (Convention on Elimination of Discrimination Against Women), 66, 99, 295
Chawla, Kalpana, 7
Chen Shiu-Bian, Pres. Taiwan, 174
Chidanandaji, 151
Child Labour, 16, 193-95, 281
- Marriage, 39, 60, 188, 242
- Marriage Restraint Act, 1929, 94
- Pornography, 16
- Prostitutes, 282
- Sex Industry, 281

China, 111, 173-75
Chipko Movement, 104
Chitrakut, 32
Civil Law, 38
Civil Liberties Organization, 228
Common Minimum Programme, 101
Compulsory Education for Children, 195
Constitution of India, 23, 38, 213
Costa Rica, San Marino and Venezuela, 112
Counselling,
- Family, 48
- Personal, 47
- Religious, 48

Cousin, Margaret, 323
Credit Schemes, 128
Crime Against Women, 43, 87, 179
- Women's Cell, 75

Criminal Procedure Code, 42, 51
Cross-Border Terrorism, 248
Custodial Killings, 275
Customary Law, 63

D

Dalit Massacre, 21
Dalit Women, 21-27, 31-34
Discrimination Against, 22
- Sexual Abuse of-, 25

Dalits, 32, 189
- In India, 31
- Slavery, 31

Dalits of India, 21
Dalmia, Aruna, 147
Darbar Saheb, Amritsar, 14
Darul-Ulum, 36
Dayton (Ohio), 122
Death Penalty, 107-08, 110-13
Decision-Making, 15, 84, 98, 161, 243-44, 293
Deen-e-Ilahi, 155
Deshpande, Ms. Nirmala, Gandhian, 273-75
Didava, 270
Dina Mata, 13-14
Directive Principles of State Policy, 213, 289
Discrimination, 5, 27-29, 32-33, 71, 72, 96, 179, 182, 185, 191, 240, 251, 290

- Policies, 230

Discriminatory Laws, 71
Disinheritance in Africa, 63
Doda, 270
Domestic Violence, 5, 182, 215, 221-22, 230
Domestic Violence Bill, 76, 145
Doraiswamy Raju and Arijit Pasayat, Justice, 49
Dowry, 38-39, 42-44, 74, 102, 217, 219-20, 242, 298
Deaths, 219-20, 249
- Prohibition Act, 42-43, 95, 219
- System, 43

Drug Abuse, 92
Drugs, 68
Dubai/Bombay, 14
Durban Conference on Racism, 28

E

Economic, 95, 252, 281
- Of Widow, 65
- Political, 84, 98

Economic and Social Organization, 110, 113
- Discrimination, 65
- Disparities, 5
- Liberalization, 280
- Policy, 76
- Reforms, 75, 200
- Rights, 15, 19
- System, 19

Economy, 16, 67, 149
Education, 15-18, 22, 31, 35, 55, 63, 68, 74, 96-97, 128, 203, 207, 211, 233-36, 240-41, 250, 252, 303, 311, 320
- Adult, 128, 281
- Compulsory, 252
- Female, 240-41
- Non-Formal, 93
- Of Women, 18
- Physical, 57
- Vocational, 93

Educational
- Ethics, 18
- Institutions, 27, 299
- Opportunities, 233
- Programmes, 212

Empowerment, 92, 95, 126, 143, 241, 252, 292, 397, 311
Equal Property Rights, 42
European Convention on Human Rights, 111-12
Eve-Teasing, 49-50, 181, 217

F

Family
- Counselling Centres, 39, 46
- Courts, 218-19
- Planning, 294

Farooq Abdullah, 276
Fatwa, 36
Female
- Circumcision, 50

Foeticide, 5, 74, 192, 249
- Literacy, 252
- Prison, 229

Fernande, George, 122
Finance Commission, 79
Five-Year Plan (9th), 235
Food Security, 101, 321
Forest Land, 76
Fourth World Conference on Women (Beijing), 244, 290

France, Canada and UK, 175
Fundamental Rights, 17, 66, 289-90
Fundamentalism, 297
Fundamentalism and Terrorism, 141
FW de Klerk, 173

G

Gandhi, Indira, 327
Gandhi, Mahatma, 21, 70, 85, 91, 102, 155, 174, 253, 289, 294, 307
- Struggle for Freedom, 5

Gandhi, Rajiv, 79, 85
Gandhi, Sonia, 7
Ganjam and Warangal Dist. (AP), 228
Gender Based Crimes, 248
Gender Discrimination, 5, 36
Genital Mutilation, 16
Genocide, 113, 167, 192
Ghana—Kenya, 65
Gillani, 275
Giri, VV, 319
Girl Child, 5, 7, 17, 194, 196-197
Global Peace Assembly, 171, 172, 174
Globalization, 24, 32, 68, 166, 250
Globalization and Liberalization, 23
- Nuclearization, 33

Golden Temple, 14
Grameen Bank (Bangladesh), 252, 303
Grossroot Employment, 82
Grassroot Governance, 74
Gujarat, 35, 117, 171
Gujarat Carnage, 159
Gujjars and Backward, 274

H

Hari Singh, Maharaja, 272
Haryana, 81
Higher Education, 236-38
Hijacking, 159
Hind-Pakistan Dosti Research Academy, 139
Hindu and Islamic Culture, 271
- Marriage Act, 1954, 42
- Marriage Act, 1955, 94
- Religious Philosophy, 27
- Scriptures, 269
- Succession Act, 1956, 62-63, 94
- Widow, 63
- Widow Remarriage Act of 1856, 93
- Women Right to Property Act, 1937, 62, 94
- Women, 19, 62, 274

Hiroshima, 306
Hiroshima Day, 301
HIV Infection, 17
HIV/AIDS, 5, 291, 295
HIV, AIDS and STD, 64
Huen Tsang, 270
Human Development Report, 1997, 243
Human Rights, 17-18, 66, 67-96, 112, 290-91, 294, 299 Act, 111
- Organization, 290
- Violations, 145-46, 276

Husainiwala Border, 139

I

ICDS Programme, 119
India and Pakistan, 143, 160, 162, 302, 306
India and Taiwan, 171
India, Pakistan and Sri Lanka, 70, 252
Indian Civil Society, 141
- Customs, 62
- Evidence Act, 42
- National Congress, 323
- Penal Code, 42- 43, 202, 225
- Population, 321
- Women, 85, 91-93, 188, 199- 200, 252

India—Taiwan, 177
Indira Gandhi Assassination Case, 109
Indo-Pak Relations, 307
Infanticide, 74, 165
Inheritance, 62-63
Injustice,
- Economic, 68
- Social, 68

International
- Covenant on Civil and Political Rights (ICCPR), 108-10, 112-13
- Communism, 310
- Cultural Society Punjabi Forum, 139
- Human Rights Movement, 289
- Institute—for Children, 175
- Labour Organization (ILO), 194, 319
- Trade, 280
- Women's Bill of Rights, 96
- Year of the Child, 194

Islamic
- Republic of Pakistan, 136
- Rules of Succession, 64

J

Jail Manual, 225-26
Jail
Bhagalpur, 227
Naini (Allahabad), 223, 292
Phulwari Sharif (Patna), 225
Sabarmati, 226
Warangal, 223
Jainism, 154
Jamaica—Yemen, 113
Jammu and Kashmir, 269, 271-78
- Constitution Act, 272
- Constitution of-, 272

Janwadi Lekhak Sangh, 139
Japan and Germany, 175
Japanese Yakuza, 68, 250
Jazia and Begar, 271
Jethamalani, Ram, 328
Judicial System, 35
Judiciary, 108, 218, 222, 240, 242, 290, 292
Judiciary and Law Enforcement Agency, 105
Justice Ahmedi, 218
Juvenile
Justice Act, 209
- Offenders, 110
- Welfare Boards, 209

K

Kabir and Nanak, 271
Kalhana's Rajtarangini, 270

KanyaKumari to Kashmir, 137
Karan Singh, 272
Kargil, 129, 301, 306, 313
Kargil Operation, 36, 147
Kashmir, 35, 142, 144, 269-73, 275, 277, 308
- Problem, 139
- to Kanyakumari, 301

Kashmiriyat, 269
Kashmir—Meghalaya, 144
Kathmandu, 159
Kerala, 92, 95, 192, 252
Kinmen Islands, 172
Kirpal Singh, 314
Kumbh Mela, 292

L

Ladakh, Skardu and Gilgit, 271
Lahore, 141, 301, 307
- Durbar, 271
- Peace Yatra, 153

Lahore, Kulu and Chhamb, 271
Lalleshwari, Kashmir Yogini, 270, 271
- Philosophy, 271

Landmines, 175
Law Commission of India, 63, 102
League of Nations, 310
Legal Literacy Centres, 278
Leh, 121
Life Expectancy, 192
Literacy, 18, 22, 31, 234, 248, 252, 302, 320
- Female Adult, 68
- in Nepal, 68

Local Training Programme, 83
Lok Adalats, 218
Lone, Abdul Gani, 275

M

Maharashtra, 51
Mahila Mandals, 6
- Police Stations, 75

Maintenance and Property Rights, 38
Manoj Devi, 314
Manu's Code, 44, 180
Marriage (Marital) Counselling, 45, 47
Match Fixing, 279
Mathura and Vrindavan, Widows in-, 118
Maulana Mandi, 36
Mexico, 96, 250
Mexico, Philippines and Venezuela, 68
Militancy, 35
Millennium Mobilization, 143
Mirza, Sania, 7
Mitakshara System, 62
Modernization, 200
Molestation, 181, 217, 225
Molestation and Sexual Harassment, 49
Money Laundering, 68
Monotheism, 151
Mortality Rates in Dalits, 26
Mountains of-, 274
- Kukernag—Sanasar, 274

Munni Khera Vill. (UP), 24
Muslim
- Community, 35-36
- Women, 35

Muslims, 24
Mutilation and Molestation, 32

N

Naidu, Sarojini, 323
Naresh Muskoh, 314

Narmada Valley, 320
National
- Academy of Agriculture Res. Management, Hyderabad, 237
- Commission for Women, 25-26, 28, 32-33, 39, 44, 71, 76, 81, 87, 107, 120, 199, 218, 236, 274, 289, 293, 295, 324
- Commission for Women (Kerala), 13
- Human Rights Commission (NHRC), 289
- Policy for Older Persons, 118
- Policy for Women, 76

Naxalites, 223
Naxalite Movement, 144
Nepal Stri Shakti, 301
Nepal, Bangladesh and Sri Lanka, 286
NGO(Non-Governmental Org anization), 16, 28, 43-44, 60, 84, 98, 119-20, 126, 128, 132-33, 144, 150, 218, 222, 241-42, 247-248, 252, 278, 283, 285, 293, 298-99, 302, 316-17
Nigeria, 61, 64-65
Non-Violence, 302
Non-Violence Concept, 174
North East States, 144
Nowpora, 270
Nuclear Disarmament, 298
Nuclear Weapons, 253, 302
Nuclearization, 153, 306

O

Omar Abdullah, 28
Other Backward Classes (OBC), 203

P

Pakistan, 122-23, 133, 138, 141-43, 153, 177, 273-74, 301, 307-09
- and Bangladesh, 301
- and India, 153
- Bangladesh and Nepal, 102
- India Relations, 153
- Indian People's Forum for Peace and Democracy, 302
- Jails, 122
- Occupied Kashmir, 273

Peace Coalitions, 301
Pakistani Border, 121, 139
Pakistanis, 139
Panchayat, 79, 83-84, 103
Panchayat Administration, 99
Panchayati Raj, 72, 80-81, 84, 93, 98, 119
- Act, 82
- Institutions, 79, 82

Panchayati Women Federation, 79, 82
Panis Ashtadhyavi, 269
Paripooran, KS, Justice, 201
Parivarik Mahila—, 217
Partition, 306
Patriarchal, 95, 103, 248, 253
Norms, 15
- Religions and Cultural, 15
- Social Order, 44

Patriarchy, 7, 58, 87
Peace and Security, 18
- Bus, 299
- Coalition, 302
- Committee, 301

Personal Laws, 35
Pervez Musharraf, Gen., 122, 307

Pir Panjal Range, 269
Planning Commission, 235
Pluralism, 160
Political Parties, 81, 89
Polygamous Relationships, 42
Population Explosion, 186
Pornography in Netherlands, 68, 250
- Markets, 281

Port Blair, 225
Poverty Alleviation Programme, 119
Primary Health Centres, 119
Prisoners of War, 122
Prohibition
- of Employment, 195
- of Traffic, 195

Property Rights, 62, 145
Prostitution, 14, 26, 64, 72, 172, 187, 188, 204-06, 208-09, 212, 214, 242, 280, 282-84
- Child, 187, 204-05, 281

Public Distribution System, 101-02
Punjab and Haryana, 5
Purana and Brahat Samhita, 269
Purdah System, 99
Pushpa Rawat, 314

Q

Queen Dida, 270
Quran, 13, 16

R

Raja Gulab Singh, 271
Rajasthan, 14, 147-48, 188
Rajasthan—UP, 314
Ram Dev Singh, 49
Ranjit Singh, Maharaja, 271
Rape, 24-25, 31, 50, 53, 181, 186-87, 217, 225, 242, 289
- Effects of-, 53
- Marital, 186
- Victim, 49

Rashtriya Rifles, 130
Ravi Karan, 314
Reforms, 271
Reforms and Policy, 101
Registrar of Births and Deaths, 41
Registration of Marriages, 39-42
Rehabilitation, 284, 313
- Measures, 128-31, 133
- Religious
- Ashrams, 16
- Fundamentalism, 15, 143, 188

Reservation, 27, 33, 88, 145, 293, 302
Reservation for Dalits, 27
Reservation for SC/ST, 88
Right to
- Employment, 33
- to Privacy, 52
- to Remarriage, 62

Rights of Women, Violations, 16
Rituals and Traditions, 16
Rituals, 61
Rotblat, Joseph, Anti-Nuclear Activists, 173
Rural
- Development Project, 93
- Poverty Alleviation Progra mme, 244
- Women, 79-80
- Russian Federation, 112

S

SAARC , 28, 69-70, 303
- Countries, 65, 68-70, 250-51, 286, 300-01
- Region, 249, 253

Summit, 252
SAFTA (South Asian Free Trade Area), 70, 252, 303
SAPTA (South Asian Preferential Trade Area), 70, 252, 303
Sati, 188
Satisaras Lake, 270
Satisaras Lake of Sati, 269
Satyagraha, 174
SC Reservation Quota, 33
SC/ST, 79, 98, 203, 324-25
- Constituencies, 88
- Population, 88

School Health Education Programme, 54
Science and Technology, 5, 217, 306
Security Measures, 128
Self-Defence, 56-58
Self-Defence Education, 55, 58
Self-Employment Programme, 128
Self-Help Groups (SHGs), 6, 284
Sex
- Determination Techniques, 102
- Industry, 56
- Ratio, 192

Scandals, 51
Shops in Europe, 68
- Tourism, 280
- Trade, 16
- Workers, 21, 204

Sexual
- Abuse, 50-51, 230, 281-82, 286
- Exploitation, 279, 281
- Harassment, 24, 74, 167, 187, 199, 201-02, 302
- Relations (Relationship), 186-87, 216, 221
- Violence, 50, 55-58

Shah Hamdam, 270
Shahid Minar, 301
Shariat, 36
Sheikh Abdullah, 272, 273
Shaiva Vedant Poetess, 270
Sikh Religion, 14
Sikh Rule, 271
Sikhism, 155
Simla Agreement, 148
Slum Development Programme, 119
Social
- Discrimination, 60, 65
- Justice, 154, 209, 238
- Legislations, 240

Security, 32, 39, 128, 147, 187, 319
Stratification, 298
Structure, 27
System, 26
Society(ies), 19, 21, 35, 38, 42, 49, 60, 62, 65-66, 68, 71, 73, 84, 92, 103, 115, 127, 141, 145, 149, 166, 168, 203, 212-13, 217, 223, 229, 231, 234, 238, 240, 242, 244, 250, 271, 279, 289-90, 294, 303, 311
- Civil, 7, 15, 42, 101-04, 153-54, 156, 160-61, 166, 174, 274, 276-78, 299
- Consumerist, 24

- Reservation Bill, 89
- Reservation for-, 71, 323-24
- Rights, 17
- SC/ST, 29
- Sexual Abuse of-, 24
- Social and Economic Status, 7, 24
- Social Status, 96

Working Conditions, 50
Women's
- Colleges, 237
- Education, 234-37
- Groups, 145, 152, 161-62, 298
- Initiative for Peace for South Asia, (WIPSA), 141-43, 153, 269, 271, 273-77, 306, 308-09
- Initiative, 269, 273, 276, 298, 305
- Movement, 73, 87, 92, 99, 143, 186, 189, 242
- NGO, 113, 162
- Organization, 83, 87, 89, 101, 104, 230, 325
- Participation in Political Process, 80
- Peace Initiative, 301-02, 309
- Place in Society, 199
- Political Participation, 325
- Population, 87, 127
- Prisons, 231
- Reservation and Rights, 84
- Reservation Bill, 101
- Rights, 219, 294, 302
- Role, 15
- Status, 244
- Study Centres, 307
- Universities, 238

Working Women, 200-01
World Tourism Organization, 286
World Trade Centre, 159
World War I, 310
World War II, 172, 310

Y

Yadav, Mulayam Singh, 328
Yaseen Mallick (JKLF), 275

Z

Zilla Sainik Boards, 126, 132, 316
Zoroastrian, 13
- Tradition, 13